S0-AIC-562

DATE DUE

PRINTED IN U.S.A.

FOSTER AND LAURIE

HV
7911
.F68
S55

FOSTER AND LAURIE

BY AL SILVERMAN

LITTLE, BROWN AND COMPANY
BOSTON-TORONTO

14188

Copyright © 1974 by Al Silverman
All rights reserved. No part of this book may be reproduced in any form or by any electronic or mechanical means including information storage and retrieval systems without permission in writing from the publisher, except by a reviewer who may quote brief passages in a review.

T 02/74

First Edition

The author is grateful to the following for permission to reprint previously copyrighted material:

Olwyn Hughes and Harper & Row, Publishers, Inc. for a portion of Sylvia Plath's poem "The Munich Mannequins," from the book *Ariel* by Sylvia Plath. Copyright © 1965 by Ted Hughes.

Jan Barry and First Casualty Press for lines from Jan Barry's poem "Winning Hearts and Minds," from *Winning Hearts and Minds, War Poems by Vietnam Veterans,* 1972.

Reed Whittemore and *The New Republic* for lines from his poem "The Mother's Breast and the Father's House," originally published in the December 4, 1971 issue of *The New Republic*. Copyright © 1971 by Harrison-Blaine of New Jersey, Inc.

The Viking Press, Inc. for a quotation from *The Kid* by John Seelye. Copyright © 1972 by John Seelye.

Library of Congress Cataloging in Publication Data

Silverman, Al.
  Foster and Laurie.

  1. Foster, Gregory, 1949-1972. 2. Laurie, Rocco, 1948-1972. I. Title.
HV7911.F68S55   363.2'092'2 [B]   73-16232
ISBN 0-316-79116-4

Published simultaneously in Canada by Little, Brown & Company (Canada) Limited
Printed in the United States of America

For Rosa

Contents

PART ONE

The Ambush

. . . The blood flood is the flood of love,
The absolute sacrifice.
It means: no more idols but me,
Me and you.

— SYLVIA PLATH

It is three-thirty, and Fifth Street, between First and Second Avenue, is as cold and gray and leaden as is the rest of New York City on this late January afternoon. It is the kind of cold that seeps into your body, chilling you, making you want to cry out, if you stay out in it too long: "Let me in, let me in." There is no blue in the sky and darkness will soon be settling in and the overcoats and the chokers and the cardigans and the long johns are never enough to keep cops warm, especially the foot patrolmen.

But despite the bleakness the street is teeming. It is always this way at three-thirty in the afternoon on Fifth Street between First and Second Avenue — winter, summer, spring or fall. It is always this way when the eight-to-four cops start straggling in, and the four-to-twelve cops begin to show up for their tour of duty. The eight-to-four cops are in a good mood because they are finished; they have survived another day in the Ninth Precinct. The four-to-twelvers feel okay, too, because the cold hasn't penetrated them yet and they are with each other, and a lot of them prefer to be with their brothers in blue rather than with their families.

There is movement on the street, almost gaiety. This block belongs to the cops. Here they are inviolate, which is more than you can say for the rest of the Ninth Precinct.

Across from the entrance to the Ninth Precinct headquarters is a row of benches fronting a school yard. Three old white women, bundled in dark coats, with shawls over their heads, are huddled together, watching the activities, cackling among themselves, a Greek chorus pronouncing judgments. Cars are double-parked along the street — patrol cars, gypsy cabs (used by the undercover Anti-Crime Unit), police trucks, private cars of the men coming on duty. A black man in a beard — a cop who works in Anti-Crime — is leaning over a car that is idling in the middle of the street, talking to a girl. He is grinning. A knot of young men, all with hard eyes but some harder than others, are gathered in front of the station house. A couple of men come out of Cal's, a below-street bar two doors from the station house, a bar that caters almost exclusively to cops. It is a second home for the men of the Ninth.

3

Anytime they want, they can go behind the bar and fix themselves a drink. The owner keeps a German shepherd in there and the dog is well behaved. He loves cops, but he still hasn't learned to love black cops who are out of uniform. He barks and lunges at them, as he has been taught to do to black people. It is embarrassing that the dog is confused, but how can you teach him the distinction between black cops out of uniform and black people in general? That would confuse him even more and there is enough confusion on the subject as is.

It is Thursday, the twenty-seventh of January, midwinter, and gray and menacing. The weatherman says it will probably snow before the night is over.

To get to their lockers the men of the Ninth have to go through the main floor of the decrepit six-story walk-up that was built in 1912. This afternoon it is very busy. Two Puerto Ricans, their wrists handcuffed behind their backs, are receiving preliminary booking. A German shepherd — the unofficial mascot in the East Village is the German shepherd — is tied to a post; his master is upstairs being booked. The phones are constantly ringing. Mounted on the wall behind a long bench that runs the length of the room and serves as the nerve center of the precinct are three plaques, three Ninth Precinct cops killed in the line of duty. One, Henry Walburger, died in 1964. "I've said this many times," reminisced a veteran cop of the Ninth, "Walburger should have been a priest. There was a *good* man, a good, kind guy." The other two, Patrolman Gerald Murphy and Patrolman Lawrence Stefane, were killed in 1970. Murphy was killed while off-duty and trying to make a narcotics arrest on Third Street. In May of 1970 Patrolman Larry Stefane was sitting on the passenger side of the patrol car. It was early morning and he had just gotten out of the car to buy himself a container of coffee. The car's operator, checking the traffic, started to pull out. As he did so, a man walked up to the car, leaned through the open window, and without saying a word plunged a knife through Stefane's heart. The man, it turned out, had recently been released from a mental institution.

One flight up is a cluster of small rooms. All the walls are painted a bilge-green, the color of a swimming pool that has not seen chlorine in months. The squad room is the largest room, with a cage

4

where squat three Puerto Ricans, their eyes rolling in their heads. They look out, watching two white prostitutes being fingerprinted. One is a skinny blond, the other a brunette with generous breasts. One of the cops, about to go on duty, hollers at the blond: "Hey! Right now, in the bathroom!" The blond wags a finger at him, the finger saying, not now, maybe later, if you're a good boy. The cop laughs. "We have the distinction," he says, "of having the ugliest hookers in the world down here." Moments later a cop goes into the bathroom with the brunette. He has a little boy's grin on his face. "Hey!" the cop who had hollered before hollers again, "a half hour, okay?"

"You know Wallace," a cop is talking to another in the roster room. "Had the best set of guns you ever seen. Couldn't hit the side of a barn door. Wallace had a German Luger, .357 magnum, under his shirt and had another gun inside his shirt. He carried four guns with him and four hundred rounds of ammunition. He had twelve bullets in his belt, one more potent than the other. You could knock over the side of a house. The thing is, the cocksucker couldn't hit the side of a barn door. . . ."

Outside a closed door a sign reads: "Anti-Crime Unit." Beside it is a word, capitalized: FAGS. There is a scrawl underneath: "Only because you wish you were in on it." Then, below, in block letters, one final word: BULLSHIT.

Adjoining the squad room is another closed door with its own sign: "Neighborhood Police Team, Operations Room." Underneath, in more decorous language, are the words — "Top Secret, Confidential, CIA." Nobody is in the Neighborhood Police Team office. The men of the Neighborhood Police Team who will work the four-to-twelve are one flight up, dressing.

Gregory Foster is just tucking his shirt into his pants. He is dressed fastidiously as usual. He has a thing about clothes. He won't let his wife press his shirts because he wants them just right, no wrinkles, so he presses them himself. His trousers — he calls them *trousers*, never pants — must have a perfect crease. His shoes must be shined to a high gloss. He is small, only five feet seven. He weighs one hundred and seventy pounds. He is stocky but not fat. He wears long sideburns. A trim black moustache sets off a full oval

5

face. His skin is a cocoa brown, he has brown eyes, alert eyes, eyes that listen and absorb messages.

He finishes dressing and hustles downstairs to the back room, where most of the cops on the four-to-twelve are congregating before muster. His partner is there already, talking to his Staten Island buddies.

Rocco Laurie is neat, too. His light brown hair is closely cropped and his sideburns are short — he does not like the longhair style of the day. He is a handsome six-foot-one, two-hundred-and-ten-pounder. He lifts weights to keep in shape and plays touch football. He is a man who takes care of his body. His blue eyes are open, warm, but there is a wariness, too, that comes through the light, a skepticism that casts his features in a more rigid mold than Foster's. He is twenty-two. Foster is twenty-one.

A neighbor of Laurie's, Larry Cummings, says, "Hey, Rock, how many passes did you miss last Saturday?"

Laurie grins. "Too many. But watch me this Saturday. I think what it was, the ball was no good. You better bring a better ball."

John DeBerry comes in the door. DeBerry is a black cop, slim, slick. He is wearing a mink coat and a wide-brimmed white hat. He is in Anti-Crime. Laurie looks up. "Ah, the pimp from Fourteenth Street."

Foster goes over and grabs for the hat. "What kind of a dude are you? I just have to get me one of these. Got to get me a big white hat."

Laurie laughs. "Oh, you'd look grand in that. Didn't I tell you, black is beautiful?"

"You just set back that saying fifty years." Foster laughs and throws on his coat. "Let's go, partner."

Before he leaves, Laurie hollers back to his friends. "Hey, what about the football game Saturday?"

They yell back. "Yeah, Rocco, we'll be there."

Laurie runs to catch up to Foster. It is four o'clock. Duty starts.

Their post is Avenue B, Fourth Street to Fourteenth Street, on the wrong side of the DMZ. The Demilitarized Zone, according to the veterans of the Ninth Precinct, begins at Avenue A. Everything east is a battle zone. Avenue B, Fourth Street to Fourteenth Street, is the middle of no-man's-land.

6

The Ninth Precinct is one of the strangest in New York City. It covers only 0.79 square miles. Yet within its borders— from the East River to Broadway, and from East Fourteenth Street to East Houston Street — reside 78,000 people. A polyglot. There are 11,000 blacks, 28,000 Puerto Ricans, 35,000 whites, 4,200 "others." The whites who live there — Italians, Jews, Ukrainians, derelicts from the Bowery, runaway girls, freaks, the aged — fear for their lives, and hate the blacks. The blacks hate the whites and the Puerto Ricans, and hatred is exchanged. Hatred abounds, and prostitution and drugs and stabbings and murder. It is Gorky's Lower Depths, Dickens's London Underworld, Joyce's Nighttown. It is the one area of New York City where nothing really works and the only thing that matters is survival.

For a precinct so small — less than three hundred uniformed personnel — the men of the Ninth keep busy. In 1971 the Ninth Precinct was the eighth highest of all seventy-six New York City precincts in robberies reported. Only two other precincts made more robbery arrests. There were forty-six homicides committed in 1971 in the Ninth, again the eighth highest of all the other New York City precincts. Two cops once compared the Ninth with the Forty-first in the Bronx, called "Fort Apache," supposedly the most "active" precinct of them all.

"Hey, man, we got rats *this* big in the Four-one."

"Yeah," said the cop from the Ninth, "we got roaches who'll *eat* your rats."

Foster and Laurie's beat is one of the worst, in that it is the center of drug activity, especially the corner of Eleventh Street and Avenue B. The Puerto Rican kids call it *la esquina de los tecatos.* The corner of the junkies.

But the two men seem to be getting along well with the people since coming together in November. Each had joined the precinct at different times — Laurie in May of 1971, Foster in July. Each had done different things and had different partners. But one day Laurie came to his commanding officer, Sergeant Fred Reddy, and asked if he could have Greg Foster as his partner. Reddy asked why. Laurie told him a little lie, that he and Foster had served together in Vietnam. They had not. They were in Vietnam at the same time, but they suffered separately. After some delibera-

7

tion, and a talk with both men, Reddy gave his okay. It wouldn't have mattered to him if they hadn't served in Nam together. They seemed compatible, they were good, aggressive young cops with excellent records, and Reddy liked to have a black and white team working together on the Neighborhood Police Team. It helped lessen tensions. So he allowed them to become partners.

The Neighborhood Police Team was organized and begun in January of 1971, a variation on an old concept, the return of the man on the beat. Basically, the idea was to try and bring the police and the public closer together.

It seemed to be working well in the Ninth Precinct, although some residents laughed at it, calling it nothing but a public relations rip-off. But, with the right personnel anything can work — up to a point at least. Foster and Laurie represented the right personnel because they were cops who were liked in the community by some and respected by many. A few, of course, hated them as they hated all they called "pigs."

At seven o'clock Sergeant Reddy comes by in a patrol car and stops on Avenue B. It is a routine visit and Reddy signs their memo books.

"Hey, Sarge," Foster says, "we got a guy who wants to give us some information about a drug haul."

"Where's he gonna be?"

"Just off the avenue," Laurie says, "and we won't be gone too long."

"What time?"

"Be after eight."

Sergeant Reddy gives them permission to leave their post briefly. He drives off.

At eight forty-five, Foster and Laurie are standing on the northwest corner of Avenue B and Twelfth Street. Two Puerto Rican kids, about thirteen years of age, come along and stop. Foster recognizes them.

"Hey, what are you doin' out in the cold?"

"It's a good night, Mr. Cool." Puerto Rican kids, who play in the Twelfth Street area, call Foster "Mr. Cool." It is a term of affection. He has played basketball and baseball with them. He has helped them out of trouble. They like Laurie, too, though they don't know him as well because he is more aloof. But he never hassles them.

One turns to Laurie, who is standing quietly, trying to draw the white cop into the conversation. "If they call you a pig, what do you do?"

"If I was a pig," Laurie says, "I wouldn't do anything. But since I'm not I would lock them up."

"You would lock them up?"

"Only when they say things about me that aren't true. If they call me a dirty name and I don't feel that I'm dirty, then I lock them up. I wouldn't call you a dirty name, right?" Laurie grins. "Where do you go to school?"

"P.S. 60."

"You know Fritz there, the principal?"

One of the boys says, "He has a wooden leg."

"You know how he got that wooden leg?"

"How come?"

Laurie says, "Did you ever hear of Guadalcanal? Guadalcanal was a very famous battle that the Marine Corps fought in World War II. That's where he lost his leg. He stepped on a mine."

"It should have blown him up."

"He was a war hero," Laurie says sharply.

"War hero? He treats us like prisoners in that school."

"You want to go to school and come out a dummy?" Foster says. "You'll end up standing around here, standing on the corner drinking wine."

"I drink wine already now."

Foster is about to change the subject but the boy, whose skin is almost as dark as Foster's, does it for him.

"Did you ever shoot anybody with your gun?"

"No, son."

"I ask every cop that, they say, 'No, son.' "

"Hey," Laurie interrupts, "you want to be a cop?"

"Nope," the boy says matter-of-factly. "Nobody respects the uniform any more."

Foster and Laurie say good-bye and move on.

9

At nine-fifteen Patrolman Peter Wocial drives to Fourteenth Street and Avenue B. He sees Foster and Laurie. He calls to them, "Hey, get in the car. Come on, warm up."

"No," Laurie says, "we'll stay out here."

"Why'd you say that?" Foster says.

"All right, take care of yourself." Wocial and his partner take off.

Patrolman Jim Liedy is cruising in a car with his partner, William Grawzo. "You know," Liedy says to Grawzo, "it's a weird night, a funny night. I can't put my fingers on it. I betcha we're gonna get some kind of a heavy job." Grawzo doesn't answer.

Patrolman Charlie D'Amodio is driving down Avenue B. He spots Foster and Laurie and honks his horn. He is reminded of an incident that happened the night before. Laurie was riding piggyback with D'Amodio for a while because of a possible disturbance between Jews and Puerto Ricans at a school on First Avenue. During that time D'Amodio gave a summons to a taxi driver. After D'Amodio had written it out and was walking back to his car, the cabbie hollered out something. D'Amodio couldn't hear.

"You know what the cabdriver said to you, Charlie?" Laurie said. "He said he hopes you get shot up in Harlem." Neither man laughed.

Mark Tuft is sixteen years old. He lives on Avenue B, in a second-story apartment fronting on the avenue near the corner of Eleventh Street. His mother runs an antique shop on the avenue. One day two people were knifed to death in the hallway of Tuft's building. The boy knows blood and he knows death. At nine-thirty he is on the street and he meets the partners. He calls Foster "Shaft." He and Foster have had long conversations, mostly about cars. Tuft likes to work with cars and Foster would tell Mark the trouble he was having with his Charger.

"How you guys doin'?" Tuft asks. He is very businesslike. "Cold enough for ya?"

"Yeah, real cold," Foster says.

"Quiet night?" he asks. Tuft likes to know what is going on.

"Quiet night."

"Nothing much happening," Laurie says.

Tuft crosses the avenue to the bodega on the corner of Avenue B and Eleventh Street. He yells, "See ya, Shaft." The partners both laugh.

At ten-fifteen Patrolman Liedy hears Laurie's voice come over the radio. There is a dispute coming from Avenue B and Tenth Street. Laurie is saying that he and Foster will handle it. Liedy says to Grawzo, "We'll take the job. We're right here." As he is driving to the spot he hears Laurie on the radio saying, "You got anything further? There's no such address."

Liedy cruises in. It is very very dark. He sees light coming from flashlights. He gets out of his car and sees that it is Foster and Laurie. Then two more foot patrolmen appear. Six cops are milling around in the dark cold night, and there is nothing. Liedy leaves. He is uneasy.

Next door to the bodega where Mark Tuft has bought some groceries is a luncheonette called the Shrimp Boat. It is owned by a man named Walter who, for some reason, is called Bill by everybody. The place is a hangout for junkies but the foot patrolmen like to jump in there to keep warm. Foster and Laurie are seen going in the Shrimp Boat shortly after ten-thirty.

The arrest log from the Ninth Precinct between 4 and 11 P.M. is not overwhelming: at four-thirty, a burglary arrest on Avenue B; at five, an attempted assault and possession of a dangerous knife at East Twelfth Street; at five-twenty, a family court warrant on Avenue B; at eight-fifty, possession of a loaded pistol and possession of narcotics at Seventh Street; at nine-fifteen, an assault and menacing with a knife at East Twelfth Street. Throughout the four-to-twelve tour there are nine ambulance cases, fourteen disputes, two fights, one "large" fight on the street, six robberies in progress, three burglaries in progress, two assaults, one purse snatch, three disorderly groups, one missing child. There is also one ten-thirteen — assist patrolman.

Nate is a large black man with a huge stomach. He is sitting on the stoop of his apartment on Avenue B between Eleventh and

11

Twelfth streets, where he is an assistant super. Foster, who is alone, passes by. The time is about ten thirty-five.

"I see you got your big army thing on," Foster says.

Nate is wearing his army coat. The collar is pulled up around his head. He is hatless.

"You still playing soldier," Foster says. "Betcha you'd like to be back in Nam."

"Sure I would. Lot warmer than it is tonight."

"I tell you," Foster says, "I was glad to get the hell away from there."

"Not me," Nate says. "I liked it."

"You're crazy." Foster looks at Nate, who is missing one hand and has only two fingers on the other. In 1970, in Saigon, he stepped on a mine. "I liked it, Greg. I'd a gone back if I hadn't got hurt."

"I tell you, you're crazy." There is a silence for a moment. The night now is very dark. "Come on, walk down there to the corner with me. I got to meet my partner."

"Naw, man, I don't feel like it."

"Come on," Foster persists.

"I tell you what, I'll catch you when you come back up this way."

But Nate goes up to his room instead. He starts to get ready for bed when he hears shots — *bap, bap, bap*. Shit, he says to himself, and he gets dressed.

The last entry in Rocco Laurie's memo book for January 27, 1972: "2210: 632 11th Street, Apt. 9. Family Dispute. 10-91. Conditions corrected."

A 911 in New York City is an emergency call to the police. Anyone can call 911 anytime, free. The police respect all 911's and treat them with the utmost seriousness.

The call comes into a control center at police headquarters on Center Street in downtown New York. Men are seated in front of a computerized machine with telephones by their side. As soon as they pick up a 911 the call is recorded. When the point of emergency is identified, the call is transferred into another room, where a dispatcher moves it immediately to the proper division. The division dispatcher then alerts all police personnel by radio.

Usually when the call is a ten-thirteen — *assist police officer* — the dispatcher will immediately drop the phone, run back, and inform the cage. But when this call comes from a woman about a shooting on Eleventh Street and Avenue B the dispatcher, in his excitement, stays with the call, not notifying the back room until the woman has hung up. Thus, precious seconds are lost in notifying the First Division, which is the Ninth Precinct's division, seconds that might have given the police enough time to reach the scene before the assailants fled.

At ten minutes to eleven the 911 regarding the shooting on Eleventh Street comes through. The dispatcher picks up the phone and hears a woman screaming.

"There's shooting! Somebody's firing shots!"

It is apparent that while she is at the phone the woman's husband is observing the scene from a window. His voice can be heard indistinctly in the background.

"They're cops," the woman shouts. "They're shooting the cops!"

The woman's voice comes over. "Oh, my God," she cries, "they're shooting the cops . . . and they're still shooting. . . . Now they're running up Eleventh Street. . . ."

A beeper is heard through the police radio, then a voice from central control: "Signal ten-thirteen, Avenue B, Box, and Eleventh Street — Avenue Box and Eleventh Street. . . . Signal ten-thirteen — a shot fired . . . Eleventh and B — two policemen shot. . . ." The voice suddenly grows louder, higher-pitched, a note of hysteria creeping in: "Two patrolmen shot, Eleventh and Avenue B. . . . Avenue B and Eleventh Street — two patrolmen shot. . . ."

Mark Tuft is now upstairs in his apartment watching television. Suddenly, he hears noises. It sounds like firecrackers. It is not unusual in the area for firecrackers to be set off any time of the day or night, any season of the year. But Mark goes to the window anyway because the sound of firecrackers on Avenue B can also be the sound of gunfire; it crosses the boy's mind that

13

maybe there is a shoot-out, cops shooting junkies or something like that.

He looks down and at first he thinks he sees two cops bending over two people lying in the street. But then he notices that the people lying in the street have on blue uniforms. He stares in horror, frozen to the spot. A black man is bent over one of the police officers, searching him, patting him down. Another, also a black man, is bent over the other cop. He has the cop's gun out of its holster.

"Oh, God," Mark says, and he starts to scream: "Shaft! Shaft!"

His mother and father try to grab Tuft but he whirls away from them, falls out the door, and runs down the stairs. He runs out to the street. He is alone. The two men who had been bending over the bodies are gone.

He looks at the men lying there. Laurie is in the middle of the sidewalk on the east side of Avenue B, just off the corner of Eleventh Street, between the bodega and the Shrimp Boat. He is lying on his side, one arm cradling his face. Foster is on his stomach, spread-eagled. He is on the edge of the sidewalk, one leg dangling off the curb. His head is toward Avenue B. The two cops, the white cop and the black cop, lying side by side, head to foot.

Mark Tuft bends down. It doesn't seem to him that Laurie is breathing but he thinks he sees Foster's lips moving. He stands between their bodies, tears running down his face, hollering for help. A police car is coming up the avenue but it is cold and its windows are closed tight and it turns into a side street without hearing the boy. The boy continues to cry.

Rich Peterson, a patrolman, is working with the narcotics squad this night. He is sitting in an unmarked car on Thirteenth Street and Avenue B, with two partners, Fred Simon and George Brown. They are watching a private social club on Thirteenth Street. At about a quarter to eleven they leave their stakeout and head for another possible drug drop. As they come up Eleventh Street from Avenue C to Avenue B — Eleventh Street is one-way, running west — they stop for a red light. They see people gathered on the corner of Eleventh Street and the avenue. This is not unusual. Then they see the two bodies lying on the sidewalk.

They all jump out of the car. Simon and Brown run over to the

14

bodies. Peterson stands behind the car to give them cover; he is worried about snipers.

In the knot of people are six or seven children. They look Puerto Rican to Peterson. There are two or three adults. The owner of the bodega is one of them. He says he ducked for cover immediately when he heard the shots. One of the bullets went through a window of his store.

Fred Simon steps into the middle of the avenue, at the intersection. He pulls out his gun and fires into the air, fires repeatedly, trying to signal for help.

Peter Wocial and his partner are driving in their radio car down Twelfth Street, which runs one-way east. At the corner of Twelfth and Avenue B, a man runs to the car. He pounds at the window and Wocial opens the door.

"There's a shooting up the block," the man hollers.

Wocial races down Avenue C to Twelfth Street, turns right on Eleventh, and speeds toward Avenue B. About ten doors into the block he hears a volley of shots that he finds out later have come from the narcotics detective. Wocial's partner immediately picks up the radio phone. "Shots fired!" he barks tersely and hangs up the phone.

At the corner Wocial sees a mass of people. There is screaming. He turns right into the avenue and that is when he sees the two cops lying there.

Patrolman Jim Liedy and his partner, William Grawzo, are parked on Avenue A and Thirteenth Street. They go up to Thirteenth and Avenue A and nothing is happening. Liedy makes a U-turn and looks up Thirteenth Street, trying to see signs of a disorder, of people massed. He sees nothing. He starts up Avenue A toward Fourteenth Street and runs into another radio car that is coming the other way. In the car are patrolmen Danny Brennan and Dominic Vetrano. Liedy, who is a friend of both men, stops his car beside theirs. "Hey, what are you doin', you dago, you stupid Italian?" Vetrano curses back. There is laughter in both cars and they move away from each other. Just then it comes over the radio: "Ten-thirteen, Ninth Precinct, Avenue B and Eleventh Street."

The first thing that hits Liedy is that it is Foster and Laurie but that it is probably not bad. He has heard over the radio that they have been covering a family dispute; maybe now they need help; maybe the man doesn't want to leave the apartment and they're struggling with him. Then another report comes over the radio: "Shots fired," and Liedy moves into action.

He makes a right turn, goes through a red light, and turns into Avenue B. He races down Avenue B in the wrong lane, the north lane. But he doesn't care. As he nears Eleventh Street he sees Brennan and Vetrano shoot out of Eleventh Street and park on Eleventh near the corner, on the west side of the street. Liedy moves down the wrong lane to the spot where he sees people congregated. He stops the car. In between the crowd's legs he can see the two men lying there. He grabs the phone and yells, "Two cops shot! Two cops shot!" and he flings open the door.

Foster is nearest to the door. He is lying there in his overcoat. The image Liedy draws is that of a man at the beach, "sunning his back." He looks over at Rocco Laurie, where Grawzo is. Laurie has his winter blouse on with a choker. He is on his side, in a sleeping position. One arm seems to be cradling his face.

Liedy looks for Foster's guns. They are gone. He hollers to Grawzo: "Laurie's guns." Grawzo looks down, then shakes his head. Jesus, Liedy thinks, it's the same guys who killed Jones and Piagentini. Eight months earlier, Waverly Jones and Joseph Piagentini, a black and a white cop, were ambushed in the Bronx. Both men were killed. Their guns were taken from them.

Liedy picks up Foster's hat. There is a hole in the top of the hat. There is blood inside the hat. He tries to grab Foster by the shoulders but it is awkward because he has his gun out. Now there is blood all over his gun so he takes the gun, reaches over, and lays it on the front seat of his car. About two seconds later he looks for his gun. He has forgotten what he has done with it. Jesus, he thinks, what am I doing? Somebody could have taken the gun. He puts it back in his holster, blood and all.

Liedy tries to pick up Foster, but he is deadweight. Finally, he rolls him over and he feels sick. The blood is coming out from Foster's face. He sees what appears to be two holes in his head. A milky substance is running out of the holes, and an eye. Liedy is

16

assailed by a great rage: junkies, fucking cocksuckers. I'll kill who-ever did this.

Charlie D'Amodio and his partner hear the ten-thirteen while they are driving on Fourteenth Street. They speed down Avenue B. It is chaos. People are running back and forth, there is screaming, doorways are jammed. Nothing makes sense. The one reality is the sight of the two men, two friends of D'Amodio's, two fellow cops. The men are lying on the sidewalk and it is very cold and blood is beginning to stain the street and he does not know whether they are dead or alive.

He bends over Foster. Blood pours out of Foster's left eye like a fountain. It is the most shocking sight D'Amodio has ever seen, just bright red all over Foster's face, the blood coming out of that eye without stopping, as if somebody has turned on a faucet. Three men — one a civilian — help carry Foster to D'Amodio's car. They put him in the back seat and D'Amodio heads for Bellevue. The civilian, trapped in the car, goes with D'Amodio.

Sergeant Reddy, cruising on Fourteenth Street, heading toward Avenue A, hears the reports of shots fired over the radio. Immedi-ately, he turns into Avenue A to get around the block to Avenue B. As he pulls up to Eleventh Street, they are moving Gregory Foster into a radio car. Laurie is still lying there.

Dominic Vetrano is hollering, "Who saw this? Who did it?" Two Puerto Ricans speak almost in unison. "White guys, white guys, we see them shooting." It takes a while to establish that what they saw was the narcotics detective shooting in the air.

Brennan, Vetrano, and Grawzo have Rocco Laurie in a sitting position. His head is back and Jim Liedy notices that he is very pale. He also sees a hole in his neck. "Get him in the fucking radio car," he yells. He thinks to himself, Foster's dead and Laurie, God, he's dead, too.

He jumps behind the wheel. The three cops carry Laurie into the back seat. There is a madness about now. Police cars from all over the city have converged on the spot. Civilians and bluecoats are milling together. The cops feel a rage and frustration, and a

17

meanness rises in them. The civilians smell it. The atmosphere is heavy.

Brennan moves into the back seat and cradles Laurie's head in his lap. Grawzo gets in beside Liedy.

"It's cold in here," Brennan yells, "close the door."

"We can't," Liedy says, "his foot's hanging out."

"Then we'll ride with the door open."

The siren is on and Brennan, holding Laurie's head gently, hollers, "Shut it off, shut it off."

"We got to get through," Liedy says.

"There's too much confusion here. Shut it off." Brennan hits Liedy on the shoulders but Liedy won't take his hands off the wheel. Finally, Grawzo moves over and shuts off the siren. They call the central dispatch. "We're on our way to Bellevue with a wounded patrolman."

Brennan holds tight to Rocco and starts talking to him. Laurie's eyes are open wide but he cannot speak. It looks as though he wants to say something, but he cannot. Brennan croons to him: "Hang on, Rocco, hang on. We're going to get you up there."

Liedy moves down Avenue B toward Tenth Street. He can't get by because radio cars are coming down and traffic is clogged. So he jumps the curb. He rides the sidewalk all the way on Tenth Street to Avenue A. He hits a bump and Brennan sees Rocco's eyes rolling in his head. He says softly, "Hang on, Rocco, hang on."

Liedy drives to Fourteenth Street, then to First Avenue. "Okay," Brennan orders, "put it on."

The siren screams as Liedy races up First Avenue toward Bellevue; Bellevue Emergency is on Twenty-eighth Street. All traffic has been stopped and he gets right through.

They drive into the emergency entrance. A crowd of people is out there waiting for them. Brennan gets out of the car first, carefully. His jacket has blood on it.

As Liedy jumps out of the car the doctors and nurses — there must have been fifteen of them outside — are already getting Laurie out. They put him on the stretcher and start wheeling him in. He rolls off a bit but Liedy catches him and places him back on. There is a desperate rush. As they run him inside, they start ripping off his clothes. Liedy sees holes in him. Laurie is naked when he goes into the operating chamber.

The two men, the partners, are together again, lying head to foot as they had moments ago on the street. They are both covered by a green cloth. Teams of doctors hover over each. A round metal disk, a defibrillator, rests on each man's chest, over his heart. Every now and then it is activated, hoping that the electric jolts will bring the men back to life. But mostly the doctors are pounding on the hearts with the palms of their hands, one hand over the other, pressing down as hard as they can.

Each man has been injected directly into the heart with adrenaline. Each has an airway in his mouth, a plastic instrument that keeps the tongue from falling into the larynx.

The doctors continue to pound on each man's chest. There is no telling whether they are alive or dead. Gregory Foster's eyes, or what is left of them, are closed. His face is no longer black. Nor is it white. It is as if he has traveled to another realm, an indeterminate realm where neither white nor black matters, where reality has nothing to do with color at all. Rocco Laurie looks very white. His eyes are still open, staring toward the ceiling. His eyes are not vacant. There are signs of fight in them, and questions. The eyes seem to be asking, what is happening to me? Why has it happened?

The doctors continue to work on both men.

I n their homes the wives waited for their husbands. The one had the television on in the living room of her two-bedroom apartment in the South Bronx. The other, in her tiny two-story house on Staten Island, was upstairs, watching television in bed. The two wives were separated by distance — by miles of water, by the tangles of bridges and tunnels and highways. And there was the other distance between them, of race, a rather more burdensome gulf than the mileage that separates the Bronx from Staten Island. The one wife was black, the other was white, and their lifestyles and their values and their inhibitions and their passions had been nurtured on separate tracks. But they were cop wives and their husbands worked together as partners and that was a bond that entwined them.

They were curiously entwined in other ways. Neither woman had known sustained affection as children. Both had grown up virtually without father or mother and been raised instead by grandmothers. And so they had grown up as loners. Then, when they married, there was distrust and fear of their husband's parents, and the distrust was returned. But they had both found men who would be good to them in a way that nobody had ever before been good to them. Even in the short time of their marriage, in only a year and a half, their husbands had become the anchors of their lives. In both instances the marriage had been like quick-changing weather patterns: one day sunny and clear, the next cloudy and threatening and turbulent. But it was slowly getting better for both women. They were beginning to adjust to the men who had brought these strange effects into their lives; stability, love of a sort, peace. In a sense, the women had overadjusted, because they had become fiercely possessive of their husbands, as well as dependent on them. Because of their loneliness as children, a loneliness that had created in them an apartness from others, both women had made their husbands the hub of their lives. And both women knew in their souls that without their husbands their existence would be threatened; their existence would be difficult, bitter, perhaps intolerable. For who else would be there to say to them: don't worry, I'm here, I love you, I will take care of you?

The TV was on but Jackie Foster wasn't watching. She liked to have the television on when her husband was working, to keep her company. Little Gregory, three years old, slim with curly black hair and large brown eyes, awareness a part of his face already, was still running around the house. It was after ten. Tyhessia, the baby, was asleep, and Jackie decided it was time for Gregory. She put on his pajamas, with a struggle.

"Don't want to go to bed," the little boy said.

"You got to."

"Don't want to."

"Gregory!" The mother's voice, normally low-pitched, turned shrill. She picked up her son and carried him into his bed.

She was in her housecoat. She was tall and slim, her body was lithe and there was a suppleness to her. She was pretty, with deep brown skin and a face that had not yet formed its character. Her full beauty was still ahead of her. She was nineteen years old. She went into the kitchen to prepare supper for her husband. She baked two sweet-potato pies because that was a favorite of his. She knew he would be hungry when he got home.

She went to the living room window and looked out. The night was cold and dark. No stars in the sky, no moon, and people down in the dark street had coat collars pulled up around their necks. She thought, I hope Gregory hurries home to get himself a nice parking space.

She always walked back and forth to the window about that time, trying to spot her husband as he drove into the street. But it was still too early. The eleven o'clock news was on the TV. Dimly she heard something about two cops who had been gunned down, then the announcer was talking about violence in Belfast, Ireland. The two cops and Belfast — it all ran together in her mind. She thought it had all happened over there.

Within herself she felt a contentment, a sense of well-being that was new to her. Lately, everything was coming together for her and for Gregory, and for little Gregory and the baby, who was five months old. She and her husband were getting along now, which they hadn't been at the beginning. It had begun to turn for them when they moved into the apartment in the fall. It got even better early in January when Gregory had come down with the flu. He coughed a lot and he had no appetite and it was then that Jackie could be a wife and do something for him. One night he was so feverish that she could feel the heat vibrating off his body.

She said, "You ought to see a doctor."

"I'm not goin' to no doctor."

She made him take aspirin and she got out a bottle of rubbing alcohol.

"What are you doing?" he asked as she came over to him and removed his pajama tops.

"I'm gonna bring your fever down." And she rubbed him, rubbing hard, and put every last drop of the alcohol on his body. And it did make him feel better and he talked a little about his work. He told her of a big case he and his partner, Rocco Laurie, were working on.

"The word's out," he said. " 'The doctor's coming to town.' " He

21

told her that the panic had been on because heroin had been temporarily locked out of the city. But now a shipment was coming in. *The doctor was coming* and Foster had found a woman, he said, who was going to help him and his partner intercept it. And if they got the bust there was a chance they might make detectives. He was excited by the possibilities, but Jacqueline Foster was afraid.

"You trust this lady?" she asked.

"Well, she's a junkie and she hates cops." Greg started to laugh.

"Oh," Jackie said, "is that all?"

"No," he laughed again, "that's not all. She's got a record, too, because she and her common-law husband, about four years ago, drowned their three-year-old daughter in the East River."

"Can you trust her, Gregory?" Jackie asked again.

"She's a junkie and a prostitute and she's all run-down. But she likes me because I could have arrested her a couple of times and I never did. That's why she told me about the shipment. Besides, her old man's still in jail. I told her we might be able to get him out soon."

"Gregory," the wife said, "just because you made it through Vietnam doesn't mean you're going to make it here on the police force. Your luck is going to run out sometime."

He grinned. The rubdown had made him sleepy. "I'm a lucky person," he said. He turned over and went to sleep. But Jacqueline Foster couldn't sleep. She worried about her husband, about this case, about the shipment, about the woman who was going to serve as their informer. Jackie Foster knew drug addicts were undependable because both her parents were addicts the day she was born.

That was on August 4, 1952. She was one of four girls and she was next to the oldest. Her father, Alfred Washington, was then nineteen, her mother, Rosemarie, eighteen. They were young and wild and Jacqueline Foster was given to her grandmother before she was three years old.

Her grandmother, Lucy Jackson, was a remarkable woman. She had twenty-one grandchildren (later she took in foster children) and Jackie always marveled that she had become a favorite grandchild. The grandmother had been married for nine years but she and her husband had been together for about twenty years in all.

Jackie liked her grandfather, too, and sometimes called him father. But the grandmother was the strong force in her life. She was a mother to the girl, very protective of her. Jackie did not find out until she was fourteen that her parents were junkies; the grandmother had always told her that they were just "sick." The extent of their illness didn't hit her until her husband, before he started at the police academy, picked up her father's files from the police department.

He came home that day with the record and threw it at Jackie. "That cat's got a package on him as big as a telephone book." He was livid. "Might keep me out of the police," he said disgustedly.

Jackie was stunned. She ran out of the house and walked in a daze for blocks and blocks. She was ashamed. She felt that she could not be hurt any more in her life. She knew that she had come from a broken home but her grandmother had always sheltered her and given her self-respect. As she walked, she thought, I had everything that I would never have had I lived with my mother and father. I had everything. I had a beautiful life as a child.

But she was overselling her childhood. When she moved with her grandmother from the Bronx to St. Albans, Long Island, she was nine years old and already a troubled child. Her grandmother was strict and overprotective. She tried to isolate Jackie from other girls because she felt her granddaughter was too good for them. She kept telling Jackie: "I want you to go to college and have a car and be somebody." There were times when Jackie hated her grandmother and she rebelled and began sneaking around.

She had a couple of fights in school with girls and when she was thirteen she became involved with a boy, her first one. He was sixteen or seventeen and at first treated Jackie like a big brother. But she was old for her age — "I carried myself big" is the way she put it — and the boy sensed an opportunity and there was a day that he jived with her. The memory of that day flooded over her as she walked through the streets, as she tried to sort out the past so that she could face the present again with her husband. The boy had taken her by force, she was not ready for it, and she remembered at the time being afraid of having a baby. Later, after she became pregnant with little Gregory, the other boy found out about it, found out that she wasn't married, and blamed himself. "If I hadn't gotten to you that day," he told her, "you would still be all right." She told him not to worry, that he hadn't messed up her life.

And he hadn't, because after that first experience Gregory had come along and it was different altogether, and it was when she started going with him that her whole life changed.

Finally, she came back to the house and tried to tell her husband all these things and they talked it out. "Look," she said, "my father and mother did their own thing. I had nothing to do with it. It was their lives. All they did was bring me into the world."

"I know that, Boop," he said (he called her Boop when he was feeling affection for her). "But you should have told me."

"But I didn't know, Gregory. When I married you — way before I married you, when I *met* you — you became my whole world. I forgot about everybody else, my parents included. You're the only one that counts."

So it was forgotten. The police department accepted Gregory's application despite his father-in-law's record. Jackie's mother enrolled in a methadone program and she told her daughter that it was because of Gregory Foster that she was trying so hard. "You married a police officer — not a drug addict — that's a big thing." A police officer to Jackie's mother was somebody with a good job, somebody to be respected. "I'm gonna get myself together," she said.

The father was another matter. He was on methadone for a while, too, but then left the program. "I don't know about him," Jackie once told her husband. "I think he has a problem. He's a smart man, very smart. It's just that he's been on the stuff so long that there's no end to it."

But, mostly, Gregory and Jackie were living their own lives, by themselves, with their children. It was what they wanted and it was getting better all the time.

She stood by the window again, looking for the car, hoping to see her husband drive into their street. There were plenty of parking spaces across the street, so he wouldn't have to walk too far in the cold. She stared into the night, thinking, I hope he comes home soon. I want him home.

It had been such a good day. Gregory had come home late Wednesday night very tired because he had gone to class in the morning at John Jay College — he was taking two courses a week, thinking he might want to become a court officer or even a lawyer — and rushed to work from there. And when he got home that night he was too tired to eat.

He woke at eleven on Thursday morning and while Jackie warmed his breakfast, which would be the dinner she had prepared for him the night before — fricassee chicken with gravy, Spanish rice, and tomato — he sewed buttons on his police jacket.

"What happened?" she asked.

"Oh, there was a riot in a synagogue. We had to break it up and some dude ripped off the buttons." He wouldn't let his wife sew the buttons because he said she didn't do them right.

He had his breakfast-dinner and when his stomach was full Jackie said, "There's a coat I want to buy at Korvette's. I really want it." He grunted something about just taking it easy.

"You promised me a coat, honey."

He shrugged. "Okay, let's go get your coat before I go to work."

"Only one thing, Gregory. I don't have enough money." He had given her three hundred dollars for the house and the bills and there was nothing left. She nuzzled close to him, "Can I have some money?"

"Okay, okay."

They dressed the kids, put Tyhessia in the car seat, Gregory in back with his mother, and drove to the department store, which was only a few minutes from their apartment.

Jackie bought the coat she wanted. Then she lingered at the wig counter. Before she could open her mouth Gregory was shaking his head. "Uh-uh. I don't want no woman around me wearing no wigs. I don't like artificial women."

So she moved to the shoe department. She saw two pairs she liked and she tried them on. "Can I have the shoes, honey?"

Gregory was holding Tyhessia, who weighed sixteen pounds and was fretting. He was beginning to feel itchy. "Come on, Jackie, I got to go to work. Buy the shoes and let's go."

She did and they rushed home. It was after three and sometimes, because of traffic, it took Gregory almost an hour to get to the Ninth Precinct. He helped carry things upstairs. He came over to

25

Jackie, who was sitting on the couch, taking off Tyhessia's snowsuit.

"I'm leaving, Boop." He bent over and kissed her lightly. "Don't get up, I'll lock the door." He kissed the baby. "See you, Minnie," he said. He had nicknamed Tyhessia "Minnie," after Minnie Mouse. His nickname for little Gregory was "Speed Racer." He looked at his son. "See ya, Speed Racer." And he was gone.

Usually, Jackie would go over to the window and watch her husband pull out of the parking lot. Now she was too busy trying to unravel her baby daughter. But little Gregory stood on a chair, looking out the window.

"Daddy's going to work," he said. "Daddy's going to work."

The little boy stood there, watching the car pull out from the parking space.

"Wave to him, Gregory," the mother said. The boy waved. He kept on waving long after the car was out of sight.

She grew tired of looking out the window, just staring at nothing. She walked back into the kitchen. And the buzzer rang.

She started. Who could that be at this time of night? She knew none of her family would be visiting, not after eleven. Then she thought that maybe somebody was playing around, because the neighborhood kids had a habit of fooling with the buzzer downstairs. So she didn't bother to press the answering buzzer that would open the door.

The buzzer rang again, and again, insistently. This time she answered it.

She looked through the peephole in her door and she saw two police officers standing there. She opened the door. All of a sudden she felt jumpy.

The cops stood at the doorway. One of them said, "Mrs. Foster, we want you to come down to Bellevue Hospital right away. Your husband has had an accident."

She didn't understand. "What kind of an accident? Is he all right?"

They would say no more.

She was in her housecoat and she said, "What do I do with my kids?"

One of the cops said, "Dress the children and bring them with you."

Did I hear right, *bless* the children? Now she was confused and alarmed. She felt a chill.

"I can't take them. The baby has a cold and I don't want to get her up and take her out in the cold. Let me call someone."

First she called Gregory's parents. She didn't even know who was at the other end of the line. "Gregory's had an accident," she said. "He's at the Bellevue Hospital. I've got to go." She hung up immediately.

She called her sister who lived nearby. She couldn't leave her kids but she would send her husband. Then Jackie called a cousin who said she would come and look after the kids.

Somehow, Jacqueline Foster managed to dress herself. She threw on a gray and white sweater and gray slacks. She pulled on a pair of knee-high boots. She flopped a blue and yellow knit hat on her head; it gave her a turbaned effect. She put on the new coat that she had just bought with Gregory's money, for sixty dollars. Her cousin came in, and then her brother-in-law. He said he would go with her.

They rushed down to the police car. The two-way radio was on when she got in the back seat, but one of the cops immediately snapped it off.

They drove to the hospital in silence. Jackie Foster slumped in the back seat. It came to her that her husband was dead, but with a great act of will she cut off the thought. He's alive, she said to herself. She kept repeating, he's alive, he's alive. She looked out the window as the car sped toward the hospital. It had begun to snow.

The pain struck her sometime after eleven. It was a weird sensation, an odd sensation. She was lying in bed with the eleven o'clock news on and, all of a sudden, the sharp pain lit up in the pit of her stomach, like somebody flicking on a cigarette lighter, a flame of pain that made her wince and caused her to ask herself — what's going on? But as quickly as it came, it passed, and she lay there thinking, that's odd, I wonder what it's from?

27

Before she left for work that morning Adelaide had told Rocco, who was still in bed, that she would wait up for him. And he had said, "Try to get some sleep, though. Wake up about twelve if you want to wait up. But try to get some sleep." But she had been unable to sleep. She had made herself a sandwich and then taken the dog out for a walk. Then she went upstairs to the bedroom, got into bed, and idly watched television. Late in the evening the stabbing, urgent pain struck her and she didn't know what it was, or why it had come as it had, or what it meant.

She stayed in bed for a few minutes, waiting to see if the pain would return. It didn't. So she got up and went into the bathroom. She removed her makeup, she washed, she put on her nightgown, and she let her black hair fall loose to below her shoulders. Adelaide Laurie had a round, moon face, an almond complexion — a legacy from her ancestors, who came from southern Italy — and luminous brown eyes that were set out on the surface, fathomless brown eyes that one could search and search and still not find bottom. She was bunched thickly in the upper torso, but she tapered down finely, a small waist and thin legs. When she was at her best, she was a striking woman.

She looked at herself in the mirror and, combing her hair, forgot about the mysterious stomachache. When she came out of the bathroom it was just after eleven-thirty. Only a half hour more for Rocco and he would be on his way home. The thought pleased her.

As she was walking from the bathroom to the bedroom the doorbell rang. Buster began to bark. She thought, who could be ringing my doorbell at eleven-thirty? She didn't expect Rocco yet, it was too soon. My God, she said to herself, who could that be? Suddenly, she felt frightened and sick.

When once Adelaide Laurie was asked, "Would you say you had a happy childhood?" she shook her head slowly and her face grew solemn. "No, no, not at all," she said, as if it was the most ordinary thing in the world to say and how could anyone possibly think that her childhood could have been at all happy?

Her father's name was Vincent Dimeo and he was born in Naples but came to America when he was eight years old. During World War II he served as an army nurse.

28

He was stationed in Europe right after the war and he went to Italy to visit his mother's second cousin, who lived just outside of Naples. The woman had a daughter, Mary Conchetta Marianna, and Vincent Dimeo fell in love with her. He came back to his home on Staten Island and told his mother and father that he wanted to marry the girl he had found in Italy. They gave their approval, so he sent for Mary. He was then twenty-six years old and his bride was a year older. They were married in 1947. Adelaide was born on March 18, 1948. A second daughter, Linda, came along almost exactly a year later.

Mary was a tiny woman and, in the manner of European wives, completely devoted to her husband. She did everything her husband asked her to. If he said, "Don't wear that blouse," she would change it for another. Mary was happy with Vincent, especially happy to be with him in America.

In the beginning everyone lived in the mother's house — Vincent, Mary, the two girls, and Vincent's unmarried sister, Anne. Anne remembers that everyone spoiled Adelaide because she was so shy and adorable and she was the first grandchild.

When the girls were very young the mother, who made all their clothes, dressed them alike, the only difference being that Linda would wear blue and Adelaide would wear pink. But the sisters were really quite different. Linda was the bigger of the girls. Adelaide was a gawky child. And Linda was always more independent and outgoing than Adelaide. Adelaide was an introverted and sensitive child. When Linda was seventeen and going to nursing school she would come home at night and, during supper, would talk about her hospital work. And sometimes Adelaide wouldn't be able to finish her supper. She never liked to hear about illness and death, possibly because there had been so much of it in her life as a young girl.

Her father was a career soldier and just after the Korean war started he moved his family to a small house in the West Brighton Beach section of Staten Island. As the war continued, he was transferred to Germany and the girls were left alone with their mother.

Adelaide remembers her mother as a pretty woman who spoke no English and was very good with beads. She remembers her sitting at the kitchen table all day and beading, making beads for bridal gowns and the fancy collars that were the style in those days. When she finished she would roll up the beads and take them into New York City to the man who paid her for the work. He would have preferred her to work in the factory but she had to take care of her daughters so he let her take the work home. Sometimes the girls would accompany their mother across the harbor on the Staten Island ferry to the city.

Adelaide loved her mother but at that age she loved her grandmother even more. Life wasn't really the same for her when they moved out of the grandmother's house and when the father was sent overseas. So she would come to her grandmother's for a day and want to stay a week and there was always a scene at night because she didn't want to go home. The family was very indulgent because they were trying to make up for the fact that her father wasn't at home. Adelaide's Aunt Anne was courting at the time and the man she later married, Dr. Matthew Iammatteo, felt the family was overindulgent toward the child. The first time he met little Adelaide he asked her innocently to do something for him and she answered back: "You can't tell me what to do." Later he told Anne, "Maybe you people don't realize it but you're spoiling her. You should watch her."

At that time Adelaide and Linda were attending St. Paul's Grammar School, which was near their house. Later they went to Blessed Sacrament Elementary School, which is affiliated with the church where Adelaide and Rocco Laurie were married. Adelaide's father believed in a Catholic education but Adelaide wasn't crazy about the school because she found the nuns too strict. She liked it much better when she got to high school, when she became involved in activities like volleyball and softball, and when she met Rocco Laurie.

In 1955 Adelaide's mother found a lump on her breast. Tests confirmed that it was malignant. Adelaide's father made arrangements for his wife to be operated on by specialists at an army hospital in Frankfurt, Germany. So the girls were taken out of school and went with their mother to Barcoli, the mother's hometown, outside of Naples. Mary wanted her daughters to see her mother and her home, and she wanted to go home, too, for she thought it might be the last time. The girls stayed in Barcoli while the mother went on to Germany for the operation. Two months later the father came and got them and brought them back to Frankfurt to visit their mother. Then he flew home with the girls while the mother flew ahead of them to the naval hospital at St. Albans. The hospital was not far from where the family of Gregory Foster had recently moved from the Bronx.

When Adelaide returned, her grandmother couldn't figure out the kind of Italian the girl was talking because it was pure Italian, not dialect. "What did they do to this girl?" the grandmother asked. "You know, I can't understand her."

The mother was released from the hospital. She had to have treatments every week but the cancer seemed to have been arrested.

Adelaide's aunt was married to Matthew Iammatteo, a chiropractor, in September of 1956, and Adelaide's mother was able to attend the wedding. And for a while she was happy. But shortly after the wedding she had a recurrence and she was sent back to St. Albans.

That Christmas she was too sick and suffering too much for the children to come and see her. She called them on the phone to wish them a merry Christmas. Then in January and February she began to sit up and the doctors thought that maybe she was improving. But all the time she was suffering terribly. She went into a coma in early March and died on March 15, 1957, ten years after coming to the United States.

Adelaide was nine years old. There was no way to measure the impact of her mother's death on the little girl. If it affected her, the signs were not visible. It was a much greater shock to both girls when their father died.

A year after his wife's death Vincent Dimeo decided he should marry again, find someone who could take care of his two daughters. The woman he found turned out not to be exactly what he had in mind.

Actually, Adelaide's grandmother and her Aunt Annie made the match. The woman lived on Staten Island. She had been married before, briefly. She seemed very nice, she was especially nice to Vincent's girls. She would take them out to eat, to a movie, to shop. She was good to them.

So they were married. They took a small apartment and the girls

31

stayed with the grandmother. It was supposed to be a temporary arrangement but Vincent's new wife, who was now pregnant, kept finding reasons for not having the girls move in with them. Finally, the father, who was stationed at Fort Wadsworth on the island, insisted: "The girls live with us or I leave." The wife gave in.

But nobody was very happy. Some nights the stepmother would lock herself in her room and cry all night.

When the stepmother had her baby, a girl, Adelaide and Linda were again shipped back to the grandmother's. The weeks went by and the stepmother made no effort to have the girls come back. Finally, Vincent Dimeo, who was normally the most mild-mannered of men, indeed a passive man, could stand it no longer. He told his wife, "I have three daughters, not just one. I want them all with me." The girls moved back with their stepmother.

There was constant tension. Very late one night Adelaide was wakened by loud voices; a bitter argument was raging between her father and stepmother. The Iammatteos rushed over. So did Adelaide's grandmother. Adelaide didn't know what it was all about but she knew it was bad. She stayed in her room and pretended to be asleep.

The next day, when Vincent came home from work, he found his clothes on the porch. The marriage was over.

He asked the army for a transfer; he no longer wanted to be anywhere near his wife. He was sent to Fort Devens in Massachusetts.

He wrote his daughters often and called them on the telephone. Early in March of 1961 he called the girls to tell them that he would be home for the long Easter weekend. The girls were overjoyed. The grandmother began to make Italian cakes for the holiday.

On Wednesday, March 29, Matty Iammatteo received a phone call. It was Vincent's wife.

"I just got a telegram from Fort Devens," she said. "Vinnie dropped dead."

It was Holy Week and the girls were at mass. When they came back they heard people crying in the living room. Their uncle was waiting for them in the vestibule.

"Girls, I have bad news for you." He paused, finding it hard to stitch the words together. Finally, he said, "Your father's died."

32

Linda screamed. Adelaide ran out of the house. Nobody knew where she went, but she stayed away for an hour and a half. When she came back her eyes were red. She said nothing. The thirteen-year-old girl was shut within herself.

The first time the girls went to the wake, the first time Adelaide saw her father, she fainted. He was only forty years old, he had never been sick a day in his life. When she recovered, she cried out, "That's not him. You're just lying. That's not him."

The girls now were brought up by their grandmother permanently. It was an arrangement that they were used to, and they loved their grandmother and grandfather. But Adelaide was thirteen and Linda was twelve and their grandparents, though they were vigorous people, were almost seventy. There was a double generation gap that was difficult to overcome.

The grandmother found herself favoring Adelaide. Linda was more independent and self-reliant. Adelaide was shy and vulnerable, and she always did what she was told. If, for instance, Linda went out on a date and was told to come home by ten she would stay out to ten-thirty or longer and not think anything about it. That was no problem with Adelaide because she never had dates.

She was quiet, a bit plump in those days, and painfully shy. Linda, who felt sorry for her, would say to her friends, "My sister is beautiful; if you could only see her, she's beautiful."

Adelaide Dimeo was a private person, introverted, meek appearing, afraid of opening relationships with people for fear of being rejected. She had loved her mother and her mother had been taken away from her. She had loved her father and he had been taken away from her. It was almost foregone that when a man like Rocco Laurie came along — a handsome, strong, self-assured young man who knew exactly what he wanted out of life — she would be swept off her feet. And it was foregone that she would react with a fierce possessiveness that would cause others to laugh at her and some to wonder about her sanity. Nobody seemed to understand that Rocco Laurie, when he brought his love exclusively to her, offered something Adelaide had never before known in her life. He brought a completeness to her life. So she overreacted. She wanted him and nobody else, and she wanted nobody else to have him. It had to be that way for her. It could be no other way.

Rocco Laurie and his partner, Gregory Foster, had been working on some difficult cases in the Ninth Precinct and Laurie came home exhausted on Wednesday night. He was in a dead sleep the next morning when Adelaide woke and dressed quietly. She worked for the telephone company on Staten Island and had to be in by nine. Before she left she bent over her husband and kissed him. She whispered, "I'll see you tonight."

"All right," he mumbled. "Set the alarm for ten." He had to take her grandmother and grandfather to the doctor for a checkup. At twelve-thirty that afternoon, on her lunch hour, Adelaide called the grandmother knowing that Rocco would be there. He answered the phone.

"What did you eat?" she asked.

"She made me steak and eggs."

Adelaide gasped. "Go ahead, get fat."

"Yeah," Rocco laughed. "Say, I'm going to pick up Frank Salt and drive him into the city." Salt was a police officer, too, and a friend.

"Okay. Listen," the wife said, "be careful."

"I'm always careful, Pest." That was his pet nickname for Adelaide. They talked a little longer and Adelaide reminded Rocco that she would wait up for him.

Straight from work she went shopping. She got home about seven-thirty, made herself a scrambled-egg sandwich and gave half to the dog. She went upstairs and tumbled onto the bed in her sweatshirt and dungarees and watched Owen Marshall. Later in the evening she went downstairs and had some potato chips and a soda. Then she came back up and watched more television. And that was when the sudden pain scorched her stomach. Pain is supposed to be a warning that something is wrong. But that didn't occur to her, because it passed so quickly. Later, in her fright, she thought of it, after her doorbell had rung and the dog had begun to bark and, in the small window above her front door, she saw the hat of a policeman.

Her first thought was that Rocco was playing a trick on her. He had done that once before. He had rung the bell and said, "Police officers, ma'am," and he had scared her then. He liked to tease her. She thought, maybe he's playing another trick on me.

She ran into the other bedroom and looked out the window to see if Rocco's car was out there. She saw a police car, and then she knew something had happened.

She couldn't answer the door. The bell kept ringing and now they were pounding on the door and the dog was in a frenzy. But she was frozen. She couldn't walk down the stairs.

Finally, she threw on a coat and came downstairs and let them in. They were from the Staten Island precinct, just a few blocks from the house.

One of them said, "Mrs. Laurie, your husband's been shot, but he's still alive."

She began to scream. "My God, my God, how did it happen?"

"Do you want to get dressed fast? We'll take you up to the hospital."

"Where? Where is he?"

"Bellevue."

She ran upstairs and threw on some clothes. She was frantic. She came down and they all went out the door and Buster ran out. One of the officers ran after the dog and finally caught up with him and brought him back to the house.

In the car speeding toward Manhattan, Adelaide sat in the back seat, crying. Like the radio car that took Jackie Foster to Bellevue, this one had its radio off, too. The only sounds were those coming from deep within her. "Tell me the truth," she cried out, "is he all right? Is he still alive?"

Under his breath, one of the cops mumbled, "We don't know that much about it. We just came on duty."

"My God, my God, he has to be all right."

Almost in unison the police officers said, "Don't worry, he'll be all right." She didn't believe them. Her crying pierced the night. She didn't notice that snow had begun to fall.

Within hours after the ambush at Eleventh Street and Avenue B police and detectives had pieced together the details. There was some question about the movements of Rocco Laurie and Gregory Foster just before it happened — but there was no doubt what had happened.

A car was parked in front of a hydrant on Avenue B, across the street from the Shrimp Boat luncheonette. At approximately ten minutes to eleven Foster and Laurie went into the Shrimp Boat and asked Bill, whose real name was Walter, if he knew who belonged to the car. Bill said he didn't know. He walked out of the store with the cops to get a better look at the car. No, he didn't recognize the car. The partners started walking up Avenue B. As they did so, three black men brushed past them. One of the men looked to be about twenty years old. He was six feet tall, around a hundred and seventy pounds. He was wearing a short dark jacket. The second man, also about twenty or twenty-one, close to six feet tall, a hundred and seventy-five pounds, had on a green fatigue jacket and a black Australian-type bush hat. The third man, a little taller and slimmer than the other two, wore a black three-quarters coat and a pea cap.

The partners were fifteen to twenty feet past the Shrimp Boat when the three men, who had just passed them, whipped around and opened fire at their backs. The men, it was determined later, used three foreign-made automatic handguns — a .38 automatic and two 9-millimeter automatics.

Neither cop had the opportunity to get at his gun.

Foster was hit first. He was hit eight times, three times in the back. He fell immediately, sprawling on the street facedown.

Laurie was hit six times. Most of the bullets struck his extremities, but one caught him up high in the neck. He staggered on the sidewalk, clutching his throat. Slowly, he dropped to his knees. Then, like a stately tree that has taken its last piercing cut, he toppled over on his side. The hand that was holding his throat moved to the side of his face upon the impact of his fall. As the partners lay there, the assassins continued to pump bullets into them. Two of the men reached down and took the cops' guns.

A car was waiting on Eleventh Street, near Avenue A. Two of the men ran down the street. The other began to do a jig in the street, firing his gun repeatedly in the air.

The automobile, a gray 1967 Chrysler, was later found abandoned near Union Square, at Fourteenth Street and First Avenue, close to the entrance to the BMT Canarsie subway line. The engine was still running when police found the car. Detectives figured later that the gunmen abandoned the car when they

36

heard the siren from the police car that was speeding Rocco Laurie to the hospital. A cop went into the subway station. He found three spent cartridge casings on the tracks and two on the platform, indication that the three men had casually unloaded their guns while waiting for the subway train to take them to Brooklyn.

Nate, the fat man who left a hand and assorted fingers in Vietnam, hears the shots — the *bap, bap, bap* — and begins to dress. Then comes the wail of police sirens. Nate runs downstairs and outside, stopping for a brief instant at the same spot where, moments earlier, he and Greg Foster talked.

"What happened?" he asks the first person he sees.

"Someone got shot down the street."

When Nate gets to the corner all he can see are cops — cops jumping out of taxis, cops climbing off buses, cops in police cars, cops on the street. The sidewalk in front of the Shrimp Boat is clear, and roped off; the wounded policemen are gone. Nate sees blood on the sidewalk. For just one moment, a startling moment when time seems to stop and run backwards, he imagines himself back in Saigon. The blood on the street is his blood — has come from his body — and he remembers how his partner has stepped on a land mine that is dead but has been wired to another mine that is not dead, that jumps up and blows off his hand and leaves five of his buddies dead on the street, flesh and limbs and blood mingling into a grotesque compost heap on that street in Saigon. And then time moves forward again.

"Who got shot?" he asks an onlooker.

"Foster and the other guy."

"They dead?"

The man shrugs. Nobody seems to know.

Nate shudders. He thinks, man, it's gonna get hot down here. They might start shootin' up Eleventh Street. I'm goin'.

He runs over to the apartment where his boss, Buddy Williams, is staying with his girl. He bangs on the door. Nate hears a sleepy voice say resignedly (it is a voice that is programmed for this kind of interruption), "Who is it?"

"Nate."

37

Buddy opens the door. Nate tells him that Foster and Laurie have been shot.

Buddy Williams, a stoop-shouldered, gentle-looking black man, and his girl, Marie, dress quickly. They know they will be receiving company before long. They are right. Buddy estimates that before the night is over thirty cops will have come through the apartment, all of them pissed. He is black and they want to know what he knows, which is nothing. They also want to see for themselves that nobody is hiding in the apartment, that Buddy Williams and his white girl friend are not sheltering any black men who have tried to kill two cops. It is a bad night but it would have been a lot worse, he knows that, except for the fact that Foster is black. That cools it a lot. Nevertheless, it hits him that he is, temporarily at least, a part of a police state, that he is living in a police state.

There are five arrests listed from 11 P.M. to 1:10 A.M. on the log of the Ninth Precinct that night of January 27. All are for possession of loaded pistols or revolvers. But the shakedowns are somewhat more extensive. Jim Liedy, who has driven Rocco Laurie to Bellevue, comes back and goes out with a number of cops who are now off-duty. They go into all the bars in the area and it is straight out of *The French Connection*. The cops walk in, holler for everyone to get against the wall, and the bar occupants start dropping everything from their pockets. That includes pills, powder, and guns.

Lenny D'Alessandro, a boyhood neighbor of Laurie's, is in the Fourth Precinct that night, working with other cops because of the telephone strike. He and George Mahoney, also a regular patrolman in the Ninth, get back to the station house at eleven-thirty. D'Alessandro sees a car, with the red light flashing, parked outside the station house. The front door is open, which is strange because it is so cold. "George," D'Alessandro says, "I have a feeling something happened in the precinct tonight."

"What is this?" Mahoney says. Mahoney is skeptical because D'Alessandro likes to fool around with him, claiming he has extrasensory perception. "George," Larry repeats, "something's happened in here tonight." When they walk in the door they are told

38

about it. D'Alessandro and Mahoney work all night. It is snowing now and it is cold, but that doesn't bother D'Alessandro, Mahoney, or the others. They search through bars, they stop people on the street, they halt cars. One of them finds a man on Twelfth Street and Avenue C sitting in a car with a girl. The cop walks up to the car, starts asking questions, and notices that the man is acting nervous. He pulls him out of the car. The man has a loaded .45 on him.

Richie O'Neill is the Ninth Precinct's Patrolmen's Benevolent Association delegate. The PBA is in effect the New York patrolmen's union. O'Neill is a man in much demand when cops have grievances. He knows everyone in the precinct and has personal contact with most of them because when they have problems they come to him. He is always available when there is trouble. This night he is sleeping at his mother's house in Yorkville. She hears the news on the radio, that two cops in the Ninth Precinct — not yet identified — have been shot. Immediately, she wakes her son. He picks up the phone to dial the precinct. This is the fourth time in two years that he has had to make such a call, and he hates it because he doesn't know what they will tell him and he doesn't want to know and the receiver trembles in his hand. And he thinks, whoever they tell me has been shot or killed, it's not going to feel better or worse; it's gonna hurt.

One of the cops of the Ninth is climbing into bed at eleven-thirty when he hears the news. He gets dressed and comes back to the precinct and immediately takes charge of the cops who are hanging around in plain clothes trying to decide what to do. He tells them, "Let's start walking around, maybe we can pick up somebody." He knows that in such situations the sooner you hit the streets the better chance you have of discovering something, a witness or someone who might open up and tell them who has shot down two cops in cold blood.

He does find a man with a gun and he makes the arrest and brings him back to the station. When he gets to the entrance, New York City Police Commissioner Patrick Murphy is there, standing by the door. The prisoner is giving the cop a hard time and the cop says, "Listen, all I want you to do is go in that cell and shut your goddamn mouth." Murphy doesn't like the tone of the cop's voice and says something and the cop answers back, not able to help himself. He is thinking, you're the commissioner, you're standing here in a nice clean suit coming off the street and we've got two cops in the hospital, maybe dead out there, and all you can think of is why mess up the guy who's carrying a loaded gun. He doesn't like the commissioner's tone of voice or attitude. If he's going to be our leader, the cop thinks, he's got to show us he cares a little bit. We care, because these are cops who work in the Ninth. They are our friends. They work with us. They play with us. They kid around with us. And all this man, the commissioner, can think about is, don't go for the prisoner, be careful with this guy with the loaded gun because he might file a complaint against the department.

Captain Edward Rogers, who has been running the Ninth Precinct for only a year, is planning to start work at seven in the morning. So he decides he will stay over and sleep in the bedroom the precinct provides for him on the top floor of the station house. At ten-thirty he goes out for a meal. He is sitting in Ratner's on Second Avenue, a restaurant that serves only kosher food, which Irish cops in the area, even captains, occasionally find diverting. As Rogers is eating, the restaurant owner walks up to his table.

"It's a terrible thing about those two patrolmen of yours."

Rogers looks up, startled. "What are you talking about?"

The owner explains what he has just heard over the radio. Without saying a word, Captain Rogers rushes out of the restaurant. When he gets back to the precinct the division inspector is there. He tells Captain Rogers to go right over to the hospital.

Darryl Anderson is off duty, driving from Brooklyn to his parents' apartment in Queens, when it comes over the radio that two patrolmen in the Ninth Precinct have been shot. That is all he hears. No names are given. It strikes him immediately that Greg Foster is in the Ninth Precinct, but he says to himself — hey, this can't happen to a friend of mine. He snaps off the radio. Darryl Anderson met Gregory Foster when they were both police trainees. Foster, Anderson, Jim Duffy and Larry Chiles were the only black men training for the police at that time. They all became good friends. Driving home, Anderson remembers a conversation he had with Foster two weeks earlier, the last time he has seen his buddy. The two were just sitting around and talking, telling about their job and its hazards. It came around to how sometimes cops did get killed.

"Hey," Darryl said, "ain't nobody gonna get us. I see you twenty years from today."

Foster grinned. "I been to Vietnam. I got shot. They're not gonna get me here."

Anderson remembers the conversation, and how Greg Foster always had these little sayings, always used to tell him and Jim and Larry: "Watch your back! Watch your back! You got to watch your back on this job."

And Anderson remembers again the last time he has seen Foster, how when they split and Greg had slapped Darryl's open palm, he said, "You take care of yourself." And Anderson replied, "Don't worry about me. Everything's covered."

Thinking back to that conversation, Anderson suddenly feels uneasy. He presses his foot on the accelerator. He wants to get home.

At about twelve-thirty in the morning, Dr. Matthew Iammatteo is awakened by the telephone. The caller identifies herself as Betty Smythe, a policewoman. Betty Smythe had gone to high school with Dr. Iammatteo twenty-five years back.

"You're Adelaide Laurie's uncle, aren't you?" she says.

"Yes."

"Well, she's at Bellevue Hospital. Her husband's been shot."

He rushes to his closet and starts dressing.

Rocco Laurie's mother is sitting in the living room. Rocco's father is in the bedroom asleep. It is quarter after twelve and the mother is listening to the news. It is a habit with her now; she has done it ever since Rocco's days in Vietnam. She sees the time and thinks, good, he's only working till twelve so he's on his way home.

She has had two teeth pulled that day and she is in pain. She gets into bed but she can't sleep. She has rosary beads in her hands and for some reason she can't understand she begins thinking about the black people who lived next door to her when she was growing up in Elizabeth, New Jersey. She lived in a tenement and her father owned the store down below and the black girl's father used to come in and buy snuff. Mrs. Laurie thinks how they were all so nice. They keep running through her mind, those black people who lived in the tenement next to her. How they used to call her Miss Anne. How they were all so nice and respectful. She has the rosary beads in her hands and she keeps asking herself, why am I thinking about Old Lady Brown sitting in her chair, smoking her corn pipe, using her snuff? And then the phone rings.

The wives reach the hospital just after midnight, a few minutes apart. Adelaide Laurie wears a gray coat. She is hatless and the back of her thick, uncombed hair sprawls over the collar of her coat. Her eyes are lifeless.

Jacqueline Foster arrives looking, someone says, like an African Queen in her fur-trimmed Cossack coat, the turban on her head. When she sees the photographers she starts to button the coat.

She is bewildered. She sees all the police around, the lights blazing for the television cameras, the photographers snapping pictures. She looks around thinking they will take her straight to Gregory. But instead they bring her to a small side room. They ask her to sit down. Monsignor Joseph Dunne, the Catholic chaplain for the police of New York, comes over to her. He is wearing his vestments.

Adelaide Laurie thinks she sees hundreds of cops around. All she can see are uniforms. She sees Murphy, the commissioner. She says, it's got to be something bad. Even though they keep telling me it's nothing, it's going to be all right, I know something is really wrong. Otherwise, why would everybody be here? And she keeps asking, let me see him. And they won't let her see him. They keep trying to make her sit down and go inside. . . . It is just awful. It is so confusing.

While she is standing there, somebody flashes a wristwatch in front of her face and says, "Is this your husband's?" She says, "I don't think so." . . . They take her into another room and she is

42

kept waiting and waiting. She cries, "Let me see him." They don't want her to see him. . . . While she is in the room she hears a lot of people screaming. She hears somebody saying, *"My brother, my brother."* She thinks it must be Foster's family but she doesn't know what to do. She doesn't know where to go. She can't sit. She can't stand. . . .

She wants to see him. And they won't let her in to see him. She is sick. She just keeps saying, he's got to make it, he's got to. They try to give her a tranquilizer but she won't take anything. She doesn't want to take anything.

The one family sorrowing in one room, the other family sorrowing in the other room, not knowing if it is life or if it is death.

Gregory Foster's father, born in the West Indies, come to the United States, married to a woman of strength and will. Driving a bus for the city of New York. Fathering a family. The one son coming into manhood before his time. The son himself fathering a child, then going off to Vietnam and returning a hero. And joining the police force and linking up with Rocco Laurie, the white cop.

Rocco Laurie's father, born in the United States of immigrant Italian parents. Faithful employee of Consolidated Edison on Staten Island. Resolute middle-class values. Married very late in life to a woman of strength and will. Fathering two sons. The one son growing up securely on Staten Island. An athlete, a good student, patriotic enough to volunteer for the marines. A hero in Vietnam, too. Then returning to become a cop, a good cop. Linking up with the black cop, Gregory Foster.

Partners. A team that works well together despite the strain of America in the 1970s on them both, especially the strain of race, the widening gulf between black and white. America in the 1970s . . . Vietnam and violence, race and drugs, and children going bad. Not Rocco Laurie. Not Gregory Foster. Merging. At the end, merged into one, their blood flowing together on the sidewalk, the flood of love, flowing in that vast urban arena of America, down there where the nerve edges of American life rub raw and the rawness can be seen so clearly. Side by side now in the hospital chamber. Merged, still. How did it come to this? How could it have come to this? "We're alone on this floating island," Bernard

Malamud's white writer tells the black writer in his novel, *The Tenants*, "full of evergreens and purple roses. We're moving with the current. Bells toll in the deep woods. People on both shores of the river are waving as we sail by."

The bells toll and Jacqueline Foster and Adelaide Laurie, sitting in separate rooms at that hospital — separate and alone in their separateness, yet linked forever by the capriciousness of life — hear the bells deep in the woods and both of them know that, for them, the bells are ringing out the past.

PART TWO

Foreign Affairs

The longest war is over
Or so they say
Again
But I can still hear the gunfire
Every night
From
My bed.

The longest nightmare
Never seems to
Ever
Quite come
To
An end.

— JAN BARRY

One day in March of 1968, when Jackie Washington was a freshman at Francis Lewis High School in St. Albans, Queens, she was tripping down the staircase on her way to her sixth-period class. The corridor was teeming but she felt a boy's shoulder touch hers. Through the crowd, through the jostling and movement of kids on their way to class, she felt the one touch of *that* shoulder. She walked on a little bit and then she turned around, and the boy whose shoulder had just brushed hers was looking at her. All of a sudden he winked at her.

That night she couldn't get the boy's face out of her mind. The next day, at the same time, she saw him again. He was in a shop class on the same floor. She asked a boy in her class, "See that kid standing there" — she pointed to the boy who had winked at her — "go find out what his name is."

The boy did. He came back and told Jackie Washington, "His name's Gregory Foster and he likes you."

When her class was over Gregory Foster was waiting again. This time he went over to Jackie.

"You want to go to the dance with me this Saturday?" He didn't even introduce himself. He just asked her the direct question, and Jackie Washington answered directly.

"Yes, but first I got to ask my grandmother."

"Where do you live?" he asked.

She told him and he said, "Oh, we only live two blocks from each other." He told her he had lived there for five years. The reason she never saw Gregory, she found out later, after she got to know him, was that he was a quiet person. He didn't bother much with other people. He never hung out on the stoop or in the streets. He was a loner. But he told her that he had seen her. And he had liked what he had seen. She was fourteen and he was eighteen but she was mature for her age and he was young for his.

They continued to talk in the corridor of the high school. "Can I wait for you after school?" he asked. She said sure. She didn't finish school until five-thirty and he was finished by two-thirty, since they were on split sessions — he started school at eight and she had to be at school at ten forty-five — but he hung around anyway. That afternoon he walked her home and after that they started seeing each other often.

She liked him from the start. She had had other boys but he was the first one, she believed, who really turned her mind. She thought he was cute. He had a little moustache, and enormous brown eyes, eyes that would just stand up and stare. Some of her friends would tell her, "Watch out for Greg, he talks with his eyes." Jackie loved his eyes and almost everything else about him. He was small and chunky and he was brown and clean. Jackie Washington thought he was a very clean person.

She did have a problem with him — he always wore sneakers. Jackie's grandmother had a rule. She didn't want her grand-daughter messing around with boys who wore sneakers. That was low-class, the grandmother felt. She told Jackie, "No boy comes into my house wearing sneakers." But that was all Gregory had. He couldn't afford shoes.

He came over to her house that first Saturday to take her to the dance. He was all dressed up. He even had loafers on instead of sneakers; he had borrowed the shoes from a friend. So Jackie's grandmother let him in, but that was as far as it went. She wouldn't let Jackie go to the dance and Greg had to leave by eight o'clock. After that, though, they managed to see a lot of each other. The grandmother was very strict and protective of Jackie, but she had to attend to a house she owned in the South Bronx and she was away a lot. And when she was gone, Jackie and Gregory were together. They became very close.

He was like a puppy dog with her. That was her expression: "he'd stand underneath me like a puppy dog." He was not that experienced. He told Jackie he had had other girls but that she was the first one he had ever really gotten close to since he was sixteen. There was one girl he had had when he was fifteen and, for a while, Jackie was jealous. It came to her later: the other girl had him when he was a little boy, and I had him when he was a man. I had more of him than she did.

She found him to be a quiet boy, almost solemn, and she never really knew what was going on in his mind. He was a good stu-dent in school and he never got called down to the dean's office and some people thought something was wrong with him; he was too good. There were even times when Jackie felt that maybe he was too good for her.

Between their lovemaking they talked. He talked about his family and she talked about hers and they discovered that there were bonds between them. He didn't have many close friends, nor did she. She didn't care about friends and he didn't either, and at the time she had the romantic notion that they were like lonely lost teen-agers.

His childhood had not been terribly unlike hers, except that drugs were not the problem. Poverty was. Half the time the Foster kids didn't know what Christmas was like or what it was to eat a good meal. He told Jackie that there were times when all they ate for a whole week was cereal — breakfast, lunch, and dinner — because there was nothing else. His father was from Barbados in the West Indies and had come to the United States when he was fifteen or sixteen. His mother's family also came from the West Indies, although she was born in the United States. Greg was the oldest of six children — three boys and three girls — and, as the oldest, he knew how much of a battle it was for sheer survival.

He lived his first twelve years in the Bronx. One who knew the Foster family at the time said that despite constant quarrels between the husband and the wife — with the husband leaving home for periods of time — it was a close-knit family, that the Fosters always believed in the concept of law and order, that they were decent people.

Darryl Anderson remembered Foster telling him that he wasn't on the best of terms with his father. "I won't do anything to hurt him," Foster once told Anderson, "but I won't go out of my way to help him, either." When Jackie got to meet Greg's mother she knew right away that the mother was the dominant figure in the family; or, as Jackie put it, "she had strong hands as a woman."

Like so many black ghetto kids of the day Greg got his real education on the street. At the police academy the black cops — Foster, Anderson, Duffy, and Chiles — told each other about their most memorable fights in the street. Greg Foster allowed as how he hadn't lost too many.

But a street kid has to be able to do more than just fight. He has to have *street sense*. Darryl Anderson once defined street sense as "the make-do of what is given to you out on the street . . . to be able to talk to the lowest form of person and also the highest, and to know what is going on out on the street at all times." The foot patrolman in the city has to have that same kind of knowledge. Greg Foster took his apprenticeship early.

When the family moved from the Bronx to St. Albans, the street kid became more of a man. Things were stabilizing for the Fosters by then and Greg was starting to form the ideas that would take him into manhood.

As the days went on, the relationship between Jackie and Greg deepened. It was the two of them, off by themselves, against the rest of the world. The day Greg asked Jackie to his senior prom was one of the happiest in her life. When her girl friends heard about it — a freshman going to the senior prom — they became jealous. One day they tried to set her up on the school bus.

A close friend of hers always held a seat for Jackie on the bus. This day, when Jackie climbed aboard, she saw the seat had books on it. She went to sit down anyway, and her friend hollered, "Stephanie, do you want the seat?"

They expected that Jackie would get all big and bad and tell Stephanie that she couldn't have the seat and then a fight would start and maybe Jackie would be jumped by fifteen girls. But she was growing up now. She had what she called a very old mind, and she refused to be rowdy on the bus. She told her friend, "Stephanie can have the seat," and went to the front of the bus, where Gregory had been taking it all in and admiring the girl's wisdom.

They almost didn't make it to the prom because the tickets were twenty-five dollars and Greg's mother was reluctant to part with the money. Nor was she very happy at seeing her son pay such close attention to a fifteen-year-old girl. But she finally let him have the money and they had a good time. They went to a beach club in Oceanside. Jackie had on a long white satin gown and Greg wore a white dinner jacket. It was just perfect for Jackie, except that Greg wouldn't dance because he didn't like to dance. Jackie wasn't too happy about that but she enjoyed herself anyway.

Right after the prom the tempo of life quickened and every-thing changed for Gregory and Jackie. During his senior year he had taken a civil service test for the police force; he had known for a long time that he wanted to be a cop. But he failed the test. He took another one and this time he passed. But he was also 1-A in the draft. If he didn't go into the service he would have to remain a police trainee until he was twenty-one, which was almost three years. He thought he would prefer to go into the army rather than just hang around until he came of age.

He went down to Selective Service headquarters with a large group of draftees. He sat in the second row. The director of the draft announced that all those in the first three rows would be drafted into the marines. Greg felt like sliding underneath the seat and crawling to the back. The last thing he had in mind was the marines. But it was too late. On June 29 he was sent to Parris Island, South Carolina. Before he left he tried to cheer up his mother and father, who hadn't wanted him to go in the serv-ice. "Don't worry," he said, "I'll come back with a chest full of medals."

At about the time all this was going on, Jackie discovered she was pregnant.

She didn't tell anyone at the beginning. Greg would write her from boot camp and tell her how much he missed her and how sorry he was that he had gone into the service because of every-thing they had to go through in boot camp. He would also ask her if she was pregnant. He told Jackie that he looked forward to being a father. But she would say nothing.

In September the New York public schools went out on strike. Jackie, at home, didn't know what to do. She was heavier and she felt that she was beginning to show. She was scared. Her grand-mother had always told her, "If you get pregnant I'm going to put you away." Jackie kept saying to herself, I don't want to go to a home. So, thinking to solve all her problems, she ran away.

She stayed with a girl friend in the neighborhood. The girl had gotten pregnant herself and was now married. The girl let her stay the night, but she called Jackie's grandmother. The next day her father came for Jackie and returned her to her grandmother's house. The grandmother wasn't mad, nor was she understanding.

51

"My Jackie," the older woman said sarcastically. "My little angel. I don't know where you found the time to get pregnant." Jackie started to cry. "Why did you run away?" the grandmother asked.

"I didn't want to be put in a home."

"You didn't have to run away. I would have understood. I wouldn't have put you in a home."

The girl couldn't stop sniffling.

"Look," the grandmother said, "it's nothing new. Girls have been having babies since the world began and you just go on and have it and just raise it as if it were your own child."

"It is my own child."

"Well, who's the father?"

Tearfully she told her grandmother.

The grandmother took her to the doctor for confirmation. She wouldn't allow the girl to wear maternity clothes and she wouldn't let her go back to school. Then she called Gregory Foster, who was now stationed at Camp Lejeune, North Carolina.

"Jackie's pregnant," she said right out, not wasting a long-distance phone call. "What are you going to do about it?"

Greg was excited. He didn't get angry, he didn't try to deny her words. He said, "Well, I'll marry her and I'll take care of the baby."

But Jackie knew it wouldn't be that simple. She was despairing. She thought, I don't know, I don't know why it happened like this. Maybe God worked it out this way for me.

Greg came home for a twenty-day leave. From there he would be sent to Camp Pendleton, California, before being shipped to Vietnam. He hoped they could marry, but he was only nineteen and she was underage, too. In New York State the husband has to be twenty-one and the wife eighteen, otherwise the parents' written consent is needed. Mrs. Foster refused to give it.

They had a good time, anyway. Greg would ask her, "Is the baby moving?" She would say, "I don't know." And he would bend down, trying to hear the beat of the baby's heart or the kick of his legs. For he was sure it would be a son. She was, too, though she told him she wanted a girl. She had a name all picked out if it was a girl, Deana Simone. "It'll be a boy," he told her.

He stayed late into the night with her at her grandmother's.

This time the grandmother didn't shoo him home. He took her into the city, where they walked the Broadway–Times Square area and went to the expensive three-dollar movies. He took her shopping and bought her maternity clothes. He told her he would figure out something. "I don't want you to go into the hospital without a man."

When he got to Camp Pendleton he sent her an engagement ring. In an exchange of letters with his mother he thought he had talked her into giving her consent. Mrs. Foster had given him an identification bracelet. On one side was his name. On the other, the words:

Love Always
Family 11-22-68

The marines gave him a three-day emergency leave to go home and get married before going to Vietnam. They made an appointment to meet the mother at the marriage license bureau. She didn't show up. She didn't show up the second day, either. Or the third. Gregory went over to Jackie's house and he was miserable. His wife was six months pregnant. He didn't want to leave her like that. Finally, he signed a notarized letter saying that he was the father of the baby and that if it was a boy it should bear his name — Gregory Foster, Jr.

Jackie and Greg's father went to the airport with him. His mother stayed home. Jackie and Greg kissed good-bye. Greg began to cry, the first and only time she had ever seen him cry. When he got on the plane he quickly closed the curtain by his seat.

Two months later Mrs. Foster called Jackie. She was crying. She said that she was sorry for what she had done. She was working at the St. Albans naval hospital and, Jackie surmised, she had seen firsthand the suffering of the wounded marines returning from Vietnam. She figured that Mrs. Foster was crying from remorse.

Mrs. Foster bought an expensive English coach carriage for the baby. She called Queens General Hospital periodically to see if Jackie was in there yet. But Jackie was late. Then, early in the evening of April 2, Mrs. Foster called the hospital. She found out that Jackie was in and had delivered the baby at five forty-five that afternoon. She was excited in spite of herself and she called Jackie's grandmother to tell her.

It was a boy. The baby's name was written on the birth certificate: Gregory Foster, Jr.

The next day Mr. Foster came to see Jackie and the baby. He told Jackie he would tell the Red Cross so that they could notify the father immediately. For some reason he did not follow through. It was a while before Gregory Foster, Sr., found out he was a father. It would have been difficult to locate him anyway. At that time he was in the bush, learning what the Vietnam war was all about.

The coming together of Rocco Laurie and Adelaide Dimeo was, in the way of white middle-class American households, somewhat more ritualized than the circumstances that linked Gregory Foster and Jackie Washington to one another. Adelaide had known Rocco Laurie, known him in the sense of seeing him around, since she was thirteen, the year her father died. They were the same age and that summer Rocco and his friends played baseball at a playground near where her grandmother lived. Adelaide would say hello to him and he would say hi to her and that was all.

Adelaide in those days, and later into high school, was what Anthony Laurie, Rocco's brother, described as "a plain Jane." She had those glowing dark eyes and that scrubbed madonna look, but she was a bit plump and she was shy. She never dared strike up a conversation with Rocco and she didn't know how to flirt.

She didn't see Rocco again until her junior year at Port Richmond High School, and then it was just in the halls and there was no rubbing of shoulders, no immediate electricity between them. By now Rocco Laurie had developed into a handsome young man. He was a six-footer with the face and look of an athlete. He played baseball and football and he was an outstanding shot-putter. Before his graduation he won the shot-put championship of the New York City public high schools and the Eastern States shot-put championship. Dr. Matty Iammatteo remembers the first impression Rocco made on him: "I noticed he had a beautiful set of muscles." Dr. Iammatteo, a chiropractor, was muscle conscious, and he lifted weights himself.

In their senior year at Port Richmond High, Rocco and Adelaide sat next to each other in the same English class. They talked a little back and forth about the classwork, but that was the extent of it. The only meaningful conversation Adelaide recalled between the two of them in those days took place on graduation day in 1965. The graduation ceremonies were held outside, by the baseball field. The girls wore white dresses and the boys had on tuxedos, with white jackets. It was very hot. The graduates were milling around after the ceremony when Rocco Laurie came over to Adelaide.

"Congratulations," he said.

She began to cry.

"What are you crying for?" Rocco said. "You should be happy."

"Oh, no, I'm sad. I don't want to leave school."

Rocco couldn't understand that. "Well, congratulations, anyway."

She managed to smile through her tears. "Same to you."

Rocco was quiet but very popular. The girls used to call him on the telephone all the time and he would tell his mother, "Hey, Ma, tell 'em I'm not home." And his mother would get mad at him. She'd say, "Come on, Rock, you've got to learn how to get along with the girls." But girls didn't matter as much to him in those days as sports.

He always loved sports. One friend remembered Laurie as the big, slugging first-baseman on the junior high softball team. "He didn't use his strength to bully people, which was unlike some of the kids at the time." That was how people who grew up with him best remembered him — strong and powerful, but good-natured and easygoing.

He came from solid, middle-class Italian stock, and he grew up believing in the same dream that had brought his forebears to this country. The neighborhood in which he lived was all Italian, consisting mostly of families who had recently come from the old country, who were confirmed in the belief that if one worked

55

hard enough he could rise in the economic class system that was so uniquely American.

Rocco's dad, Anthony, worked all his life for Con Edison on Staten Island. He married late in life, at forty-six, and that, plus the fact that he worked shifts and slept much of the time when the boys were awake, made him the lesser influence in the household. Under the best of circumstances, however, he would have undoubtedly had to take second place to Anne Laurie. A big woman, bluff, outgoing, authoritarian, devoted to her family, she made all the key decisions and it was she who orchestrated her childrens' destinies. She was, like Gregory Foster's mother, the matriarch of the family.

The Lauries lived in a small house in the Willowbrook section of Staten Island. Until Rocco was seventeen, he and Anthony slept together in a double bed. But, unlike Greg Foster, there was never any question of where the next meal was coming from. The boys never felt disadvantaged in any way. Their Aunt Connie, who was very close to them, often took them into New York, to the Statue of Liberty or to an Easter or Christmas show at Radio City.

The boys were raised as devout Catholics, attending church regularly. Rocco became an altar boy at Our Lady of Pity Church, a chubby little blond boy with a saintly look on his face.

The chubbiness disappeared once he started to play sports and lift weights, the saintly look also, although he always had an open face. He was a model boy in every way. He was a good student, though he had to work hard for his grades. He would come home from school, eat supper, and immediately do his homework. When he was finished he would read the sports magazines of the day and cut out the color photos and the stories, especially when there was one about a shot-putter. He saved a story on Randy Matson, who was the Olympic champion of the day. Matson, an apostle of clean living, personified the American dream to Rocco Laurie.

After high school he went off to Iona College in New Rochelle, New York, on a track scholarship. Adelaide went to work for a bank in the Wall Street area of New York. Despite his good looks and winning ways he stayed mostly aloof from girls.

There were a number of romances before Adelaide but these were of a minor nature indeed. She never went out much, either. She did ask a boy to her junior prom because she thought he was nice and he came from another high school, which gave her a cachet of sorts. But it was a disaster. She found the fellow so repulsive that she didn't even let him kiss her good-night. And there was no one else until Rocco.

One day in June of 1966 Adelaide and an aunt were driving in the aunt's car. They saw Rocco and a friend waiting for a bus. The aunt lived near the Lauries' and she knew Rocco, so she stopped the car. "You kids want a ride?" she said. They got in. Rocco's friend was going to see a girl and Rocco was off to a party for a friend who was going in the service. Later Rocco told Adelaide that that was the time he made up his mind he wanted to take her out.

A few days later Rocco's mother went into a five-and-ten to have lunch. The girl behind the counter came right over.

"Aren't you Mrs. Laurie?" she said.

"Yes, I'm Mrs. Laurie. Who are you?"

"I'm Linda Dimeo."

Linda had lost a lot of weight since Mrs. Laurie last saw her. She knew Linda because of the aunt that lived in the neighborhood.

Linda and Mrs. Laurie talked and then Linda said, "We're having a pool party at my aunt's. She's put in a new redwood pool. Will you ask Rocco to come?" The mother did and Rocco said okay.

Linda thought that she would like to date Rocco, but that day at the pool, when she noticed that Rocco was watching Adelaide, who had slimmed down and looked lovely, she decided she would encourage it. Not much encouragement was needed. By the end of the day Adelaide and Rocco were holding hands.

That whole summer they were together. Their first "official" date was at a beach party on Staten Island. There were a number of couples there, including Anthony Laurie, Rocco's brother, and his girl friend, Kathy. The evening was made vivid for Adelaide by the rats that swarmed over the blankets. She would be sitting there and she would hear the scratch, scratch, scratch and in the light of the bonfire she could see the little black things scurrying all over the beach. She was nervous anyway because it was her first date with Rocco and she wanted it to go well. The sight and sound of all those black rats was almost too much for her. She began to relax finally when they heated the marshmallows and started throwing them at each other. Everyone got marshmallow-sticky and Rocco laughed a lot and started calling Adelaide by different names — Buster, Boss, Nose (he told her she had a big-Italian shnozz) — and he was tender toward her, and Adelaide thought she was in love.

Adelaide remembers exactly when they started going steady: July 16, 1966. They would either meet at her aunt's house, where they would watch TV while they baby-sat for the children or they would walk around together, hand in hand. They were in their own orbit, locked in together, and everyone else was on the outside looking in.

Rocco's mother saw all of this and she was uneasy. She knew Adelaide was crazy about Rocco and that he liked her, too, but he was only nineteen, he was in college and she didn't want anything to change. Mostly, she didn't want to lose him. One night she confronted her son.

"Gee, Rock," she said, "you're only a kid."

"You got to meet her, Ma," the boy said. "You'll like her."

"Sure, I'm sure I will. I just don't want you to get serious yet."

"What do you want me to do?" His voice began to rise. He was agitated.

"Go out with other girls. Give yourself a chance, Rock. You're too young to know what you want."

He yelled at her. "Mom, I have my own life. You can't always keep telling me what to do, so don't try." He stormed out of the house.

Adelaide understood what was happening and she was terrified of meeting Rocco's mother. One night they made a date to see a movie. The movie house was on the other side of the island and Rocco didn't drive yet so the Lauries volunteered to drive them. It was a very informal date. Rocco was wearing a blue and white striped sweatshirt, white Levi's, loafers without socks. Adelaide had gone out and bought a pair of bell-bottoms for the occasion, navy bells and a red and white striped tank top. Rock brought Adelaide into the house. "Ma," he said, "this is Adelaide."

The mother stood there towering over the girl. She said hello, looking her up and down, then added, "Oh, I can't stand bell-bottoms."

Adelaide felt faint. She wished she could melt away. The mother continued in that deep, gruff voice. "I see those kids on New Dorp Lane with those wild bell-bottoms and, oh, they're so horrible."

Adelaide swallowed and said something about how bells were the style of the day and Rocco hustled her out of the house.

The movie they saw was *Lady L* with Sophia Loren and Adelaide remembered that it was a terrible movie, but she didn't know whether it was the movie that was so bad or whether it was the encounter with Rocco's mother that just made it seem bad. She did know that she could never ever feel completely comfortable with Mrs. Laurie, no matter what happened.

But Rocco's mother made no attempt to stop them from seeing each other. They went to movies, they baby-sat at the aunt's house, they walked the beach hand in hand. Three or four weeks into their relationship, Rocco told Adelaide, "I think I love you and maybe someday we ought to get married."

"Oh, really," Adelaide said, trying to act casual, not believing his words. Her heart was pounding like a trip-hammer. "It's too early to start talking about anything like that," she said. But, still, they kept talking.

He went off to school but he came home every weekend and they were together. Adelaide preferred to have him come over to her house rather than for her to have to face Mrs. Laurie. But her grandfather and grandmother were very strict. They would all be watching television in the living room and when it came to ten o'clock the grandfather would get up from his chair and walk around the room. He would point to Adelaide and say, "You go to bed." Then he would point to Rocco and say, "You go home."

One night in the winter they came back from the movies after eleven. It was cold and Adelaide said, "Come in for a hot chocolate before you walk home." The grandmother heard the stirring in the kitchen and she came downstairs and sat with the couple. "If Grandpa comes down," she said, "he can't say anything because I'm sitting with you."

They missed each other during the week when Rocco was at

Iona but they made up for it by writing to each other. The tone of his letters was lighthearted but, increasingly, Rocco was becoming dispirited by college. Iona had given him a thousand-dollar athletic scholarship because of his shot-putting abilities and his family paid for books and room and board. He felt he owed them something but he just didn't like college. He didn't like the courses he was taking — he would have preferred to major in physical education but it wasn't offered at Iona — and he didn't like the atmosphere. He wasn't the college type. He didn't like to go out drinking, he didn't smoke pot, and he had a girl friend at home. In addition, kids were questioning values he believed in and he never really felt close to them. The war in Vietnam was unpopular among Iona students and Rocco felt at the time that the United States was right being in Vietnam. He was conservative by nature, anyway, and the whole college scene jarred him. He liked sports and that was all. He was just getting by with his grades and he began to feel guilty. He felt he was cheating his parents and himself.

He came home one weekend in the late winter and went right over to see Adelaide. "I have something very important to tell you," he said.

They went for a walk. He was silent for a while. They walked without talking. Then he got it out. "I'm quitting college and I'm going to join the police department."

Adelaide was stunned. "Why?" she asked him. "I don't understand."

"I just don't like college, you know that. And I never wanted a job where I would have to sit at a desk all the time. I want a job where I can be active. I want to be a cop."

After a while she said, "If that's what you want, fine." She squeezed his hand. "But you better tell your parents."

They took it hard. He told his father first, and Anthony Laurie said, "You're going to break your mother's heart."

She heard him out and when he was finished she said, "College is so important, Rock. Without college you got nothing. What are you going to do with your life?"

"Well, I'm going to try to be a cop."

A week later he took his test. He finished his second year at

Iona and then, in June of 1967, he became a trainee with the New York Police Department.

A few months later he and Adelaide had their first fight.

The body of a friend of theirs, John Brown, was shipped home from Vietnam. Brown was only nineteen, the same age as Rocco. They had all gone to high school together and John Brown had played ball with Rocco. He was the first boy Adelaide knew personally to be killed in Vietnam and she was very upset.

The second night, she went to the wake with Rocco and her sister, Linda, who had once dated Brown. At the door to the funeral parlor, Adelaide stopped. "I can't go in. I can't bring myself to go in."

"I'll be with you," Rocco said. "You can just go in and kneel down and go up to his mother and then we'll leave."

So she walked in. Immediately, she felt oppressed by the atmosphere. The coffin was closed and they had John Brown's picture over it and the coffin was covered by the American flag. Seeing the flag reminded Adelaide of her father. She began to scream. She screamed so loud that they heard it across the street at the gas station. Her knees felt weak and Rocco had to hold her up. He was embarrassed and angry. She went over to the boy's mother and instead of consoling her, found herself being consoled by the mother.

When he got back to his house Rocco was furious. "Ma," he said, "I don't go for that. Maybe I'm hardhearted but the way she acted was unnecessary."

The mother was surprisingly conciliatory toward Adelaide. "You're not hardhearted, Rock, but then I can understand her. I know how she was brought up. The Dimeos are very emotional people. First they all hate each other and then they're kissing and hugging all over each other. I don't go for it, but that's the way they are."

Adelaide wanted to go to the wake the next night but Rocco refused to take her. "You get too upset," he said. "It's not worth it for you to get all upset."

"Then I'm going alone."

"Fine. If you want to go alone, go alone."

She did. She also went to the funeral by herself. That night Rocco called her.

"Did you go to the funeral mass?" he asked.

"Yes. What did you do all day?"

"I went to the mass and then went skating with my friends." She was livid. "Oh, you did, really?"

"Hey, Pill" — that was a nickname he gave her when he felt she was leaning too hard on him — "I'll call you tomorrow."

"No, don't bother. Don't ever bother calling me again." She was aggravated by what she felt was his callousness and by his lack of respect for her. Mostly, though, she found it hard to accept his independence. Already she wanted him for herself; she felt he should do what *she* wanted to do, just as she tried to do what he wanted. It was irrational, perhaps, but it was something Adelaide could not control.

"All right," he said, relief in his voice, "I won't call you."

And he didn't.

It was a peculiar time. They didn't see each other for almost two months yet Adelaide would come over to his house every Saturday night to do his mother's hair. That had been going on almost a year, beginning when Adelaide was going to beautician school at night. Mrs. Laurie had asked her then to come and set her hair and it had become a habit. So Adelaide still came to the house on Saturday, arranging to have a boy pick her up each time. Rocco managed not to be around but his mother would tell him that Adelaide was seeing another boy and he would just laugh about it.

Then he decided to enlist in the marines. The reasons were complex. Breaking up with his girl was part of it. But also, like Gregory Foster, he didn't want to spend all that time — he was only nineteen — as a police trainee. He wanted action. He could serve his country and come back, if he was lucky, and go right into the police department. He chose the marines because he felt it was an elite group and it would test him in many ways; it would test his manhood.

She found out about it and she called him. "Before you go," she said, "my grandmother would like to have you come over for dinner." He said all right.

So it started again. They talked for a long time that night.
"Will you write me?" he asked.

"If you write to me first, I'll write to you." The petulance was
still there. She still had to extract a concession from him.

"I'll write to you."

"All right, I'll answer your letters."

They talked about the future. "Look," he said, "you know how
I feel about you, but I don't want you to wait for me. I'm going
to Vietnam and you never know what can happen. I don't want
to tie you down while I'm gone. If you want to go out with
someone, that's up to you. But as soon as I come out, if you
still want to, we'll get married."

"I'll wait for you," she said.

"No, I don't want you sitting around waiting."

"If you tell me to go out, I'm going to sit home and wait. And
if you tell me to sit home and wait, I'm going to sit home and
wait. It doesn't make any difference." He was the one she
wanted to marry, nobody else. She was going to wait for him,
whatever happened. In her first letter to him (she wrote first,
after all) she said: "Please don't stop loving me because I know
I love you and I know I always will."

When he graduated boot camp at Parris Island, the Lauries
took Adelaide with them for the graduation ceremony. They all
came back together. It was on that leave that they decided definitely they would marry. But there would be no engagement yet.
His drill instructor at Parris Island had told the men: "If you
have any plans of getting married or engaged, put it off until you
get back from Vietnam because it's really not fair to the girl if
something should happen."

So they put it off. In September he came home from Camp
Lejeune for a month's leave. They spent most of the time quietly
together. He would come to her house and she would make him
homemade macaroni. And they would play double solitaire, and
they would go to the movies, and they would stay close to each
other.

He was scheduled to ship to Vietnam on November 1. But
when he got to Camp Pendleton, California, he dislocated a
shoulder playing football. So he stayed at Pendleton. He came

63

home again in June of 1969 knowing that would be his last leave.

She picked him up at the airport. He looked strong and handsome in his marine greens. But there was a seriousness in his face, a solemnity she hadn't remembered seeing before.

"We're going to get engaged," he said. "Tomorrow, we'll go and get the ring."

Adelaide was startled by his change of mind, by his assertiveness.

"Why?" she asked.

"It doesn't make sense to wait any more. That's all." They kissed. She felt an overwhelming sense of happiness.

They went to his home first. His mom and dad and brother were there waiting for him. He came in laughing. "Hey, Ma," he said, "you better sit down. We've got something to tell you."

She sat down.

"Adelaide and I are getting engaged."

"So what?" she said quickly. "Did you think I was going to be shocked? I expected it." She began to cry. She hugged Adelaide, thinking, be nice to me, don't be jealous. A mother's a mother, a wife's a wife. It's two different things.

They went home and told her grandmother and she refused to believe it. Even when they showed her the ring the next day she wouldn't believe it. "It's a fake," she said. Finally, they convinced her and she cried, too.

Once when he was in college, Rocco had given Adelaide a ring he had gotten out of a Cracker Jack box. It was a round fake diamond, very plain. He had brought it home as a joke and she told him then: "When the day comes, this is the one I want."

The real ring looked the same. They bought it in a diamond exchange on the Bowery. Then they walked to a restaurant in Little Italy that he had been to when he was a police trainee.

Arm in arm, they were laughing. "This restaurant I'm taking you to," he explained, "is a front for gangsters. It has to be because the place is always empty no matter what time you go in there."

They walked in the big room and the waitress came over to them and said, "Let's see, which table shall we give you?" All the tables were empty. Adelaide and Rocco burst out laughing.

She wouldn't put the ring on right away. She was wearing a

ring he had given her the first Christmas they were dating. She had on a gold locket, too. In the restaurant she took off the ring and removed the locket. "Now," she said, "you can put the engagement ring on me." And he did, and they looked into each other's eyes, each trying to fathom their future.

They finished lunch and started walking. It was a beautiful warm day. The buses kept passing and Adelaide would say, "Should we take a bus?" And he'd say, "No, let's walk." And they walked all the way to the ferry that would take them back to Staten Island.

It was June 5, 1969. In a month he would be in Vietnam.

The column was moving single-file, which is the way you always moved in the jungle, one marine spaced behind another, with enough air in between so that if they caught you in an ambush there might be a reaction. And there might be some survivors. The trail was along a ravine and there was a stream flowing along the bottom. The temperature was in the mid-eighties, not as hot as usual, but that was because there was no sun, just thick fog and humidity that warped minds.

Foster was beginning to adjust, though. He was in the rear of the column, carrying his M-60 machine gun, which weighed twenty-two pounds, plus his ammunition and assault pack and his personal equipment, and all that weight and that heat was not quite as unbearable as it had been when he first came into the bush six weeks earlier. He was getting better at humping hills.

Ahead of him was William Henry Brown, a black marine, a tall man, powerfully built and well regarded by Sergeant Riepe and Sergeant Fiore and Sergeant Lester and all the officers in the command. Brown and Foster had become good friends, having in common, besides the color of their skins, mutual skills as machine gunners and mutual bewilderment at the human condition as it seemed to them in late February of 1969 in the Republic of Vietnam.

"What the fuck are we doing here?" Brown grunted, sweat

65

soaking through his green fatigues. He was from Blytheville, Arkansas, and he normally deferred to his big-city brother.

Foster chose to take the question broadly. "I don't know about you but I'm here because I sat in the wrong fucking row when I got drafted."

"No, no," Brown said agitatedly. "You told me that. I mean *here, now.* What are we lookin' for? No NVA here. Nothin' round but mosquitoes and snakes. Don't make sense, man, chasin' phantoms."

Foster was about to answer when the explosion stunned him. As he hugged the ground, he saw smoke rising from the middle of the column.

The other machine gunner, Ralph Ike, had gotten it.

Seconds passed. Minutes passed. There were no further explosions. The silence, the gray sour jungle silence, was unbearable.

It was a Claymore mine. Both the North Vietnamese and the Americans used Claymores extensively. The American Claymore was a rectangular high-explosive device with pellets on one side of it. It was used to spray a large area, inflict as many casualties as possible. The NVA Claymore was round, almost the same shape as a land mine. They liked to put theirs in a corner, where a trail came up and made a sharp turn. They hung their Claymores on trees or put them on a post about chest-high behind a bush. They used Claymores for psychological reasons — hit the first man and cut him in half and demoralize the Americans. Only this time, for some unaccountable reason, the NVA soldier who held the wires waited before tripping them. He let the platoon leaders — the lieutenant, the sergeants and the radiomen — go through first. Then he detonated.

By a roll of the dice Ralph Ike got it, the first KIA Foster and Brown had witnessed since their arrival in the bush.

Operation Purple Martin, it was called, and if Foster and Brown had known the origin of that term the irony would have struck them immediately. The Young Men's Business Club of Lake Charles, Louisiana, all white, had built the Louisiana Memorial to Peace, a one-hundred-and-twenty-nine-foot tower that looms over the city and the surrounding countryside. It was dedicated to the Americans who were serving in Vietnam, one of the

66

few expressions of patriotism over a war that had, by now, given a majority of Americans acute spiritual discomfort.

Due to its height, the tower attracted large flocks of purple martin swallows each winter as the small, dark purple birds migrated to warmer climates. The patriotic men of Lake Charles requested that an operation be named Purple Martin. Since all operations in Vietnam had code names, to distinguish one from another, and the names tended toward the colorful, it was not difficult to grant that rare patriotic request.

Operation Purple Martin was begun on February 23, the responsibility thrust on the Second Battalion, Fourth Marines, of which Foster was a member of G, or Golf, Company, as it was known phonetically. The mission basically was the interdiction of enemy infiltration routes leading into the Republic of Vietnam. It was also aimed at preventing enemy forces from massing for attacks against forward fire bases and preventing the buildup of large supply areas in the rugged, triple-canopied mountain jungles of northeastern Vietnam, which are all within sight of Laos.

The Second Battalion, Fourth Marines, had a certain tradition, and a taste for such activities. The 2/4 had come into being in 1932, in Shanghai, China, when the marines were helping to keep China safe for democracy. During World War II the 2/4 saw action on Guadalcanal and later at Guam and Okinawa. Marines of the 2/4 were the first American combat troops to set foot in Japan. The 2/4 was deactivated after the war but came back into existence during the Korean war, not in time, however, to become involved in combat. But there was plenty to do in Vietnam, beginning in 1965. The 2/4 was steadily in combat through 1966, '67 and '68 and, at times, sustained heavy casualties. Its last mission before Purple Martin, before Greg Foster joined G Company, was in early December near the DMZ. The battalion, with assistance of artillery and air strikes, succeeded in overrunning a massive, fortified NVA bunker system. They earned the further distinction of killing an enemy battalion commander, a singular achievement in this peculiar war.

The marines of the 2/4 in 1969 were quite different from the career marines who stayed in Shanghai, even from the idealists who fought in the Pacific in a war everyone believed in. Vietnam was infinitely more complicated. Not only was the enemy elusive, there were the complications of race and drugs and guilt about killing Asians in a land that meant nothing to them. The same major elements that were afflicting the nation at home were being exported to the tiny country that had become a touchstone for all human misery. Notwithstanding the good intentions of the young businessmen-civilians of Lake Charles, Louisiana, few young marines in Vietnam were patriotically motivated. All most of them wanted, Foster included, was to serve their thirteen months and get the hell out in one piece.

Relations between black and white marines were almost always tense but Gregory Foster seemed to get along with everyone. He even made it with his staff sergeant, Ray Riepe, who was the most traditional of all marines, who by 1969 had served seventeen years for his country. A commanding officer of Sergeant Riepe once characterized him as being "lewd, crude, loud and profane — and the toughest marine alive."

The commanding officer remembered the day in Vietnam when a marine in Sergeant Riepe's platoon had the poor judgment to fall asleep on post. Sergeant Riepe was carrying a sack of peaches at the time — he loved canned peaches — and he used the sack as a weapon on the errant marine's head. The next day the marine reported Sergeant Riepe and that made the veteran even angrier and he went out again and this time beat up the marine with his fists. When pressed for an explanation from the captain, Riepe said, "Well, goddamn, Skipper, he broke my peaches."

Out in the bush Sergeant Riepe had a nickname. They called him the "Rock Ape." Rock apes were plentiful in the craggy, mountainous area where the marines of Foster's platoon were then operating. When Riepe went weeks without shaving and he had all the fuzz on his face going in nine hundred different directions he looked, according to all reports, like a rock ape. "And," said a sergeant who worked with him, "he kinda acted like one sometimes."

Foster was attached to the First Platoon, which was Sergeant Riepe's platoon. "He was a real fine guy," Riepe remembered. "He was a little colored boy but he was a real good guy. Good to talk to.

"I was always talking to him. When he was on the hills he looked like heck. I mean, you know, he was slow going and

68

nothing seemed to bother him and everything. When you got him out in the field everything seemed to be all right. Nobody had no problems with him. I mean, just because he was colored. A lot of times you'd have problems with 'em. Not him. He was different. I never met one that cooperated like he did."

The implication of course was that most "colored boys" did not cooperate. Riepe's feelings were perhaps more naked than most, but the white marines who served with Foster regarded him — although in less of a stereotyped way — as Riepe did, as an asset to the company.

What went on in the rear was something else again. There were fights constantly between black and white. There were fraggings, grenades thrown into tents of white officers. There was bitterness on both sides, and hatred. Blacks resented the institutional racism of the Marine Corps as a unit and the more elemental racism of the white marines individually. Whites resented blacks because they hung together, because they "dogged" it — they were lazy — and because they were "different." But none of these resentments applied to Foster who, from all accounts, went his own way, offending no one, doing his job in exemplary fashion.

Nor was he ever hung up on drugs. Another buddy, Roland Radford, said, "A lot of cats went for dope and junk. Foster never did. If I'm not mistaken, he didn't even drink beer too much."

The marines in Nam, according to Dale Duke, who was with Foster in the bush, needed pot when they got to the rear. "It was the only high we had, that and hot beer. We got to the point where toward the end of my duty the corpsmen were teaching the guys how to squeeze each other's jugular veins until they passed out for a high."

After coming out of the bush, after fighting the heat and the mountains and a mostly unseen enemy, many marines felt need of a high. Another buddy of Foster's, Mike Brown, went from Vietnam to R and R in Australia. It took him two days to hold a cup of coffee without spilling it. His nerves were shot when he finally did get home.

"Pot was something you didn't do when you might be in combat," Duke said, "but in the rear the whole tent would get together. One time there must have been forty people in there, all in a line. Everybody was lighting a joint and passing it on. You took a drag on one and you had another. But I can say I never remember Foster smoking pot."

One would have to assume that the pressure on black marines, the pressure to prove themselves as men, must have been intense in Vietnam. The pressure on Gregory Foster, slight, boyish, and black, must have been extraordinary. But he was up to it.

When he first joined the company, which was lying at an abandoned artillery base called LZ Stud (it was later renamed Vandegrift Combat Base) in the northeastern corner of Nam near the Laotian border, he created a mixed impression. To Sergeant Gerald Lester, the platoon guide, he seemed a little small. Sergeant Lester, a career marine, stood only five-foot-eight, and Foster was an inch shorter. Lester knew that Foster had to carry a machine gun and ammo all the time and he worried about that.

To Lieutenant John Strange, Foster was that "smooth-complexioned marine." Most marines became muddy and bedraggled in the field, with a couple of days' growth on their face. But, Strange noted, Foster was always clean and fresh.

Dale Duke remembers Foster having problems at the beginning. "He had trouble humping the hills. Each guy in a machine-gun unit — generally three men to a gun — carries four hundred rounds of machine-gun ammunition. Plus some poor devil's got to carry the gun. And then somebody else carries the tripod. And that pretty well weighs 'em down. And we were all in a mountain area and when you first get over there it can take your ass out. So he fell out on a couple of marches and I guess his leader had to knock him around a little bit. In the mountains up there if you fall out you're really tired. You know, no guy's really faking it. But you're not leaving any alternatives. Either the whole unit has to stay in a nonstrategic place to guard you, or they can leave you. Or we can kick your ass and tell you to get up that hill. And kicking your ass to get you up that hill was the way that usually worked the best.

"But after a while he did the job. I remember Foster ended up being the leader of a machine-gun team. And he was damn good. When I had a squad and I had to have a machine-gun team

I always liked to have Foster's team. When I had a patrol that had to go out at 0700 and I wanted that machine-gun team there, all I had to do was tell him how many rounds of ammo I wanted and what time we were leaving and how far we were gonna be going, so he could tell his team how much water and stuff like that to bring. And he always had them right there on time with what they needed. Foster was a little guy but he wasn't afraid to kick ass to get people to keep up."

After the death of machine gunner Ralph Ike, the First Platoon of Golf Company stayed at Fire Support Base Cates, which was down toward Khe Sanh. H (Hotel) Company was up on Fire Support Base Neville and E (Echo) Company was nearby at Russell. Early in March Neville and Russell were hit simultaneously by sapper attacks. They were hit hard. The next morning the weather turned bad and they were socked in and couldn't get their dead out. So Golf Company was relieved at Cates and moved up to try and relieve pressure on the other two companies. The NVA was lobbing mortars every time battalion headquarters tried to get helicopters in to remove the dead and wounded. It began to get desperate for the two companies.

The battalion commander told G Company that it would be a four-day operation. Golf would just go up and clear the ridge lines leading to Neville and Russell. The company was flown up to an old-line support base. From there they searched the hills in the area. There was no contact with the enemy.

The weather was still bad and they couldn't get any supplies in and there was no food.

"Goddamn," Willie Brown said to Foster, "I'm hungry."

"Be cool. They'll drop us in supplies."

"How the hell are they going to do that?" Brown looked up in the sky. It was eerie, a smoky gray. You couldn't see the tops of the trees.

"I tell you what I'll do," said Ronald Radford, who was from Chicago. "I'll bake you a cake."

"You'll bake us a cake," Brown said incredulously.

"And invite the gooks to join us," Foster laughed.

"We'll just eat it amongst ourselves," Radford said. The Marine Corps used dehydrated cake mixes and two of these had

71

found their way into Radford's pack. He stirred a mix and put it in an enamel can and lit a fire, and it burned.

"Shit," he said, "what I do wrong?"

"Get a bigger ammo can, dummy," Foster said. "Get an ammo can that M-16 ammunition comes in. Put some water in it, then take a smaller can like an M-60 machine-gun ammo can, put the cake in that, and put the water inside. That way you'll keep the temperature down."

"Where'd you go to school to learn that stuff?" Radford said. Foster grinned.

The cake got them through the night and then Hotel Company gave them one·C ration per man. But otherwise there was no food. It had taken them four days to get to where they were and now they were told to stay in the area. And they were out of food.

Finally, a C-130, guided by radio communications on the ground, swooped in low and dropped three pallets of C rations.

The next morning Golf Company got its new mission: to go up Catapult.

Catapult was an old fire support base that had been opened by the Ninth Marines a year earlier and then abandoned. It was five or six clicks from the demilitarized zone, on the Cam Roh river. Catapult was just an objective, a piece of high ground that the marines wanted secured.

On March 7 the First Platoon — Foster, Willie Brown, Mike Brown, Radford, Duke, and thirty others — was assigned to patrol the higher ground and valleys leading up to Catapult. They went around a big hill and the fog was so thick they couldn't see where they were going half the time. The patrol spent the night at the top of the hill near Checkpoint 4, on top of a little finger. And they set out ambushes for the evening. The strategy was for the marines to set up ambushes at night because the NVA moved at night. Since the marines moved during the day, that's when the NVA set up their ambushes.

It was warm and humid and overcast. Haflway down the finger the ambush point man, Dale Duke, stopped. Sergeant Lester moved in to find out what was going on.

"I hear movement out there," Duke said.

"You sure?"

"Yes. Sarge, why don't you let me throw a grenade?"

72

Duke wore thick eyeglasses and that made Lester hesitate. "Okay," he said at last, "just make sure, for Chrissakes, you don't hit a tree."

Duke threw the grenade. He hit a tree. The grenade bounced back and the marines hit the deck. Nobody was hurt.

They moved into a hasty defense, forming a three-sided line on top of the hill. A voice could be heard outside the perimeter, from atop the ridge line they were on. Sergeant Lester decided to go and take a look. He took Sergeant Lou Fiore with him. If anybody was there, Lester thought to surprise him and get it over with.

Immediately, he saw him. "Gook," Lester said unbelieving.

He was walking down the trail toward them. He had blood on his face and an AK-47, the NVA assault rifle, in his hands. Lester and Fiore opened fire immediately. The soldier was cut to pieces.

Then the shooting began. Foster and Duke and Brown and the others stripped off their gear, tying their shirts to their waists. They dropped the packs on the trail and took the high ground. They called in mortars. The attack was brief. A point man was grazed in the shoulder, a lieutenant was wounded in the muscle of his right arm and had to be medivacked.

By radio the battalion commander told them to move back to Checkpoint 4, set up ambushes in the area that evening, and await the arrival of the rest of the company.

At Checkpoint 4 the body that Lester and Fiore had wasted was still there. There was blood on the trees, too. And they found their packs had been ransacked.

"Look at that," Foster said. "While we were fightin' the mothers were sittin' around eating our food."

Brown went over to his pack. "Sonofabitch, they took the best food. They ate my pineapple, they ate my pound cake, and they left the beef with spicy sauce and the other lousy stuff."

"We'll have to bake another cake," Foster said.

At one point in the night Foster was staring into the bush and everything was stone quiet. He noticed a sapling sticking out over the bush about fifteen feet from him. Then, all of a sudden, the sapling was bent over, pointed right at Foster. The PFC opened up with the machine gun, spraying the whole area.

The next morning they went up to Checkpoint 5, which was an old abandoned marine position with holes that had already become overgrown. They spent the night at Checkpoint 5. They could hear the NVA walking around outside the perimeter. There was fear among the marines. It seemed to Foster, to Brown, to Lester and the others, that the enemy was trying to figure out how many marines they had to contend with. If the patrol had opened up, they would have found out how small a unit it was. What the marines didn't know at the time was that the North Vietnamese had a whole bunker complex in the valley — battalion strength.

In the morning the patrol started back down to Checkpoint 4, to the site of the first ambush. In the meantime, the North Vietnamese had come up and set another ambush for the Americans. Halfway between Checkpoint 4 and Checkpoint 5 the marines were hit.

The fighting continued for forty-five minutes. Four men from the First Platoon were wounded. One was extremely bad. He had a hole about two inches in diameter in the middle of his chest. The battalion commander ordered the platoon to pull back on top of the hill; he said they would bombard the area with whatever they could get hold of. The weather had begun to clear and some fixed-wing reconnaissance planes came in low and offered a little fire support.

A jungle penetrator had to come in to get the badly wounded marines. The terrain was so thick with rocks and trees and heavy vegetation that it was impossible for a helicopter to land. The penetrator, a big crablike device with legs on it that fold out, was lowered from the helicopter. Gregory Foster helped buckle the wounded marine to the penetrator and they started him up.

The North Vietnamese opened fire. They didn't seem to be aiming for the wounded marine but for the helicopter, trying to knock the chopper down. But they finally got him into the helicopter and it roared off.

The platoon moved to Checkpoint 3, set up a perimeter, and called in medivac to come and get the other wounded. The next day, on March 10, the rest of the company joined the platoon.

The lieutenant in charge was smiling. "Men, there's a blueline [stream] at the bottom of the hill. We'll be taking a bath in the blueline by tonight."

It took the company six days to get down there.

At eight o'clock on the morning of March 11 the First Platoon had the point (was the lead element of the company) and started out of the perimeter, with Lieutenant Wooten in charge. The platoon was shaped like a U. On the left side was a team of three people for flank security headed by Dale Duke. On the other side was another three-man team from Duke's squad, also for flank security. In the middle was the machine-gun team — Doysey G. Miller, the leader, Gregory Foster and Willie Brown, side by side, his assistants. At the head of the U was Lieutenant Wooten and his radioman. Another squad, behind the U, served as a tail.

Outside the perimeter was a ridge line and down from the checkline the ridge line forked into two other ridge lines. One of them turned right to Catapult, which was the First Platoon's objective. The other went straight down to the blueline. It turned out later that the North Vietnamese had their bunkers down by the blueline and that's what they thought the marines were after, not Catapult. And they were going to fight until they had time to evacuate.

It was hazy and a light rain was falling. "Look around you, man," Brown said to Foster. "If the gooks don't have us hemmed in, the fucking terrain does."

"I know what you mean." Foster felt enveloped: steep mountains, thick, almost impenetrable vegetation, no visiblity. All he could see in the morning mist was looming gray shadows, the occasional top of a gray, scarred tree — all pinching in on him, making it difficult even to breathe.

From one of those trees ahead a rocket-propelled grenade whooshed in. The front squad hit the ground and fired into the trees. Nobody was hurt. There was no further firing. It was an isolated sniper, or, perhaps, a warning to comrades back in the gloom.

But nobody knew what was in those trees. Lieutenant Wooten called in for 60-millimeter mortar fire.

The mortars were sitting back at Checkpoint 3 and the first round landed beyond the trees. The mortar tubes were set up in

75

muddy ground and in that first round the recoil sunk the base plate about an inch.

"Drop fifty," Lieutenant Wooten ordered. That meant that the next round would be fifty meters closer. But they hadn't realized that the base plate had sunk an inch and the next round came in a hundred meters closer.

One large tree loomed out of the darkness, fifty to sixty feet higher than any others. A mortar shell hit the tree and the shrapnel sprayed down and caught Wooten in the ankle.

He tried to continue but he couldn't walk. Sergeant Lester and two other marines took him back to Checkpoint 4, which was clear at the time, to be medivacked. And Sergeant Riepe assumed command of the platoon.

Now it was silent. The First Platoon lay on their stomachs, guns cocked. Moments passed. Suffocating heat rose from the ground. The stillness was suffocating, too. Then Sergeant Riepe stood up. He motioned to the others. "Let's go," he barked, and the platoon moved out.

They crawled down the ridge line in that tight U, through thick-canopied jungle, throwing grenades in front of them. They reached a saddle, where the ridge line came down to a little flat area and started up again. "I think I see a hooch," said Duke. "Sit down right here." That's when the NVA hit them.

The ambush began with Claymores exploding. Then they were sprayed with RPGs (rocket-propelled grenades), chicom grenades, and small-arms fire. The NVA hit the First Platoon on all three sides at once. And the front end of that U — Miller, Brown, and Foster — sagged and collapsed.

Nobody knew who was dead or who was alive. Through the fire and smoke Sergeant Riepe hollered, "Is anybody hurt?"

Only Doysey G. Miller answered. Doysey G. Miller of Tyler, Texas, had been named for a buddy of his father's who had been killed in World War II. Doysey G. Miller cried out, "I am, I am, oh God, I am."

But it was too soon to attend to Miller or the others who had fallen down there. For ten minutes there was no communication at all. Firing was going on, heavy from both sides.

Dale Duke remembered: "It was up to the squad in the rear, the tail-end Charlie, to go for the wounded, because we were

76

fighting our own fight. This guy Button got hit on my team. And Ozzie — it was his first fight — went a little goofballs and I had to wake him up. And we were in a bomb crater covering the flank. And it was just a matter of making sure that nothing could live, you know, downhill from you. Throwing grenades and spraying the area, just killing anything that might be in a clump of bushes or so."

Gregory Foster had escaped the first onslaught and had crawled back to join the others. He was waiting for tail-end Charlie to go in and help evacuate the dead and wounded, the men lying out there unprotected, one of whom was his buddy, W. H. Brown. Foster was crying. He knew Brown was hurt bad. He needed help. But nobody moved. There was no way to get to the dead and the wounded because of the heavy fire and because it was impossible to see them in the thick brush. And it was not possible to call in fire support for fear of hitting your own people.

A great rage welled in Foster, a great bitterness, a great anguish. "What are you bastards doing down there?" he cried out. "Why don't you help?"

Nobody moved. He could contain himself no longer. He stood up, grabbed an M-60 machine gun, and ran down toward the men who were lying there, firing from the hip. Completely exposed, he sprayed the area until he ran out of ammunition. He scrambled to another position and picked up an M-16 rifle. He moved closer, to within twenty feet of the enemy. He fired until the barrel of his weapon burned out. He was berserk, out of control.

And, suddenly, the enemy stopped firing, and Foster, falling on his hands and knees, crawled over toward Brown. Brown's eyes were closed. Foster didn't know if he was dead or alive.

At last the others came to help. Dale Duke rushed down and he and Foster lowered Brown into a poncho to carry him up the hill. Sporadic fire came from the brush, fading away. On the poncho Brown's head rolled and it was then that they saw that half his neck was gone and that he must have been killed instantly.

A corpsman went down to get Doysey Miller. Miller's head was filling up with blood. By the time they got him to the top of the hill he was dead.

77

Four others in the platoon were wounded. They started carrying out the dead and wounded. Duke was in a bomb crater watching everything. Then the Second Platoon came in to relieve the First and they put a two-man machine-gun team in the crater.

Duke scrambled out. He went over to a sergeant from the Second Platoon. "Can I return to my platoon, Sarge?" he asked. "I want to help carry the wounded up the hill."

"Sure," the sergeant said. Duke walked off, looking back at the men in the bomb crater who were setting up their gun.

Huey gunships came in and raked the area with rockets and machine guns. The fighting got heavy again and the company commander, worrying that the position might be overrun, called for artillery support.

Battery G at Fire Support Base Neville started lobbing in 105-millimeter howitzer shells. But there was a miscalculation and a 105-millimeter shell landed in the bomb crater that Duke had just abandoned. The two men in there were blown apart. They were a black marine and a white marine. After they were hit there was no way of telling one from the other.

Miller and Brown were flown out that day but they couldn't remove the machine gunners of the Second Platoon because the clouds had come back in. Foster and Duke and the others were exhausted from the long hump up the hill with Miller and Brown and the wounded. But now they had to carry the new bodies. They went back and forth between Checkpoint 5 and Checkpoint 6, waiting for the enemy to let up and for the weather to clear. For four days they carried the bodies with them, three legs in one poncho, assorted parts in the other, the gagging, rotten-egg stench overpowering. Finally, it cleared and a helicopter came in and took away the remains.

The day after the ambush the Second Platoon went past the saddle where the First Platoon had been hit. They found fifteen fresh graves just on the other side of the line separating the Americans from the Asians.

And because he had "saved the lives of numerous marines and inspired other leaders of the platoon to regain fire superiority over a numerically superior enemy . . ." and for his "uncommon leadership, courageous actions and selfless devotion to duty," Gregory Foster was awarded the Bronze Star.

But it didn't mean a helluva lot to him because he had won it at the expense of his best friend in the bush. And, sitting there on Fire Support Base Catapult, which they had finally taken, Foster knew it was not over yet.

G Company reached Fire Support Base Catapult at the cost of seventy-seven casualties. Nobody yet realized what the company had gone through: that it had been up against a numerically superior enemy, that it had battled the equivalent of an eight-hundred-man regiment of NVA soldiers. All of those facts came out later (along with the inevitable statistics — sixty enemy dead, seventeen hundred pounds of rice taken, thirty-nine enemy Claymores, seventy-one mortar rounds, twelve individual rifles, one light machine gun, and a hundred and fifty A-frame bunkers destroyed). Meanwhile, Foster and the others helped tidy up Catapult, clearing the area of Claymores and booby traps. They set up their 60-millimeter mortars and started to go on patrol from there.

The company continued to have contact with the enemy every day. If one platoon went out on patrol, another platoon was in reserve. Every day a platoon either had to go out on patrol, relieve another patrol, or help pull a patrol out of a tight situation.

One day, soon after the company had established a command post on Catapult, the Second Platoon was hit hard. It lost five people, including its platoon commander. The dead were torn apart from Claymores; the point man was decapitated. It was the First Platoon, Foster's platoon, that helped get the others out.

The fire fight on March 18, the loss of his best buddy, William Henry Brown, had changed Gregory Foster in some ways. Though he still laughed a lot, he was now more reserved; there was a gravity about him that had not been there before. Never a mingler, he seemed more withdrawn than ever. He had turned into himself.

79

A more profound change developed in the attitude of other marines toward him. Before the eighteenth, Foster was largely unproven as a marine. He was a black man and, therefore, had to play to the music composed by the white man. Now the other marines recognized him — at least out there in the bush — as one of them, a fighting marine and only incidentally a black man. So, while Foster literally retreated into his own skin, other marines came out of theirs. The breaking down of the ethnic stereotype, a strange and sometimes ironic process that seems to succeed only on a battlefield — whether it be a boxing ring, a basketball court, a patrolman's beat, or a war zone — has always been a part of the American mythology. It was no different in Vietnam. Sergeant Lester, for instance, who had not been in the fire fight, remembered Sergeant Riepe coming back shaking his head. "That's all he talked about," Lester recalled. "Foster, Foster, Foster."

Afterward, old Rock Ape became more friendly toward Foster. He went out of his way to talk to him, trying to draw him out. One night he went over to Foster, who was sitting by himself.

"What you gonna do when you get out?"

"I'm gonna go back to New York and become a policeman."

The Rock Ape laughed a booming laugh. "Hey, you can't make it, you ain't big enough."

Foster looked at the sergeant coolly. "Well, size don't really mean that much."

Riepe changed the conversation. "Foster, you got a girl friend or something?"

"I know a couple." He smiled tightly.

Riepe remembered those conversations, but mostly he remembered that Foster didn't do much talking. There was, he recalled, more action than talking.

On March 23, a clear, hot day, the First, Second, and Third platoons of Golf Company went out on patrol. The Third Platoon's mission was to go down into a ravine, where there was a small spring, and then move up to high ground on the other side. If it met any resistance, the First Platoon would be sitting on the hill just above it as a reactionary force.

The Third Platoon went out. It was still within earshot of Catapult. The men on Catapult heard mortar cans being rattled around. The company commander, Joseph Dwyer, went over to Sergeant Lester.

"Pick up some people," he said, "and go find out what that noise is."

Lester walked around the perimeter asking the men, "Does that sound like water cans from our hill to you?" They all said yes. He went back to Captain Dwyer and told him.

The CO was unimpressed. "Take out a patrol the other way," he said.

Lester picked out eight marines. Before he left he said to Captain Dwyer, "I wish I had more people."

"Better to have eight than eighty," Dwyer answered. Stealth was the reason. It was a reconnaissance patrol, not a combat patrol. (When he did get down there, Lester decided that eighty would have indeed been better than eight.)

He started to move out with his patrol. The day before, he had run a patrol down in the same area and he had found a block of North Vietnamese TNT and left it there. He figured he would take the patrol down into the area he knew was clear and pick up the TNT. That would make his company commander happy.

They crept single-file. The heat was oppressive. The air was still. It was noiseless, like sitting alone in a cork-lined room. Nothing moved.

Lester was in the middle. Ahead of him were Private Felker, Private Bebrin, Corporal Ouellette, and the radioman, Kelly.

They reached the area. The TNT was still there. They picked it up. Lester motioned for them to turn around and start back. They were moving back up in the same order when they were hit.

From higher ground, from the brush and from up in the trees, the North Vietnamese opened up with automatic-weapons fire. All four men in front of Lester caught bursts.

Felker fell, his face slashed by automatic fire that hit him at almost a forty-five degree angle. He was split wide open from his lower lip to his upper lip, across his nose, missing his eye but out through the skin on his forehead.

Bebrin, the second man, went down with six rounds in the left side of the chest, the abdomen, and the legs.

81

KALAMAZOO VALLEY
COMMUNITY COLLEGE
LIBRARY

Corporal Ouellette, the squad leader, took four or five rounds in the shin of his left leg.

Kelly, the radioman, was hit in the shoulder.

Lester was safe. He moved quickly and helped grab Ouellete and dragged him back to cover. And he radioed the company commander, who was already on his way with the rest of the platoon. The other three men who made up the rear of the patrol were safe. Lester was caught out there alone.

I was sitting behind a little-bitty tree, about as round as the bottom of a Coke bottle, just very small. All I had on me was a .45-caliber pistol. (By the way, it wasn't loaded.) And here comes Foster. And if it hadn't been for Foster — well, there was enough of 'em where I couldn't have held 'em off. Because everyone else was wounded and out of action. There were two people down there. I didn't know whether they were dead or alive. Foster came down and he just cleared out the entire nest. With just a regular rifle, an M-16 rifle. He just walked down there with it blazing. And if it hadn't been for Foster coming down there, we'd have all been gone.

Within five minutes the rest of the platoon was down there, two hundred and fifty yards ahead of Lester and the wounded. Quickly they set up a perimeter.

Staff Sergeant Riepe saw the wounded men, Felker and Bebrin, lying there exposed. He saw Lester, helpless behind the three. He heard the vicious cross fire from NVA guns. A move had to be made.

"Get the fuck down there," Riepe told two men in the platoon, Corporal Michael Brown and Corporal Joseph Barbagello. They started down, crawling on their hands and knees. They reached the wounded men and lay next to them. But the enemy fire became more intense. There was no way they could get out the two men without counter fire.

Gregory Foster, back with the others, could stand it no longer. "To hell with it," he yelled. "People are hurt. There isn't time to wait." He got up and ran down to the ravine, firing bursts from his M-16, blasting away, shooting at anything he thought might be the enemy. Gerald Lester couldn't believe what he saw.

He was a one-man army. I mean, he, alone, kept the NVA's heads down. It may not sound like much except for the fact that he was about twenty feet from the enemy — face to face with them — all by himself. And there was no order for him to do it, and nobody would have ordered him to do it. It would have been suicide. But somehow he did it.

About fifteen meters down the trail Foster made contact with Brown and Barbagello. "Okay," he said, "I'll cover you when you're ready to move."

Brown and Barbagello each put their hands under the armpit of a wounded marine. "Now!" Brown cried.

Foster stood up and began firing as the two men pulled back with the casualties. He had magazines loaded back to back, taped together (there are eighteen rounds per magazine) and he continued to fire. It got so hot that the bolt of his weapon actually welded itself right into the chamber. He threw the gun away and picked up an M-16 belonging to one of the wounded. He continued to fire. That weapon got hot too and he was having cook-offs; the heat from the gun was causing the rounds to go off by themselves.

When the two men were out, Foster picked up all the weapons and equipment he could and ran back to the platoon's position.

After the First Platoon got out all of its people, the men moved back on top of the hill, set the platoon in a perimeter, and called in for emergency medivacs to come and get Felker and Bebrin, the two most seriously wounded. It was not over yet. A helicopter came in directly in front of the perimeter at a spot referred to as the razorback (there was a series of razorback hills in the vicinity) and the NVA peppered the chopper with extremely heavy fire.

By now Greg Foster was back to his machine gun, and he was needed. The platoon came under a frontal attack by the enemy while it was trying to get out the wounded. Foster was one of those instrumental in keeping the perimeter from being overrun. But 50-caliber machine-gun fire from the North Vietnamese troops wounded another in the platoon, Michael Morbert, and also hit the pilot of the copter. Despite critical injuries the pilot was able to take off, under very heavy fire. But the bird was hurt. It couldn't retain its power. It went down a few hundred meters from its original landing area. However, the companion helicopter that was circling with it was able to set down and get everybody out. Felker and Bebrin made it back all right but the hero pilot of the first helicopter died en route to the hospital.

Members of the platoon had to carry Morbert and Ouellette back to Fire Support Base Catapult. They did so under lessening enemy fire. Most of the NVA force, it seemed, had cleared out. At Catapult, the wounded were medivacked, and the First Platoon continued to run patrols.

I wrote Foster's mother a few days later to tell her what I thought about her son as a marine. I mean, I had the highest regard for Foster as a marine and as an individual and, I don't know, I just felt I wanted to tell somebody about it and I thought I'd tell his mother. After all, he saved my life. I praised him extremely high in the letter and I still do today. He was one of the finest individuals I think I've ever known and I only wish I had a whole platoon of Fosters.

So, five days after receiving the Bronze Star, Gregory Foster added another medal to his collection, and a more prestigious one — the Silver Star. The last sentence of the citation reads:

"By his courage, aggressive determination and unswerving devotion to duty in the face of extreme personal danger, Corporal Foster [he was then a PFC] contributed significantly to the defeat of the North Vietnamese Army Force and upheld the highest traditions of the Marine Corps and the United States Naval Service."

It was a dirty war, a meaningless war, an unjust war; in so many ways, a shameful war, a dreadful dark stain on whatever heritage we claimed to have possessed. My Lai, massacre, rape, looting, napalm, burning: perhaps Vietnam will be remembered for these assorted horrors. But some men still did their duty. There were men who fought in the old-fashioned, traditional way, cleanly, honorably, for high purpose, whatever the motivation. The record shows that Gregory Foster was one of them.

But it was not over for Foster. He still had to serve his time in the bush. There were skirmishes continuously at Catapult, though they were of a reduced scope. Finally, Fox Company moved in and Golf Company went off to a new position, securing that, and then doubling back to Fire Support Base Neville.

Now the heat was as much of an enemy as the North Vietnamese. Every day the temperature soared over a hundred degrees. And the humidity was unbearably high. The combination of the heat and the humidity and the gear they had to carry and mountains that seemed to grow steeper and steeper caused intense suffering among many of the marines. Foster and the other veterans, having been in the bush awhile, had built up their endurance to the point where they could fairly well withstand the heat and humidity. But it was difficult for the new men.

One day at the end of March, G Company was ordered to move to a new position, sixteen hundred meters from its present base. The air force was going to vacuum-clean the area; the term they used was *Arc-Light*. It would be a massive bombing raid in which B-52s and other planes would come in and cover every square inch of land with bombs — arc-lighting as an art form, special effects created for the land of Vietnam.

That day, the First Platoon, which was down to eighteen men, picked up six new people. The First Platoon was the point again, though Sergeant Lester kept the new men toward the rear, where they wouldn't have to work quite as hard and might have time to get used to the climate. For most of the way the platoon had to cut a path through thick underbrush. It seemed like an easy movement to the old-timers. But to the new men it was misery. With the temperature over a hundred the men were continuously perspiring. They had salt tablets and each person had a ration of a canteen of water — about a quart for the day — but in that heat and with the activity they were engaged in, it wasn't enough for many of them.

The objective was upground, a little razorback-type hill. Before they were halfway there the company commander noticed the condition of the men. "Turn right and head for water," he hollered.

Already two of the new men from the First Platoon were in very bad shape. Sergeant Lester, walking behind one, gave him all his water and dumped some on the man's head to cool him off. Foster shared his water with one of the other new marines. "Come on, man," he said soothingly, "we're almost there. We get there, everyone'll have all the water they need." But the new men — almost all of them — were tottering.

They got down to the ravine, to water, but it was too late. One of the rookies went into convulsions and died. A few minutes later another one died the same way.

Doctors conducted autopsies. Opening them up, they found the men were as dry as cotton. The doctors said they were so dehydrated that it looked as though they had been dead for about a week.

When the battalion colonel heard about the deaths he screamed that the men had been pushed too hard. But a few days later another man died of heat prostration in the rear, without having marched a foot. The heat was killing people.

Still, Greg Foster persevered. He was one of the most resourceful of the men of the First Platoon, so resourceful in fact that Sergeant Riepe began calling him "Jim Dandy." There was a story in the marine newspaper *Sea Tiger* (it was later picked up in United States newspapers) and it was all about Foster. The headline read: "JIM DANDY TO RESCUE." In the story Sergeant Riepe was quoted as saying, "When we get in tight jams in the bush Foster seems to save the day for us." The story went on to tell about Foster's heroics, which had earned him the Silver Star. But there was more.

"When Jim Dandy isn't in the bush saving the day," the article went on, "he has been known to pull various forms of heroics in the rear.

"One of Foster's abilities is to get food for the platoon at times when it would otherwise be unobtainable. 'No matter how much they have improved C rations,' Riepe comments, 'troops still get tired of them after being in the field for a while. One thing you really look forward to when you return to the rear is a good, hot meal. And we always get it, thanks to Jim Dandy.'

"Riepe went on to explain that sometimes the platoon gets back to the rear after their mess hall is closed for the day. 'I don't know who he knows or how he does it,' Riepe admits, 'but when Foster goes to the mess hall it isn't long before the rest of the platoon is inside eating hot chow.'

"In the bush and in the rear, Jim Dandy's ability to 'deliver' is going to be missed when the marine moves his operation to the New York plains."

Several years later, his memory of Foster still fresh in his mind, Sergeant Riepe said, "He was an outstanding marine, one of the best ones I ever served with."

The entire Purple Martin operation was a success, in marine terms. The North Vietnamese regiment had been cleared out of the area; it was firmly in marine hands. (But the NVA did return. As late as December 1972, when Henry Kissinger was trying to button up a peace with North Vietnam, *South* Vietnamese troops were trying to recapture terrain near the DMZ — the same terrain that had been secured by the marines three years earlier at the cost of so many dead and so many more wounded. Michael Brown, who also received a Silver Star for his part, with Foster, in the March 23 mission, said about that operation: "We would leave and the next thing you know we were back on that same hill trying to take it all over again. It didn't make sense. Has it ever made sense since then, anything we've done there?" Then Brown answered his own rhetorical question: "Not really.")

As time went on it got easier for G Company and Gregory Foster's platoon. He was promoted from PFC to lance corporal and then to corporal. They gave him his own machine-gun team. And he began to loosen up again. He made new friends. He tried to forget the trauma of battle, the nature of war in that steamy, mountainous, indecent jungle. He tried to forget about the dead, about losing his buddy, Brown. Of course, he never could forget completely, he never could forget anything. For weeks and months after he got back home he was subject to frightful nightmares. Once in the middle of the night Jackie crossed over him to get to the other side of the bed. He jumped up, grabbed her by the neck, and started to choke her. She had to scream to wake him up. And, she remembered, he couldn't drink at all. Every time he drank, Vietnam would come back to his mind. And he would start talking about his buddies over there, particularly about the ones who had died.

While in the bush his correspondence with Jackie was sporadic.

87

He was thrilled to hear about the baby and that it was a boy and that it bore his name. Almost at once she sent him baby pictures and he showed them around. He would write her and say: "You don't know what life is like until you've been over here." He told her how many men he had killed and how many of his friends had been killed by them. He was unsparing of the details. In his early letters he also promised to send her money. But he sent it to his family, asking them to pass some on to her for the support of the baby.

Then her letters began to get sharper. She wrote that she wasn't getting any money. She asked Gregory what kind of a father he was. In turn, he got mad. He wrote her one letter that started with a flood of colorful, off-key language. His complaint was that she wasn't writing enough.

All this time G Company, First Platoon, had been circling the area, just moving from mountain to mountain making sure they were secure. They were in Quang Tri Province now, toward the lowlands. Enemy action was light and scattered.

One day late in September they were helicoptered into a landing-zone area to relieve a marine company that was going out on a sweep. The idea was for G Company to hold the zone until the other company returned.

The day before the operation, Greg received a letter from Jackie. He started to laugh because in it she called him every name she could think of. She enclosed a picture of the baby. On the back of the picture were the words: "Ain't ever sent me anything all my life."

One of Greg's buddies grabbed the letter from his hand. "Give it back, give it back!" Foster yelled, running from man to man as they read it and passed it on.

They all laughed uproariously. One of them said, "I got a good name for that cat, Greg. You got to call her 'Runaway Child.' " Runaway Child it was for a long time after that.

The one thing that got them all was Jackie's last line. It read: "I hope they shoot your black ass."

The next day Greg was sitting out on the perimeter watching the incoming helicopters. Suddenly, mortar fire started from the brush. The NVA was shooting at the birds. Foster set up his machine gun. He was about to fire when a burst from a 60-millimeter shell hit near him. Fragments burrowed into his shoulder and his right arm.

He slumped down in pain, fingering his dog tag. He looked at it, muttering: "Foster, G. P., 2467323 — Catholic." He stared at the red, white, and blue border with the words "land, sea and air" on the outside. He stared at the cross in the middle. He prayed to himself.

As soon as the attack stopped he was medivacked out and put on the naval hospital ship *Sanctuary*. He stayed on the ship for a month. The wounds were not serious, but serious enough to earn him a Purple Heart in a shipboard ceremony.

He asked that his family not be told what had happened. But a buddy wrote his mother and she became frantic, not knowing the extent of his injuries. She sent a letter to her congressman:

"I am the mother of a U.S. Marine. . . . It is extremely distressing to know that lives must be lost in this country when civilization is supposedly at its highest standards and men are aiming for planets in outer space.

"It is very depressing to receive news of one's son, Gregory, being wounded in action from a buddy on the stationery of the American Red Cross without any form of confirmation from the Marine Corps. On October 4, 1969, I received a short letter from a marine friend of my son stating that Gregory had been wounded by 60-millimeter mortar shells in both arms and was unable to write. No confirmation was ever received from the Marine Corps. . . ."

The marines wrote back a letter of apology, stating that Foster had requested that his next of kin not be notified. Had the wounds been serious, the marine colonel wrote, she would have been contacted immediately. What bothered her the most was to find out that her son was going back to duty in Vietnam.

He stayed there for three more months, but saw little combat. He had done his share. Others could hump the boonies. He was thinking of the future now: about his girl, about his son, about his chances of becoming a policeman. The future would be complicated, he knew, but that was okay. He was looking forward to going home.

Mr. and Mrs. Laurie's only concrete memory of their son as a marine came out of the trip they took to Parris Island, South Carolina, for Rocco's graduation from boot camp. They hadn't seen him for eleven weeks and they were both shocked at his appearance.

"I almost dropped dead," the mother said. "He looked tall and skinny. He was some two hundred and ten pounds when he left."

"Two-ten," repeated the father, Anthony Laurie, Sr.

"And he was only a hundred and eighty then because he had been sick and he didn't want to tell them that he was sick. He had the diarrhea."

The father nodded. "He was going to get through the training no matter what."

The mother, Annie Laurie, couldn't understand. "I said, 'Why didn't you tell them you were sick, Rocco?' He said, 'What are you, crazy?' "

She shook her head. "That training. 'Rock,' I said, 'do they hit you?' He goes, 'Yeah.' "

"That's all you could hear down there," the father remembered, "hit, hit, hit."

"They slap you, you know." The mother wavered at the memory, losing her thread of thought, and the father picked up on it, as if he were winding a new reel into the home movie machine.

"Talk about the heat. The day we got there they had the black flag out. That meant you weren't supposed to march because it was so warm. And I think one of the boys died and there was hell to pay. I think it was in the newspaper."

"I was surprised he held his temper," the mother said. "But he said, 'Well, Ma, it's for your own good.' "

"We went down there for eats. I could never forget that. The eats were terrible. Rocco said, 'Well, Pa, it's either this or nothing.' You ought to have seen him eat it. He ate it."

The mother chuckled. "He said, 'This is good.' 'Rock,' I said, 'when I pay for food and I don't eat it, it's got to be bad.' It was horrible."

"We went to a store. We found a delicatessen and we bought ham, cheese, a couple of loaves of bread, some fruit, some soda, and we went in like a little park and we ate it under the tree. That's the way we ate. Oh," the father said, "it was much better."

"I thought he'd be fed up with the marines," the mother said, "but, no. And I was proud of Rocco."

In the progression of letters to his brother and to his girl, one can trace the development of Rocco Laurie from man to marine, or at least into the marines' conception of what a marine should be. The whole thrust of that eleven-week boot camp, with its emphasis on physical toughness, unquestioning obedience, and fear, was to turn men quickly into disciplined fighting machines. And the chief instrument of that transformation was the DI, the drill instructor. The DI was the rookie's mommy, daddy, school-master, and local bully. In the 1950s there were scandals involving sadistic DI's who literally worked their recruits to death. When Rocco Laurie hit Parris Island in late May of 1968, the DIs were as tough as ever, but they were more in control of themselves, more self-disciplined. They had been taught to understand psychological as well as physiological factors in the training of their young men. As one DI put it not too long ago, "When you're through with them, you have men with values a lot different than those they had when they started." If that was true of boot camp at Parris Island, it was doubly true of the experience of Vietnam.

In a letter from boot camp, Rocco wrote his brother: "About that last letter I wrote, telling you that I didn't want to mention some of what goes on down here, well disregard it. It was just from the initial shock of the place. For the first two or three weeks you're scared shit (pardon the expression) and that's what I was, I guess. Now nothing fazes me anymore. . . . Well, anyway, the third night we were here, in the middle of the night, one guy slit his wrist with a razor blade. What a mess, blood all over the place. There was something wrong with the kid, though, he was real nervous and all that. He didn't die, though. It's funny how people attempt to kill themselves, but make sure that they don't."

91

On July 28 he wrote his brother from Camp LeJeune, North Carolina: "It sure was good to see everybody down at Parris Island. . . . Only thing was, after they left I got lonely as hell. I didn't let them know it, though, and that was good. . . . All this time with nothing to do is a pain in the neck because all I think about is home and the Pill and that stuff. . . .

"Well, Parris Island was tough as hell and although there were times when I didn't think I'd make it and times when I hated it, believe it or not, I miss it and I miss the three drill instructors, too. . . .

"I've got things planned pretty good now, I just hope they work out this way. When I get to Vietnam, there is no tax at all on my salary, plus ten percent interest, so I'll take all the money I have plus what I earn and put it in the bank. That and the money I have will give me a good start. I'll go back to the police department and a short time after I get settled, I'll probably marry the Pill. That is, if nobody else does."

On August 10, Rocco wrote his brother from Camp Le-Jeune about his combat training. "So far I've fired a bazooka, machine guns, threw grenades, the whole bit. We also had to go into a gas chamber — ich. We had this class, on gas masks and all, and in the middle of it the instructor threw a tear gas grenade into the bleachers we were sitting in. Let me tell you, it is terrible. It burns like hell. But I got my mask on in time, so I just sat and laughed at everybody coughing and throwing up and running into the woods. Then we had to go into this gas chamber, still tear gas. Inside we had to take our masks off and give your name, rank, service number and date of birth. Then we put our masks back on to get a good breath of air. However, I didn't get mine on right so I choked. Then — get this — we had to take our masks off and run around the chamber singing the Marines Hymn . . ."

On Christmas Day 1968, Camp Pendleton, California, Rocco wrote the girl he liked to call "Pill," Adelaide Dimeo. "How are you this Christmas? I'm not too well. It's not that I'm having a rotten time, it's just that it's like any other day only it's a day off. It's not like the way I like to spend a Christmas, but I can bear it quite easily. Just think of all the guys in Vietnam this Christmas. I'm sure they got it a lot worse than me. Can you imagine cold C rations for Christmas dinner?

"I was just watching a program on TV. It was a news essay. I don't know if you could see it or not in New York. It had pictures of people celebrating Xmas with carols being sung in the background. It also had flashbacks of the Vietnam war, guys getting wounded and stuff. It was a very touching and pointed show, I guess to show how wrong war is, and it's true. It's really a shame that people have to go into some country they don't give a damn about and get shot at. I told you once that a lot of the guys here were wounded over there, they don't even care about it, they are just glad to be alive. One guy is scarred from head to foot and lost an eye when a mortar landed near him. He had an eye transplant and he's about the happiest, jolliest guy here. He's always smiling and laughing and all, but I wonder if he really feels that way. . . .

"About what Tracy said about the Marine Corps, it *is* a machine. Don't you see, all that's drummed into our heads is kill, kill, kill. Don't misunderstand now, we're all individuals, but when it comes to fighting we're like a machine that knows one thing. I'll tell you one thing, as proud as I am to be a marine and all that, I think it's a shame that a country as good as the U.S. is supposed to be has to even have a Marine Corps. Wouldn't it be a much better world if there were no armies, marines or any other fighting forces? Well, all I can say is that I hope that day comes someday. I doubt if it'll be in my lifetime, though."

On New Year's Eve he wrote Adelaide again. "Don't tell my parents this, but since I left home from leave nothing has been the same. Remember how I liked it and always talked about it and all? Well the whole thing is different out here. Nobody likes it. They're just serving their time. I think it's influencing me, too. It's kind of boring out here, but then it's better than dodging bullets, right? So, I don't like it any more, but don't tell them because they tried to talk me out of it, remember?"

Then it was Vietnam. On July 31 he wrote his brother: "Last night we got rocketed at about two in the morning. It scared the hell out of me. It was funny in a way seeing everybody running around and jumping into bunkers. Half of us weren't even dressed, but as soon as someone yells 'incoming,' you just run like hell for the nearest hole. No one got hit, that's why it was kind of funny. One guy ran into a wall in the dark, that was a

93

riot, and some of the guys slept through the whole thing. Not me, though. I was one of the first ones into our bunker. You can't fight rockets, you just have to wait it out. . . . Don't tell Annie about this, okay? She'd probably get worried, but I'm just fine."

He went into the bush as a corporal with Echo Company, Second Battalion, Third Marines. He should have been a squad leader right away but when they asked him he backed off. He had no field experience and he said he would just as soon work with somebody and get used to it a little bit. So they put him in the Third Platoon's Alpha Squad.

He joined the platoon in May of 1969 while it was doing security duty just south of Con Thien in Leatherneck Square. Because of his size and strength Rocco was assigned to carry the squad's M-79, a 40-millimeter grenade launcher. The man who lugged the M-79 was expected to carry a satchel of forty to fifty grenades. Laurie usually carried about seventy with no problem. About a week after he joined Alpha Squad the platoon's commanding officer, Lieutenant Marvin De Vries, asked the squad leader how the new man was working out.

"We've got him tagged as a 'gungie,'" the squad leader said. That meant that Laurie was eager for action.

He didn't get much at the beginning. At one point Alpha Squad had to go recover the body of a man killed from the Third Platoon. They found the body had been booby-trapped with Claymores. They disarmed the mines and got the body out safely. Another time they had to help recover a downed CH46 helicopter. It was a danger area and De Vries, thinking ambush, told Laurie to sweep the area with his M-79. He did. There were no NVA around.

They patrolled the area for two weeks and then were trucked farther west, to the Ki Gee Bridge, near a spot called the Rock Pile, which was north of Vandegrift Combat Base. The platoon spent a week west of the bridge and placed ambushes along the road. On their last night there Lieutenant De Vries placed Alpha Squad, under Corporal Steve Breneisen, at the bottom of a large rock formation known as the "witch's tit." They were overlooking the road as it passed between the witch's tit and the Rock Pile. At about 0200 they spotted four or five NVA soldiers planting mines in the road bed. The whole squad opened up with Laws (antitank rockets) and M-16s but only blood trails and one enemy mine were found the next morning. The squad patrolled the area for a couple of weeks, the only casualties being men who had relapses of malaria due to the intense heat and humidity and steep hills.

Steve Breneisen, who ran the squad while Rocco learned, was serving his second tour in Vietnam. (Breneisen recalled later, "It seemed to me Rocco wanted to make things right before he took over a squad. By God, he asked questions.") Breneisen was from Muncie, Pennsylvania. He had joined the marines in 1966 and gone to Vietnam immediately. He had seen a great deal of action on his first go-round, working search-and-destroy missions near Da Nang. Between tours he had his nose broken in a bar-room fight at Guantánamo Bay in Cuba. He was a tough, hard-nosed, jungle-wise marine, and he was calloused by combat. Already on his tour he had seen more action in Vietnam than the first time around. Two months earlier he and a fellow Pennsyl-vanian, Brooks Matyi (who would later become Rocco Laurie's closest friend) were thrust into a precarious situation.

Breneisen, Matyi, and five other replacements were choppered from a staging compound into Khe Sanh. As they were moving up toward Laos, the front element of the platoon walked into an NVA ambush. The NVA threw grenades and an ammunition cache blew up and the marines lost fifteen men. Only Breneisen and Matyi, of the seven replacements, survived that fight.

On the first of August, Echo Company moved up to three thousand meters from the DMZ in Quang Tri Province, but in a different area of operation from where Gregory Foster's outfit, G Company, 2/4, was serving. The 2/3 was on a nine-hundred-foot jungled ridge line, moving by platoon along an area known as "Mother's Ridge." It was near the Cam Lo Valley, which the marines called the Valley of the Tubes because there were so many mortar positions there and it had been hit by so much shellfire. The maneuver was part of Operation Idaho Canyon, but not nearly as impressive as that title. It consisted mostly of field maneuvers to see whether or not there were NVA soldiers around. The order was given to establish platoon patrol bases.

95

Day after day they ran patrols, checking out different areas and setting up ambush sites.

The Second Battalion, Third Marines' history was not quite as colorful as Foster's 2/4. Laurie's battalion did not come into being until 1942. But then elements participated in the battles of Guadalcanal and Guam. The 2/3 did not see action in the Korean war, but it was seeing plenty in Vietnam.

In November of 1965 the battalion fought around Da Nang. In the next two years it engaged in various search-and-destroy missions, with such bravura names as Beaver Track, Bear Chain, and Kangaroo Kick. The 2/3 returned to Quang Tri in 1969, conducting operations around Khe Sanh and the A Shau Valley area.

The last time any NVA force had tried to come across the DMZ in strength was in 1966. Then the Ninth Regiment of the North Vietnamese Army tried to take Khe Sanh. The siege of Khe Sanh lasted seventy-three days before the marines were finally overrun. But the NVA regiment was so badly battered that it limped back and was written off by American intelligence officials as inoperative as a fighting force.

It was called back to Hanoi to be rebuilt, and the soldiers were used as a policing force during the heavy bombing of the North Vietnamese capital. Then President Johnson stopped the bombing of North Vietnam and the rebuilt NVA regiment, freed of its duties in Hanoi, prepared to strike south again.

All this was later determined by an evaluation of evidence, including papers found on the body of a young NVA soldier, the first man Rocco Laurie actually saw die in Vietnam.

It happened on the afternoon of August 9 and it was a traumatic experience for Laurie. Each platoon in the company was moving independently of the other, and one of the patrols found caches of weapons and explosives, indicating that the North Vietnamese were in the area in force.

Breneisen's patrol moved northward about two hundred meters. Then, before turning back, he called for a break. When a patrol takes a break on the trail everybody moves back about five meters off the trail. One person sits on one side, another on the other side, and they face each other. The last man faces the rear and the first one faces front. That way, everyone is covered in case of trouble.

That was the way they were all sitting when, suddenly, they heard rustling in the weeds. And out popped a North Vietnamese soldier. He looked like he might be a teen-ager, if that. He was wearing a fresh uniform and he was walking down the trail alone, unconcerned, his rifle on his shoulder. And everyone opened up on him at once.

Other patrols in the area heard the noise — the *bam, bam, bam* — and to them it sounded like an ambush. And then there was nothing. Brooks Matyi saw Rocco Laurie and told him that he really looked shook up, that he was white, that all the color had drained from his face.

It seemed puzzling that the death of one NVA soldier — who was the enemy, after all — would affect Laurie quite that way. It was better understood when Peter Wood, who was in the adjoining patrol, explained: "They mutilated the body a little."

"In what way would they do that?" Wood was asked.

"They cut his throat."

Later Steve Breneisen was asked about the incident.

"Somebody said that the NVA soldier you saw that day had his throat cut."

There was a pause.

"Had his throat cut?" Breneisen said.

"Yeah."

"Well, he mighta had."

"Was there much of that going on?"

"What's that?"

"You know, taking NVA bodies and cutting throats and multilating them and things like that."

"No, there wasn't. There wasn't too much of that going on. There was marines that had ambushes out at night that were found — five of them — with their throats slit. And there was some times when a marine would leave it go to his head and cut into one, right."

Peter Wood, who later became a good friend of Rocco Laurie, who won money on Laurie for Rocco's feats as an arm-wrestler, sought to justify the throat-cutting. "That's nothing compared to what they did with ours. It wasn't anything, it was a common

97

thing to do. You either did that or you went up there and shot him right in the head.

"So we got back that night and we really got hit bad. And, later, they tried to say that the reason we got hit bad was because someone had mutilated the body. I don't know, none of us felt that way. We didn't figure that a whole goddamn battalion of gooks — I think they said that there were two battalions of gooks, I can't be sure, I didn't take a nose count of the gooks but there was a lot of them, lot more than us — I just don't believe they'd move out one or two battalions just to hit us on account of one guy. It was a plan. And we were in the way and we got hit. Okay, a lot of the guys were saying that the gooks were yelling a lot of things — 'those dirty marines, them Americans. . . .' We were supposed to be famous for that, for mutilating bodies. The Ninth Marines maybe, the one-nine; the Walking Dead, they called them. But we were the Third Marines and it didn't happen that much that I could see."

Brooks Matyi explained it another way. "It goes back to the attitude you get over there. Before Rock got there we got hit by NVA. They had partially overrun our perimeter and there were two men in the hole wounded, and two others pulled back and left the two wounded there. We could hear them scream — 'No! No!' — and the NVA pulled back and shot 'em. I guess cutting the one guy's throat was an act of rage and futility."

So Rocco stood and watched the blood flowing out from the boy's throat while others searched him. He had a radio, he had a cartridge case, he had on a new uniform, and he had papers on him that were sent to marine liaison and indicated that the young soldier was part of the rebuilt NVA Ninth Regiment.

The death of that soldier shook a lot of people in different ways. "We knew we were out on the Rock Pile," Breneisen said, "and we were in the northern territory just below the DMZ and you just don't like to run into anybody out there. That gook had been with us out there, walking the hills, for about a week. And he was the first sign that anybody else was in our vicinity, and that indicated they were out there."

They were more than out there. The NVA had in effect surrounded the company.

Later that day Phantom jets streaked in, dropping two hundred-and-fifty-pound napalm canisters, and the marines could hear screaming from the bottom of the hill.

Peter Wood recalled: "Now Fox Company, our sister company, was working down the valley. And they had hit the area for three days. The story was they had walked into a battalion of gooks down there that was the point element for the regiment. So they were really going at it down there. It was only a matter of time before we got it. So we were moving up the ridge and everything like that, trying to get a good observation of the situation, calling air strikes, artillery, what have you. So we moved around up there.

"Well, we set up that night and we just set up our watches and I had first watch. So we're sitting there and that was about eight-thirty. First Platoon was set up away from us, about a couple of thousand meters away on another hill. And they started catching some crap. We could see it, tracers going up, red tracers going down, and a fire fight going on over there. So they really got hit for about an hour. We were all over there laughing. We thought it was funny. 'Cause the First Platoon always skated; they never got hit. They'd walk through and the gooks never hit them. They always hit the Third Platoon or Second Platoon. I don't know, it sounds weird, but we were all over there laughing. *Look at those bastards, you'd better fight now.* The fighting stopped for a while; it calmed down. We figured it was our turn now."

The platoon was dug in on top of a hill at a landing pad called LZ Echo. Scuttlebutt had it that Echo Company had been up a year or two before and been hit bad. *Somebody* had been up there for sure because there were foxholes everywhere. ("Most of the holes on those hills had been manned time after time," Breneisen observed. "Every month somebody ends up on those hills eventually, one side or the other.") The hill was oddly shaped, with two steep sides and two narrow fingers running up both ends. And there was no real grade to them, so it was easy to walk up them.

The platoon was set in an oval-shaped perimeter. Breneisen and Laurie were in a hole together at one side of the perimeter, toward the middle. Brooks Matyi was in a hole on the opposite side. Next to Matyi was a young man named Brian Wolfe, who had joined the platoon only three days earlier. Next to him was

99

Peter Wood's hole. The command position was at the stubby end of the perimeter.

The holes were four to five feet deep, and three and a half to four feet wide. The men of the platoon dug them out and reinforced them, some with sandbags, others by piling dirt in front of the holes. And Laurie and Breneisen erected a small hooch behind the hole. It was simply a poncho on sticks so that they could keep dry, because it was raining. One would stay in the hole for forty-five minutes while the other one kept dry in the hooch.

"During the night, then," Breneisen remembered, "we had our positions all set in and our holes dug and it was raining misty rain. And I had a starlight scope with me at the time. We used them for night action. You can see in the dark and you can pick up any light objects and, if the moon's out, it will make a hillside two or three hundred yards away look just like an early afternoon. Well, there was no moon. It was raining and it was dark and the wind was up.

"Earlier during that night I remembered we heard what sounded just like a party going on right below the hill, and this was even before midnight, a couple of hours before this ever started. And we knew they were down there, that they were gathering down there and that was just the way they gathered the two tours I was over there. They'd gather right around your position.

"After we heard the noise we walked around the hillside and we had an ambush site out. And we kept walking the hills and we picked up different sights, flashlights and things in the woods. Through the starlight scope you could just pick up different lights coming through the woods, moving. You knew it was flashlights because we picked 'em off. They just cover up the globe with paper and then put a pinhole in it. That's how they follow each other at night.

"It was raining harder now and that caused a lot of problems, not being able to see any stuff. And Rocco'd take a turn in the hole and I'd take a turn and we were running about every forty minutes to an hour in the hooch. But there was no sleep.

"And we found out later, evidently, that we had a little problem up on the hill there. Those North Vietnamese got into our perimeter. Now I have no idea to this day how they did it because we were supposed to be on one hundred percent alert. But somebody didn't do the job or we would never have gotten battered up as bad as we did. Because that main attack came off of one finger and those chicom grenades came through there and they were throwing charges *down* the hill at us. And I had my doubts about why that finger was that way and there was one reason I thought about: there was an ambush site down off that finger and those people — if anything comes through there — would have to see it and radio back to us so we'd be ready. Someone was supposed to run an LP [listening post] out on the finger, maybe fifty meters off the hill we're on. I understand the LP never went out, never went outside the perimeter that night. I mean, that's no way to talk about anybody on that hill because there was only one or two on that hill who made it off the end of the finger anyhow, who survived.

"But before it all happened, Rocco, he kept talking about it, wondering about getting hit, what it was like at night. After that afternoon, coming across that North Vietnamese soldier and all, he wasn't going to get no sleep, there wasn't no doubt about that, because that was his first encounter. But it was nothing to what came in the night.

"It was quite a surprise. I mean, it was a hit like I'd never been involved in over there. I never encountered anything quite that bad ever in my life and I don't think I ever will. And for somebody like Rocco to have to start out like that was pretty bad. But he was pretty calm about it. You couldn't ask for a better man in the hole with me, I'll go along with that idea."

That same night Annie Laurie, the mother, sleeping in her bed in Staten Island, had a dream about Rocco. She dreamed that she had her rosary beads in her hand and she was praying and Rocco was saying to her, "Count down on those beads, those three beads, Ma."

She woke up and sat on the edge of the bed and tried to find the third bead, or whatever he had tried to tell her, for she had fallen asleep with the rosary beads in her hand. And she said, "Oh, God, please watch over these boys. I'm not praying for my own, I'm praying for the others, I swear." And the next day, Sunday morning, it came over the radio that there had been a

*terrible battle near the DMZ and that the North Vietnamese had
inflicted the heaviest American casualties in six months. And a
neighbor ran over and said, "Gee, the marines took an awful
shellacking on some hill." The mother knew it was Rocco's outfit and she looked out the back window and she said, "Oh, God,
he's out there in that thing and, oh, God, please watch over them
all."*

Rocco had just exchanged places with Steve Breneisen —
moving into the hooch to keep dry while Breneisen
took his place in the hole — when it started. It was three-thirty
on the morning of August 10, and it started with a satchel charge
or a rocket-propelled grenade, just one loud explosion that
alerted everybody. Rocco rolled down from the hooch into the
hole.

"What's going on?" he asked Breneisen.

Breneisen motioned for Laurie to be still. He heard noise out
there. The wind was blowing very hard, toward them, and men
were talking, in Vietnamese. It occurred to Breneisen: there's no
Vietnamese out there but bad ones.

"Be quiet," he whispered to Laurie. "Sit tight and we'll see
what happens now." But he knew what was going to happen. He
knew the Vietnamese had gotten inside the perimeter, that the
enemy was on high ground looking down at the holes in which
scared American marines huddled and waited. Breneisen knew,
too, that all the marines were within grenade range of the North
Vietnamese.

The first enemy grenade blew apart the hooch Laurie had just
crawled out. Shit, Breneisen grumbled to himself, it was a mistake
to put it up. That gave them the location of our holes. I'm the
squad leader. I should have realized that.

But there was no time for self-recrimination. They were being
hit on three sides — by grenades and dynamite bombs and satchel
charges and small-arms fire and even, Breneisen was to find out
later, rounds from an M-60 machine gun, the marines' own
weapon. In the initial charge, NVA sappers had hit the listening

post, wounding all four men and forcing them back through the perimeter. One of the wounded marines opened up on them with the machine gun but, immediately, a sapper threw a satchel charge into his hole and the American was killed. Another marine attempted to retrieve the M-60 but he was driven back as a point squad of sappers poured through the gap. The NVA sappers stayed in the hole, firing the M-60 into marine holes.

Two of the wounded marines, a black man named Graves and a white man named Germany, both suffering head wounds, piled into Peter Wood's hole.

"What the hell's going on over there?" Wood asked.

"They overran us," Graves said.

Four men were crowded in that hole and then Woods saw two silhouettes five feet away. The silhouettes were crouched over and were carrying rifles. And Wood and Graves and Germany and Wood's partner, Dan Row, blew the two men away.

"Well, that was a mistake," Wood recalled. "Cause it called attention to us and our hole started getting the crap. Consequently, we had to jump out of our hole four times in the course of about twenty minutes. The chicom would land in the hole and as soon as they heard the thump, guys in the hole would yell, 'Get out!' Finally, it was getting too damn hot. We're catching all kinds of crap, RPGs and stuff. So I told Dan Row, 'Move the goddamn gun over to the next damn hole. Try to move it and we'll try to keep you covered.' So he gets going and Graves and Germany and me keep him covered. But Domingo in the next hole over thought we were gooks and he's shooting at us from the back. So we're getting it from the front *and* the back. 'Domingo, you goddamn fool. It's Woody' — they called me Woody over there — 'oh, Christ, it's Woody.'

"As we were moving the machine gun the skipper, Lieutenant De Vries, came down. He always carried a pump shotgun. And De Vries yelled, 'Woody, is that you? Is that you?' I said, 'Yes, Lieutenant, get down.' As soon as I said that — *boom!* — an explosion went off right between him and me. That was the last I saw of him that night. I thought he was dead. But I found out the next morning that he was hit in the back of the leg and he somehow had reorganized a new perimeter.

"When we got back to that hole we really started working out with the gun. One guy was shooting so much he burned the barrel out of his gun. Our gun was the only machine gun working in that spot. But the gooks were all over the goddamn place.

"I remember there was one gook up there. He had us pinned down. He was on top of the hill and he must have had a couple of satchels of grenades. He'd throw them in the knoll, then he'd throw them down the hill. And I got so damn mad and I had it with this shit. I just couldn't take it any more. That gook was really doing the job. He was behind the tree stump and he kept really intense fire right on top of us, and there was no way you could get a shot at him. So I told the guys that I was going to get this son of a bitch.

"I started out of the hole and water was running down the hole and it was all mud. I'm slipping and sliding. It just seemed like I couldn't get up that goddamn bank. It was really steep up there. It had all turned to mud from the rain and I couldn't get up the hill.

"Well, I finally get up there, I start crawling and I run across Phil Gates. Sergeant Gates was hit already in the back. Shrapnel. He said, 'Where the hell you goin?' And I said, 'There's a gook up behind a tree stump up there.' So I went up there and the gook didn't even see me. He was popping his head above the thing and I just blew the top of his head right off.

"So I started moving back toward the hole again. And then artillery started right on top of us — our own artillery. Well, we had a flare ship come in, a plane that rides around and drops flares. It was really windy that night, too, because I remember the flares were popping right over our hole. In no time at all they were getting blown all the hell down in the valley. And the gooks started shooting at the flare ship with *our* machine gun. The guy in the plane was chicken crap. He just took off. He wouldn't drop any more flares. If it wasn't for the artillery, I tell you, I wouldn't be here now. The gooks were pouring all over us."

Brooks Matyi had grabbed his gear when the explosions started. He took an extra bandolier and ammunition and went down into the hole. There were two other men in the hole and, looking down the hill, they could see Vietnamese not more than twenty feet from them.

"Open fire on them," Matyi yelled. And they did, two of them with M-16's, the third man throwing grenades.

The North Vietnamese started lobbing chicoms back at them. The grenades landed in the hole twice and they jumped out each time, then jumped back in the hole after the explosion. They were able to move fast because they saw the grenades coming at them — Chinese grenades leave a trail of sparks from the fuse. But one of the men jumped out of the hole when he should have been in the hole and a grenade went off and his face was shredded by shrapnel.

Finally, Matyi considered the situation untenable. "Let's move to another hole," he said. "They got our number in this hole."

As Matyi started to climb out of the hole a grenade landed in it. It went off and blew Matyi down the side of a steep hill. And that was when American artillery started coming in, coming in right on top of him. Matyi was just lying out there in the open and .155 rounds were going off all around him, the concussions lifting him off the ground repeatedly. He dared not move, so he stayed there until the barrage stopped.

Two holes away, Brian Wolfe, who had been in Vietnam only a week, and in the bush only two days, and his partner, Phil Cox, were under the same intense fire. But their luck ran out. A chicom grenade landed in the hole between Wolfe's legs and went off. He was still alive and Cox propped him up on the side of the hole and kept firing at the North Vietnamese, who were coming up the hill. Another grenade landed in the hole, resting momentarily on Wolfe's shoulders. The explosion took off most of Wolfe's head. The bottom of Cox's foot was torn away, someone said, "like somebody had just come along and peeled it off." The next morning they found Wolfe's remains. There were two dead North Vietnamese in the hole with him.

Later both Rocco and Brooks Matyi wrote letters to Brian Wolfe's mother, who had never received a letter from her son while he was in Vietnam. Rocco's letter, which described his relationship with Brian Wolfe and his heroism in that battle, brought tears to the mother's eyes.

Through it all that night Rocco Laurie was thinking (when there was time to think) about his own death. He thought about it continuously because he felt sure he would die before the night was over. A calmness filled his mind. Anticipating his death he was unafraid. Only very practical thoughts filtered through to his core. How would they notify his mother and father? Would they be terribly upset? What would be their reactions to his funeral? That was all that bothered him, really, the idea of the grief his death would cause his mother and father.

In the midst of it all, Laurie and Breneisen had gun problems. Breneisen's gun jammed and Rocco found himself out of ammunition. So he crawled out of the hole, up the hill — in the face of unrelenting enemy fire — and picked up an M-79 grenade launcher. He brought it back down and then Breneisen crawled out and in one of the abandoned holes picked himself up a rifle. "And," as Breneisen remembered, "it just turned into one big party that night. And it kept going right until daybreak."

Their side of the perimeter was slightly better off than the other side, where Matyi and Wood and the others were fighting. Laurie and Breneisen were in a hole on the upper part of the hill and nobody could climb up it without being seen or heard, and Laurie and Breneisen had the advantage because they had a straight-down velocity of fire. But there was a time when a lone Vietnamese was shooting into their position. He had green tracers on his gun and the United States does not use green tracer rounds, so Laurie knew it was a Vietnamese. He was being careful whom he shot at now because he knew the Vietnamese were mixed in with the marines and he didn't want to hit any Americans. Rocco would get up and shoot at the NVA, then the enemy would get up and shoot at Laurie. Finally, Laurie's bullet hit target, for there was no further shooting from that position.

Freakish things were happening on the hill that night, and atrocious things. Not until the morning would Laurie know the extent of the fight, how most of the hill had been overrun by the NVA. But the NVA was apparently so sure that they were going to take the whole hill that, during the night, they set up an aid station on the LZ and they brought in female nurses to tend to the wounded.

During the fighting a black marine was seen running down the hill with three NVA chasing him. His hand was blown off and his flesh was stripped from his arm, from his elbow up, with only the two bones showing. He was running for his life. And he did outrun them. He was found alive the next morning.

Another marine was down there and had his legs blown off. The NVA came up to him during the night and a female nurse felt his pulse and said something to the soldier beside her. And they put a satchel charge underneath the marines' legs and pulled it. The concussion apparently cauterized the marine's wounds so that he didn't bleed to death. The next day he was able to tell his rescuers what had happened.

There were marines up there who played dead and yet were still clubbed to death by NVA soldiers who decided to make sure. Other marines hid in holes and pulled bodies on top of them. And there was one marine — Sergeant Gates — who had his thumb almost bitten off in hand-to-hand combat. Steve Breneisen saw it and heard about the details later from Gates himself.

"The two of 'em were rolling in the mud on the side of the hill. We couldn't shoot at 'em for fear of hitting Gates. But the Vietnamese below the hill, they didn't seem to mind. They were throwing chicoms up at 'em. They couldn't care which one they got, I think.

"What happened was that a Vietnamese went down the hill and Gates came up. They locked and the only way I think Gates got off him was when he tried to put a thumb in his eye and when he had him down. He evidently had the gook down in the choke hold and was just going to gouge his eyes out — when you're in hand-to-hand combat that's the one thing they teach you, put a thumb in where they can't see out. And he said he was going to try that and that was the last time he tried that. I remember him telling me that.

"He put the thumb in the gook's mouth instead and that Vietnamese just wouldn't let go — that's quite a story to believe but it's the truth." Breneisen laughed tonelessly. "And Sergeant Gates is one guy, one thing about him, he wasn't gonna make up no story like that. Because this was his second tour of Nam and he just about lost his life the first time around when he got shot in the chest.

"The thumb was a mess, it looked like a big golf ball. It was really swelled up, you know. When he was in the hospital (he came back to us after that) the doctors wouldn't believe it. They asked him how it happened and they just wouldn't believe it. I guess from the way he talked he everything but picked that gook off his feet trying to get his thumb back out of his mouth."

"I wonder how many people are left besides us." It was an idle question for Rocco Laurie to ask because Breneisen had no answer. The fight was well over an hour old now and the firing was as bad as ever and there was no way of knowing who was dead and who was alive out there. The night was impenetrable and you could not see the other holes unless there was an explosion that lit up the area. "Maybe it's only us left," Rocco said. "Maybe everyone else is dead." Breneisen didn't answer.

It was a night of horror for Laurie, his first combat experience, facing the enemy under the worst possible conditions. Yet he remained cool throughout. Breneisen, the veteran of two tours of Nam, was glad to have Laurie with him.

One chicom grenade landed outside their hole and blew something on top of them. "What is it?" Breneisen asked nervously, thinking that maybe it was a piece of some marine's flesh.

"Just a piece of sandbag," Rocco said. "It's all right." He brushed it away. "How long are they going to stay around here, Steve?"

"I have my doubts how long *we're* gonna be around here," Breneisen giggled. He wasn't joking. They were lobbing chicoms around. "This guy's gonna get lucky one of these times and one's gonna come in this hole."

"What do we do?" Laurie asked.

"If you feel just anything drop in this hole, Rocco, get the hell out of it and down the hill."

"I can't believe they'd throw one in here."

"It can happen. And if it does, just roll out of the hole and, as soon as it goes off, roll back in it. You can't sit out of the holes too long either because you're too susceptible to getting shrapnel. There's an awful lot of shrapnel flying up here."

The night seemed to be lasting forever. Rocco asked again, "How long are they gonna stay out there?"

Breneisen blew on the bolt of his rifle. "They'll stay right to daylight."

That's what happened. Early in the morning — at about 6 A.M. — when light came through the rain to the devastated area, the firing stopped. Laurie and Breneisen left their hole. They walked up the perimeter and the first one they saw was Brooks Matyi. Breneisen walked over and shook hands with Matyi. He said, "Least us guys from Pennsylvania are still around."

They looked all around them. "Kee-rist," Breneisen exclaimed, "between the wounded and the dead we're pretty well hurting."

The perimeter was perhaps half the size of a football field. It was a mass of bodies. There were nineteen dead Vietnamese lying in or around the perimeter. The NVA usually dragged their dead with them. This was a sign that they were hurting, too. The estimate was that at least double the amount of dead found had been killed, and twice as many wounded. The estimate, too, was that a force of over five hundred North Vietnamese had assaulted that hill.

Against them were ninety marines. Of those, only seven were not either dead or wounded. Nineteen marines were dead, sixty-four were wounded. There had been twelve men in Matyi's Charlie Squad. He was the only one to come out whole. Three men were left in Bravo Squad. Alpha Squad, Corporal Breneisen's, was intact. Seven healthy men left out of ninety.

Laurie and Matyi were put up for the Bronze Star but only Breneisen received it (Lieutenant De Vries got the Navy Cross.) Breneisen's citation read in part:

"While occupying a night defensive position near the DMZ in Quang Tri Province, Corporal Breneisen's platoon came under a vicious ground attack by a North Vietnamese company reinforced by sappers, utilizing automatic weapons fire, rocket-propelled grenades and satchel charges during the initial moments of the assault. The momentum of the hostile movement enabled the enemy soldiers to penetrate a portion of the marines' defensive perimeter on Corporal Breneisen's left flank, causing him to be surrounded on three sides. Although having thus become the most forward element and a natural target for grenades and satchel charges, Corporal Breneisen repeatedly exposed himself to North Vietnamese fire as he moved among his men, shouting fire directions and encouragement to them, and on frequent occasions pulling casualties from the line of fire. His heroic and determined actions throughout this fierce fire fight inspired his squad to exert maximum combat effort and engage in a vigorous defense of the friendly position. Corporal Breneisen's courage, aggressive leadership, and unwavering devotion to duty at great personal risk contributed significantly to the defeat of the North Vietnamese Army company by the tactically outnumbered marine platoon. . . ."

"I don't think I earned it any more than any man up there," Breneisen said. "Like I say, it was something every man on that hill should have been cited for if they were gonna cite one. It should have been a platoon achievement."

He has never forgotten the sight that greeted him that Sunday morning when the battle eased, he and Rocco standing there with Matyi, looking out at a field littered with blood and bodies and friends now lost to them forever. "It really put a choke on me for a while. I encountered a lot of dead bodies over there but I never encountered anything like that. It affected everybody. We all pretty well had tears in our eyes. Because here was a group of men you walked the hills with, stayed up every night with, ate out of cans with every day — and now we had to carry them down in ponchos."

Brooks Matyi (pronounced Matey) lives in a large, sprawling white house in Newtown, Pennsylvania, at the southern end of Bucks County. It is his parents' home. His father is an executive for the Sunbeam Company. Brooks's father is forty-nine. He dropped out of high school, went into the service in World War II, came back to finish high school and complete a college education at Texas Tech in three and a half years. "I think he's quite a man," Brooks says of his father. "I've got a lot of respect for him."

The land is open in Newtown. The Matyi house stands between farm acreage and there is room to ride horses and the soil smells lush and Matyi appreciates the contrast between the richness of his home and the barrenness of Vietnam, a land that has shaped his life in so many ways.

He is a small man, perhaps the size of Gregory Foster. He has put on weight since his return from Nam. He has a small black moustache, his curly black hair is worn a bit shorter than the fashion of the day. His brown eyes show fatigue, and bewilderment, too, a restlessness that seems to match his personality. As he admits, he has not yet gotten himself together.

It is nine-thirty in the morning and he has just woken. He excuses himself from his mother and his girl, who are still puttering in the kitchen. He takes me into the den, a long, stylish room with a picture window facing out to open, tree-studded land. And he sits down and tries to put into perspective his friendship with Rocco Laurie and their experiences together in Nam and what effect those experiences may have had on him as a human being.

"I went into the marines in January of 1968. I wanted to see if I could do it. You know, they always had a reputation for being hard. And I think another reason was that I wanted to prove something to myself. I was going to school at the time — the community college — and I just wasn't doing anything. Going to classes, putting in my time, and that would be it. I had just turned twenty and there was a lot of friction here at home. I didn't know what I wanted and I was miserable and everything started building up on me. I just had to get away and it was playing in the back of my mind. So I walked out of school two weeks before finals. I said, that's it, I can't take it. So it was a combination of things, really.

"Once I got to Vietnam, it changed for me. First off, I found the Marine Corps wasn't exactly what everyone said it was. And I got burned a few times and it kind of disillusioned me. And when I got to Nam, right away I was thrust in a combat situation. My first day in the bush we took fifteen casualties, my second day we took seventeen. My platoon was decimated and here I figured I wouldn't last longer than a week at the most. But I went through it and I didn't think that much about it — you can't, really. You can't really sit down and analyze things while you're there. If you do you're just liable to go out of your skull."

He sat back on the chair, relaxed, trying to put his thoughts together. He spoke in a matter-of-fact voice, no inflection, no rise in pitch, almost a dull monotone. The words and ideas seemed to come easily.

"It was after I came back that I was very confused. It took me six months or so to straighten out my thoughts. People would ask me, 'Well, you just came back, what's it really like back there?' The peace movement had really gained steam and people wanted to know: 'What's it really like there? Is it true what they're saying, that there's no purpose there?' And I had so many mixed feelings about it. I was so confused. I'd just say, 'Well, I don't know, I'm not sure.' The only thing I felt at that point was, after all, my friends had been killed there. If they had died for no reason I was going to be a very bitter person.

"The longer I thought about it, I finally came to the conclusion that the only thing I could do for my buddies that were killed there — the *only* thing I could do — was to help get the guys who were still there out, before they ended up the same way. So I became active in the antiwar movement. I'm a member of the Vietnam Veterans Against the War. I have been for about a year and a half now."

"Did Rocco share your point of view?" My question seemed to catch Matyi off-balance. He pondered a long while. The women in the other room were talking; their chatter drifted into the den like aimless wisps of smoke.

Finally, he said, "Rocco was a different person than me. We got along, we were very close. I think it took him a long time to sort out his views, too. I think underneath — when you got him alone and just talked — basically, he was thinking along the same lines as me. I'm not a radical. I just wanted to get the people out of there because I couldn't believe in what we were doing and I think he felt the same way. I know he felt the same way about all the people we had lost there as I had felt when I first got back, that if they died for nothing that was going to be bad and he'd be very bitter about it. But at the same time I think I said, 'Well, look, I feel the same way.' And he said, 'Well, I guess you're right.' He said, 'There's really nothing you can do for them. And I said, 'Well, Rock, we were there, what did we do?

112

Did we accomplish anything?' And he couldn't give me an answer. He said, 'Well, I guess we didn't.' 'Well, I said, 'don't you think it's wrong to be there?' He said, 'Yeah, but I'm still mixed up about it.' "

"He knew you had joined the Vietnam Veterans Against the War?"

"Oh, yeah, he made a couple of cracks about it. You know, he didn't think less of me for joining it. In other words, he wasn't upset that I had done that. He just made a couple of wisecracks about it. We both laughed and we just let it go. And, too, we had been through one traumatic experience, really, on the hill, and when you get together, sometimes you just don't want to talk about it. You know what each other is thinking, but you really don't want to bring it out again. So when I went up there to see him we just kinda let it slide. We'd talk about *now* instead of *then*. It was a lot healthier, I guess."

But it has been hard, almost impossible, for Brooks Matyi to forget *then*. It is on his mind constantly. "I think about it, I still think about Nam every day," he said, his voice quavering for the first time. "Every day something comes up that reminds me of something in Nam. Rock did the same thing because I asked him. I said (because I thought I was going out of my mind), 'Do you think about it, still, every day?' And he said, 'Yeah, little things, like something will happen, or you'll see something that will flash you back, flashes you right back.' So in that aspect I know it was on his mind constantly as it was mine. In a way it relieved me to know I wasn't the only one. And I was very, very troubled for a long while."

He was beginning to sweat now and I tried to turn the interview to other directions. "When did you first meet Laurie?"

"I met him in the rear toward the end of July. I had just got off the hospital ship. I guess I had malaria or jungle rot or something like that. I was an old salt by then and I came back to the rear and he was in the rear with about, I'd say, eight or nine other replacements. He was a very quiet guy. I met him and we talked a little bit. We stayed in the same hooch, a Quonset hut. It was pretty crowded in there, about twenty guys. I met him there and talked to him a little bit and he seemed . . ." He broke it off for a bit, trying to remember what he had felt about Rocco that first meeting. "Like, a lot of these guys were kind of cocky. He wasn't. He had just come over from the States. He just sat back and took things in and I knew the first time I met him that he was going to be a good person."

They moved into the same platoon together but Brooks didn't see much of Laurie before the fight on the hill. He was closer at the time to Steve Breneisen because they had fought together before. It wasn't until he and Rocco became survivors together that their friendship deepened. And even then not right away, because the morning after the fight they were still in much peril.

"They were mortaring us periodically that morning," Brooks remembered. "By this time they had flown in another company to us, Alpha Company, First Battalion, Third Marines. They flew 'em in as reinforcements because we didn't know if we were going to get hit again or what. And, what the hell, there were only nine people there that could defend themselves.

"In any event I was sitting there with two guys I was very close to." Brooks let out a sigh. Sweat glistened on his forehead. Outside the window the Matyi land looked pastoral, serene. "One was Lindsay Turner; we called him Snake Turner. He was from Rocky Mount, North Carolina. He came over from the States with me. The other fellow's name was Pete Christoff, from Massachusetts. We were sitting there — this was after everything was done, more or less; they were still cleaning up and we took a break because the other company had been flown in by then and we were pretty exhausted. And we opened up a can of fruit cocktail and we were sitting there eating it and just talking about how lucky we were to be alive. And we heard the *pop* from the tubes somewhere in the distance. You can hear the mortar tubes pop. You have about half a minute to get covered before the rounds hit. So we heard the tubes pop. Somebody yelled, 'Incoming!' and we all three scrambled for foxholes. There were two holes together. Rock was on the other side of the hill still. Basically, we maintained the same positions as we had during the night.

"So there were two holes together, more than a foot apart. One was deep and large, the other wasn't quite as deep. All three of us made to jump into the big hole. All of a sudden I stopped and jumped in the other one. I don't know what it was, something

114

made me jump in the other hole. Turner and Christoff jumped into the big hole.

"Well, a round landed right between them. And it dazed me because I was so close when it went off. And when I finally collected my head Christoff was dead — he was killed outright — and Turner was still alive. The side of his face was blown off but he was still alive. I couldn't believe it. He was fighting like crazy. I pulled him out of the hole, took him to the top of the hill, and called a medic over. The medic said, 'Just keep him quiet. There's nothing I can do until I get a chopper.' He died right in my arms. He couldn't talk. Like I said, half his face was gone, he had shrapnel in his brain. It was just amazing that he lived at all."

Matyi was taking deep breaths now. His face had gone white. He would talk for a sentence or two, then sigh deeply. He was becoming increasingly agitated.

"So we got out. We collected our materials and left the hill. We left our dead there and we moved to a position where the people who were mortaring us couldn't see us. There were seven of us left, not including Turner and Christoff. They were still there when we walked off the hill. The other platoon, and what was left of our platoon, moved down the trail about fifteen or twenty meters. And we waited for the mortar fire to stop. Then, when it got dark, we went back and picked up our bodies, which was a freaky experience in itself because the NVA was massing down at the bottom of the hill for another assault. I didn't find that out until we started to get shellfire in — our artillery, in other words. They were spotted down there and somebody, one of the officers or somebody, called for artillery, and it went flying right over our heads and struck at the base of the hills.

"And we were just walking back and forth along those two hilltops, carrying the dead back and forth, which was quite an experience. It was a complete, total physical exhaustion I had never before known. We just kept going. The guys from Alpha Company, they didn't want to handle the dead because they were badly torn up and they had been sitting out there all day and had started to decompose. And we made some litters and ponchos and two poles wrapped around ponchos and that's the way we carried them, all of them.

115

"We had started walking about six in the morning, and we carried them all day, till about two in the afternoon. We carried them, I guess, for about seven hours. Rock and I were together. We carried some together.

"It was pretty bad. From there, we finally got to this position that was safe, where we weren't being mortared. They brought choppers in and took us all out. They took us to an R and R center at Cua Viet, at the mouth of the Cua Viet River and the South China Sea. They had a nice white beach and they had tents set up and a little stage. After R and R they brought in all new replacements and we went on a small operations in Cua Viet Plains, which was very secure, really. I think it was more to break in the new people because there were so few old-timers there that were left. We ran a couple of operations after that but we didn't see any real combat. And it was after we got off the hill that Rock and I became very close, really. Rock was made my squad leader, so I was in Rock's squad and we really became friends from then on.

"That was kind of an odd situation because I had so much more time than Rock. Here I was over the Rock with more experience and yet less rank and under his command. But it worked out fine. He had a good head on his shoulders.

"I remember the time we were near a bridge, at Mai Loc. Our squad had gone out on a brief security patrol. We ran two-team patrols: one team stayed at the bridge, the other went on patrol. I had the afternoon patrol. So I took my team out — there were four or five of us — and it was a secure area, so I thought. Well, I never did figure out if we were ambushed or if it was some Arvins — South Vietnamese Army — because they had an encampment not far away. But, anyway, all of a sudden, we started getting all this small-arms fire. It was coming at us, so I just put everybody down behind these big trees. We had no communication, no radio, no nothing. We just sat tight. Only thing you could do in a situation like that because you couldn't see anybody, you couldn't see where the firing was coming from, and you just had to sit tight. And Rock and the rest of the guys heard this fire and it didn't take them too long at all. You could see them pushing across the paddies. As soon as they came out the firing stopped. There was no two ways about it. As soon as he heard fire he just picked up everybody and came out to us. They had to run across an open area, too, about a hundred yards of open land, to get to where we were. But Rock was gonna do it, and he did."

Matyi got up from his chair for the first time. He was composed once again. "Want to see the slides?"

He had a carousel all set up on the machine. He closed the drapes and set up a screen over the bar. And it was Vietnam. There were pictures of Laurie and Matyi together, stripped to the waist. "That's the Cam Lo Valley," Matyi explained. "A hundred and twenty-seven degrees there, hottest ever." There was a picture of Steve Breneisen lying in a hospital bed, his nose all bandaged; they were fixing the nose he had damaged in the barroom fight in Cuba. There was a photo of four men, including Lindsay Turner and Pete Christoff. The other two had died on the hill, too. There was Rocco on the Fourth of July, 1969, swimming in the river. There was a stark photo showing gray, scarred trees. "That's where we were hit that night," Brooks said. "It was completely desolated. On the maps the area was once classified as a national forest preserve." He chuckled. "Now there's nothing above three feet living." There was another photo of woods being lit by fire. "Napalm," Matyi explained.

He showed a photo of Rock standing beside a young boy. "He had befriended that kid, from Cua Viet village. Hai was his name. I gave him one of my dog tags and Rock gave him a Marine Corps pin. He used to march around with us and give us Popsicles and food. He hung around Rock all the time. The kid cried when Rock left. Rock told me if he could have taken the kid home he would have."

There was a picture of Rocco dragging his bedding out of the tent. "He came down with the GIs," Brooks said. "Every ten minutes he had to go, in full gear. Toward the end he was really dragging ass. I took this picture because I woke and Rock wasn't in the next cot. Neither was the cot. There was a full moon out. I saw a naked figure bathed in the moon glow. I said, 'Rock, is that you?' 'Yeah, that's me.' 'Rock, what are you doing?' He was looking for another cot. He had ruined his cot because of his rear-end trouble."

Matyi snapped off the projector and opened the curtains and the morning light from the Pennsylvania countryside flooded back into the room. Showing those pictures seemed to relax Brooks and he started to tell stories about his friend.

"Adelaide used to send him packages from home, and it was funny. He loved rice pudding, and when you got a package from home you didn't keep it to yourself, you shared it. We all used to get packages and you'd open them and just distribute everything among the guys. And I liked rice pudding, too. I said, 'Come on, Rock, give me some of your rice pudding.' And he said, 'Matyi, you can take anything you want from me, you can have any kind of pudding, any of the food that you want, you can have anything — but *don't touch* my rice pudding.'

"When we were back in the rear, when things were breaking up, when we were waiting for assignments, we were at Quang Tri. Rock got hold of a pair of barber clippers and he was lining up guys in the squad for a haircut. The guys said, you know, did you ever cut hair before? 'Sure, sure I cut hair before,' he said. 'I used to be a barber back in Staten Island.' I'm laughing my head off. Oh, did he butcher those guys off; he'd chop down here, chop down there. They'd say, 'Where's your mirror?' He'd say, 'I don't have a mirror. You don't need to look at yourself, it's gonna be a good haircut.' So he would do one and send him out and then send another one in so the guy who was coming in wouldn't see what the other guy that went out looked like. And he did three or four of them like that before they finally caught on."

"By then there was a very strong bond between us. We just liked each other tremendously. He was so gentle and he never got mad and he was a very easygoing type person. And the minute you got around him you just had to relax. He made you relax. I just felt very much at home with him."

In their last days together, Brooks remembered talking to Rocco about what each was going to do when he got out. "He said something about the police," Brooks recalled, "but we really didn't talk about it that much. We were more or less worried about just getting out of Nam, getting back to the world. Because Vietnam was one place and the world was everywhere else but Nam."

They separated when Rocco went on to Okinawa and Brooks went directly back to the States. But Brooks got a letter from

Rocco, from Okinawa, asking Matyi to be in his wedding party. "I wrote him back and said I'd love to. But I was kind of surprised he was going to get married so fast. I wrote him and told him he should wait a while, get back and get his bearings, settle down and become a human being again, before he got married. Because you're different when you come back."

"How are you different?" I asked.

"Well, war does that to you. It's hard to explain." He sighed. "You're more pessimistic, you're more jumpy. . . . I don't know, it's hard to explain, it's hard to put in words how you're different. . . . Everybody notices it when you come back from something like that, and it takes a while to readjust. You snap at the least little thing. Ah," he sighed again, "I still . . . still, with me, noises, strange noises, loud noises . . . I jump.

"I came home — I remember this — I think it was my first night home. My dad came into my room the next morning, he opened the door and" — Brooks snapped his finger — "I was awake like that. I was up. Another time somebody else had come in and woken me up and I reached over and grabbed for my rifle. Things like that."

I told him how Gregory Foster had grabbled for Jackie's throat when she tried to slide over him in bed. "I did the same thing to my sister," Matyi said. "I don't know what it was. I'm extremely ticklish and I'll do anything to get away from being tickled. I think she was trying to tickle me or something, I don't remember exactly. I just turned around and grabbed her by the throat. BEFORE I KNEW WHAT I WAS DOING." His voice had risen, for the first time, to a high pitch. "Like, my mother was sitting there, she was sitting on one side of me and my sister was on the other. Even before I knew what I was doing I just grabbed her. I didn't hurt her because I pulled away."

A question hung in the air, about Nam, about his experiences, about what a war like that does to people. "You think it brutalized you a little?" I asked.

"Yeah, yeah. I've become very fatalistic. Death doesn't mean anything to me now, it definitely doesn't. Things that would have moved me before still leave me rather unemotional. Of course, I've improved quite a bit but I guess it just takes time. Seeing a bad traffic accident or something, or hearing somebody's misfortune doesn't faze me in the least."

"Do you think Rock felt the same way?"

"I think he changed but I don't think he changed as much as I did. For the simple reason that he wasn't there that long. He didn't see that much combat. And he didn't really have time to become as affected as I did and as a lot of other guys did, guys who were there for six or eight or ten or thirteen months. That was a big change, after the experience of seeing guys you've been so tight with, seeing them just blown away. When they're killed you don't break down and cry — you feel *bad*, in a way — but you're glad it wasn't you and life goes on and you have to go on, too. That's it. And when it starts to hit you is after you've come home, six or eight months after you've come home. All these things start coming back and you start getting fatalistic again. And you start to feel things.

"You know," he went on, talking very slowly now, "I used to lay in bed at night and just cry, I would get so worked up. I know I've been on the brink of just flipping out so many times. I could feel it inside of me just welling up, and I couldn't talk to anybody. I couldn't talk to my folks about it. The only people I could talk to were people who had been through it — Rock, Steve Breneisen — the people who went through the same thing with me."

He got to talk about it with Rocco when they were both civilians, when he went up for Rocco's wedding. "I had a great time. I drove up to New York one Friday afternoon, stayed at Rock's house. I had never met his parents. This was the first time I'd seen him since we had said good-bye together at Dong Ha, where I got on a truck and he was on the other truck and we went in separate directions. So, naturally, I was really looking forward to it. His folks were great and I met Adelaide and she was nice, very sweet. She was the type of person I could imagine him with."

"Did you talk about Nam?"

There was a silence in the room. The women had long since left the kitchen. Brooks stared out the window, lost in thought. "The night of his bachelor party. That's when I found out that Nam had just affected him the same way it did me. We had gotten kind of drunk and on the way back from the party we were sitting in the back of the car. We were cold sober now. We talked about our friends, the ones that were here and the ones that weren't. I started to cry. He broke down and started to cry, too. And we sat in the back seat and I just held his hand and we cried."

PART THREE

Domestic Affairs

To achieve faith one must suffer for decades
And to suffer one must get up early in the morn-
    ing and raise a family and go to work
Suffering is middle class
It was invented by Benjamin Franklin
It begins with the search for a loaf of bread and
    ends with funeral expenses
                                    — REED WHITTEMORE

The returning Vietnam veterans, Gregory Foster and Rocco Laurie, came home with a sure knowledge of what they were going to do with their lives. They would get married, and they would become policemen. Basically, that was all both wanted. They wanted to get out of their *war* skin as fast as they could, they wanted to forget what they had seen and what they had endured in that strange, silent, green country of death. Laurie once expressed the source of his longing for home in a letter he wrote to his mother. He was very basic: "You know what you think about when you're here? You think about the faucet. You don't know how lucky you people are. Just think: you go to the faucet, you open it up and you get water. You think about the toilet flushing most of all." The regularities of American life were what he missed the most — the faucet, going to the bathroom at the regular time every morning and then being able to flush the toilet. That was what he — and Foster, too — most looked forward to on their return to America. They came home seeking the resumption of a kind of order in their lives. The faucet, the flush toilet, a wife (which implied a regularity in their sex lives) and a career as a police officer — this was the American dream for Foster and Laurie at that time in their lives. The dream was heightened by the fact that, for reasons beyond their understanding, they were survivors while some of their friends had come back home in aluminum boxes.

Foster returned first, in December of 1969. Laurie arrived in May of 1970. Neither man yet knew the other. Their units had fought within miles of each other below the DMZ, but there had never been a connection. They would enter the police academy at different times. The linkup would not occur until mutual need brought them together in the Ninth Precinct. But the paths of their lives, it seemed, had always been charted in the same direction. In so many ways what one did, the other did; what happened to the one also happened to the other. The parallels in their lives were startling.

Jackie Washington was living with her grandmother in St. Albans, not far from the Foster family, trying as best she could to raise her baby, who was nine months old. She knew that big Gregory was due home soon, but she hadn't heard from him — not since the exchange of letters that had bristled with profanities and recriminations and ended with Foster's buddies calling the girl "Runaway Child." She didn't know if he would come to see her when he did get home, if he wanted to see her and the baby. She knew his parents didn't like her and certainly hoped that Gregory wouldn't marry her. She wasn't even thinking of marriage. But she did long to see him again.

One morning in the first week of December, Jackie woke up with the clearest, surest feeling that Gregory was home. She told her grandmother. "Call and see," the grandmother said. She called his home. The father answered.

"I haven't heard from Gregory," she said. "Do you know when he's coming home?"

"No," the father said, "I don't know."

But Jackie knew. There was something in the father's voice that told her that Gregory was home, that he was probably standing by the phone.

"Well," the grandmother said impatiently.

"He's home, I'm sure."

"What are you gonna do about it?"

She shrugged. "If he comes, he comes. If he don't, he don't. If he doesn't come by a certain time it's all over with us."

An hour later Jackie was looking out the screen door when she saw a young man, wearing a marine uniform, coming toward the house. The man had a funny walk that she found hard to describe; it was almost a lope. She knew that distinctive walk. She knew who was inside the uniform. She jumped back from the door, hoping he hadn't seen her. She ran upstairs.

Her grandmother let the young man in. The first thing he said was, "Where's the baby?"

When Jackie came downstairs with the boy in her arms, Gregory Foster just stood back, looking. He looked at her and he looked at the baby. His face (it was an older face, she thought; he looked a lot older) split into a grin.

"Gimme my baby," he said.

The father took little Gregory into his arms. He was still grinning. "I was expecting to see a smaller baby than that." Little Gregory was big and round and the father held him almost all day until Jackie's grandmother left the house. When the grandmother went out and they were alone, they put little Gregory back in the crib and then they went to bed together.

Afterward they talked about marriage. "You're young, Gregory," Jackie said. "You still have a whole life ahead of you. You don't have to tie yourself down with me, you're going to be missing out on a lot. You won't be able to hang out with your friends, and you're going to have two people to support. You won't be able to do the things you want to do."

"Uh-huh," Greg murmured dreamily.

"I'm serious, Gregory," she said, her voice rising. "You don't have to marry me if you don't want to."

"What if I want to?"

"Well, that's different."

"Whether I want to or don't want to, Jackie, I got to. It's my job to marry you. Besides," he said, running a finger down the side of her face, "love is there. Right?"

Originally, Adelaide Dimeo and Rocco Laurie planned to marry on July 18, 1970, which would be as close as she could get it to the fourth anniversary of their going steady. (Adelaide was incurably romantic. She made a shrine of everything that concerned their relationship. She kept a record of every movie they saw together, she saved all his letters as a marine, tying them neatly into bundles with red ribbons.) Then they decided to move things up. Rocco would be getting out in May and he figured he would be wasting time if he hung around until July. Get married in May, go on a honeymoon, come back and start at the police academy as soon as possible. So they moved up the date. It was what Adelaide wanted, anyway.

She was at the airport waiting for him the night he came home. Because it was late and her grandmother didn't like her to be out by herself at night, Adelaide stole out of her grandmother's house, not telling her where she was going. She drove to John F. Kennedy airport and was there an hour ahead of time.

It was one-thirty in the morning when his plane came in. He

had been gone eleven months and when she saw him it was like he had been with her all the time. He had on his marine uniform and he looked immaculate except that his tie was off. She had written him that as soon as she saw him she was going to run up to him and hug him and kiss him. And that's what she did. He stood back, admiring her. "You look so good," he said. "You look thin."

"So do you," she said. He had two duffel bags with him and she helped carry them to the car. She drove him to his parents' house while he sat back, smiling, telling her how good it was to be home.

The days before the wedding were a whirlwind of activity. While Rocco was trying to get accustomed to civilian life, Adelaide was working on the wedding plans. One night her Uncle Matty took her to hear a rock band he thought would be right for the wedding reception. Dr. Iammatteo was a lusty sports fan and participant (softball and weight lifting) and he had spent his honeymoon, much to his wife's discomfort, listening to the 1956 World Series. He tried to explain to Adelaide that Rocco was probably inclined the same way.

"Adelaide," he said, "Rocco seems to be a real gem. I'm going to give you bits of information which I feel should help you. He happens to be very sports-minded. Don't choke him off sports, leave him alone, enjoy sports with him. Because if you give a man your love, he will give it back twofold. I know you're not interested in sports. I know you're not interested in weight lifting. You're not interested in discus, shot-put. You don't like baseball, you don't like football." Reeling off these negatives seemed to freshen Dr. Iammatteo's enthusiasm and he spoke forcefully, rising to an occasional malapropism in an effort to get across his message.

"Make him happy. These things make him happy, he will in return make you happy double-fold. Don't strangulate him from all these things. Don't possess him that he has to be home by a certain time because he doesn't." Dr. Iammatteo was worried over tendencies he had always noted in Adelaide. He wanted the marriage to breathe freely; he was concerned that in her love for Rocco, she might try to smother him. Adelaide told her uncle that she agreed with him and that it would all work out fine.

But just before the wedding, Rocco himself was filled with doubts. His friends had wanted to give him a bachelor's party. Adelaide had said no, there was no time, there was too much to do. On the Friday night before the wedding, when the rehearsal was over, Rocco's friends in the bridal party decided to take him to a bar for an informal party. With two girls from the rehearsal, Adelaide said, "Let's follow them." At first it seemed like a joke. But as she drove after them, trying not to lose them, she seemed to get angrier. "Just wait," she mumbled. "He's going to Bermuda by himself. . . . Who does he think he is?. . . . I don't ever want to get married to him. . . ." And the madder she got the more recklessly she drove. The other girls were terrified. She gunned the car down quiet streets, racing to keep up with the men. Finally, they eluded her and she slowed down, her anger drained, and took the girls home.

That night at the bar Rocco, for the first time, expressed his misgivings about the marriage to his brother, Anthony. "Maybe it's all a mistake," he said. "Maybe I shouldn't get married." He was uneasy, but how many brides and how many grooms share that state of mind on the eve of an event that will so profoundly change their lives? In that way, Rocco was no different than the others. They filled him with drinks and that helped lift his gloom.

Originally, Jackie and Gregory planned on a quick, quiet wedding. She was just going to go to the preacher and get married. That was what both she and Gregory wanted. But Jackie's grandmother wouldn't have it that way at all. She wanted her granddaughter to step out. She insisted that they "do it nice so that everybody can see that you're married." So it was planned for February 14, St. Valentine's Day, at her church, Christ Gospel Baptist church in St. Albans.

They had only a week to get ready and the preparations went on right up to the last minute. Jackie waited at her grandmother's house while the grandmother completed her chores. It was almost five o'clock when she arrived at the church.

Gregory was so angry that he almost took off. But his first sight of her coming into the church changed his mind. She was wearing an opulent white gown (it had cost her three hundred dollars) with a long train hanging down the back. This surprised people, because after all she did have a baby and some thought it was inappropriate for her to marry in a white dress.

But she looked beautiful. She was slim and her tawny skin shimmered against the white of her gown. Her maid of honor, a cousin, moved ahead of her as the organ played the Mendelssohn wedding march. There was a bridesmaid and a flower girl and even a ring-bearer, a little boy who lived next door to the grandmother. By the altar Gregory waited. His younger brother, Michael, was with him; his cousin, Nathan, was the best man.

Jackie glided down the aisle proudly, her head erect, and Gregory, who had been so angry with her, was now smiling. It was a double-ring ceremony, and as it proceeded she dropped his ring out of nervousness.

On Saturday, Adelaide and Rocco had a little fight. She had packed for Rocco. She asked him to come over and help her close her suitcase. He couldn't believe she was taking so much. There were words. She started to cry.

The morning of the wedding Adelaide's phone rang. It was Rocco. "You're not supposed to call me before the wedding, Rocco Laurie." She feigned anger. "What do you want?"

The voice on the other end laughed. "I'm just calling to find out if you're going to be there." But he was half serious. After their quarrel he wanted to make sure.

"Be where?" she said innocently.

"At the church."

"Yes, I'll be there — unless you keep calling me."

"What do you mean? Don't you like me to call you?"

"Not on my wedding day. You better watch out or I won't marry you after all."

"See you at the church, Pill." Rocco hung up, relieved.

It was a nuptial mass, scheduled for three-thirty in the afternoon at Adelaide's parish, the Church of the Blessed Sacrament on Staten Island. Father Alvaro Arguello, an old friend of the Dimeo family, was to officiate. Rocco's brother Anthony was to be best man. (Rocco had told Anthony beforehand to shave his moustache and cut his hair or else he would get another best man; Anthony complied.) Brooks Matyi was one of the ushers.

Anthony's wife Kathy was maid of honor and Mrs. Anne Iammatteo was matron of honor. Adelaide's grandfather stood up for her, and her grandmother started sniffling the moment the organ music began, the soprano began singing "Ave Maria," and she saw Adelaide start down the aisle.

As for Adelaide, she was shaking, as nervous as she had ever been in her life. The nervousness fell away from her when she linked up with Rocco at the altar and he whispered to her, "You look beautiful." After that it was all right.

I am a man, Gregory repeated, whom God has blessed. Through His grace I met Jackie and offered her my love. Through His grace she accepted my love. I am a man, Gregory concluded, whom God has blessed.

Adelaide: I pray to You, oh Lord, I rejoice in You my saviour. How great is Your name throughout the earth . . . Through God and his grace, I have accepted him and I am about to become his wife. Blessed be you, oh Lord, blessed be You, for ever and ever.

It is fundamental to the Christian life, Gregory Foster, that we shall sacrifice our life by losing it.

Today Rocco and Adelaide are going to meet Christ, are going to have an encounter with Christ. No man, no woman, comes out of an encounter with Christ unchanged.

Look with love on her. Give her grace of life. Give them grace. May they live to see their children be born and flourish. Grant them fullness of life — in the kingdom of heaven.

The wedding service for Jackie and Gregory Foster lasted about half an hour and after that the newlyweds, Jackie remembered, didn't stop kissing all that day. They held the reception at her grandmother's house and everyone came. Her grandfather went around blowing a horn all the time, celebrating as though it was his own daughter who had just gotten married. Despite their reservations about the marriage, Gregory's parents came, too, along with his sisters and brothers. And everybody contributed to the cooking. They had potato salad, they had soul food, they had collard greens, baked macaroni, turkey, and ham. Neither Jackie nor Gregory drank, except for a little champagne; they were too excited about everything. But Jackie danced. She danced with all her cousins, but not with her husband. He didn't know how to dance.

Later, during a quiet moment at the reception, Jackie asked him, "This what you want?"

"This is what I want," her husband said.

They left the reception at eight o'clock. All day the weather had been beautiful. Now it was snowing.

"It's good luck," the grandmother said to both of them, sprinkling confetti atop their heads. The confetti mixed in with the snowflakes and they ran out to the car, the snow and confetti and rice whirling about their heads in a kaleidoscope of color.

They were going to spend their honeymoon in a hotel across the street from LaGuardia airport. It cost them twenty-five dollars a day but they didn't care. They stayed there for three days and all three days were beautiful.

In the limousine driving away from the church Rocco slumped back in the seat. "Are we married?" he said. "I can't believe it."

"We're married." Adelaide cooed in his ear, brushing his cheek with her lips.

The reception was held at the South Shore Country Club and they had cocktails, then dinner, with two bands — music playing all the time. Adelaide was so exctied she couldn't eat a thing. Rocco ate everything. When he was finished with his plate he leaned over to Adelaide and said, "You want your meat?"

"No, you can have it." She didn't even get to taste the wedding cake.

They stayed around until eleven, then changed. When they came out Adelaide threw her bouquet and a cousin of Rocco's caught it. Then Rocco took his wife's garter and threw it straight over his head, but with calculation. Brooks Matyi had told Rocco the night before — "I want that garter." He caught it.

They ran outside, people chasing after them with handfuls of confetti. It had been beautiful all day but now it was drizzling.

"Don't worry," Adelaide's grandmother said in Italian, "that means good luck when it rains on the wedding night."

They spent their first night, like the Fosters, in a motel near the airport. The next morning they left for Bermuda. It was warm and sunny when they got there. They had a beautiful honeymoon. They liked it so much that on the day they returned to New York Rocco promised Adelaide they would come back to Bermuda for their second wedding anniversary.

Right away, Gregory Foster reapplied for the police force. He had passed the police exam before he went into the marines, but there was no assurance he would be taken. Just to cover himself, he took a civil-service examination for the post office. And he waited.

In the beginning he just loafed around the house. He and Jackie and little Gregory were living with her grandmother at her home in St. Albans, and Gregory tried to adjust there. He still had nightmares about Vietnam. He couldn't bear to hear a firecracker go off or a truck backfire. Loud noises of any kind disturbed him. He was jumpy and Jackie was concerned about him becoming a police officer.

"Don't go into the police," she begged. "You had enough over there. You seen enough killing, you got yourself hurt. Why do you want to risk getting killed again?"

"I want to be a cop, Jackie, that's all there is to it, baby."

"Didn't you get enough of that jive in Vietnam? Gregory, I don't understand you."

"That's right, you don't understand a thing." He tried to explain to her. He told her that being a police officer meant a degree of security for her and her children. It was a good job, you were looked after, they could not fire you unless you did something bad. He came from a family that had had no security, where money was scarce and the future was always a question mark. He told her, in his own words, that wearing the uniform in New York City was an expression of manhood, and there were precious few ways black Americans could express their manhood.

He started to tell her that being a police officer meant helping people, too, was one way for a black man to help contribute to the stability of black people. But he stopped when he saw her eyes glaze over. All she understood was that he was going to be carrying a gun. That meant to her that his life would be in constant danger, almost as bad as it had been for him in Vietnam.

They argued about it back and forth, but by that time they were arguing about a lot of things.

At first it was okay between them. There was a sort of feeling-out process and Gregory was around all day, anyway, playing with little Gregory and listening to records. His favorite then was Marvin Gaye, an album called "What's Going On?" Jackie would jump around listening, dancing off by herself, and Gregory would lie there, just listening. "That tells you about the world itself, doesn't it, Jackie?" he murmured. "It tells people what's really happenin'."

> . . . Oh, you know you've got to find a way
> To bring some understanding here today.

She went over to the couch and tried to pull him up. "Come on, let's dance."

"Go way. You know I can't dance."

"I've seen you dancin' around here when you thought I wasn't lookin'."

He smiled. "That's different. You'd just laugh at me if I got up and danced."

After a while he began to get restless. They were living off the money he had saved in Vietnam and it was beginning to stretch thin. He went looking for a job. He tried being a guard for the Burns Detective Agency. He didn't like it and stayed for one day. Then he got a factory job in Queens working for Aurora Plastics, at fifty-three dollars a week. Finally, the post office called. He went to work as a mail handler in a Queens post office.

And his troubles with Jackie began to multiply.

He expected certain things of a wife and they were not always forthcoming. He had to be at the post office early in the morning and he wanted his wife to get up at 5 A.M. to cook him breakfast, and she wouldn't do that. She was not yet eighteen years old and

134

she wasn't interested in being a housewife. "Ain't nobody goin' to get up at five o'clock in the morning to cook no breakfast," she would say. He would holler at her and stomp down the stairs and the grandmother would get into it.

Jackie's grandmother was of two minds about the whole thing. She had wanted the marriage to give Jackie's baby a name, but she also wanted Jackie for herself. Looking back on it some years later Jackie would summarize the problem succinctly: "My grandmother didn't want me to have Gregory and Gregory didn't want me to have *her*. I was stuck right in the middle."

There was an occasional sex hang-up, too. Some nights he was ready and she wasn't. "I'm tired, Gregory," she would tell him and he would get mad. And she would taunt him, "Gregory, you can't get enough of me, can you?"

He would stutter and say, "I don't think it's right. Here I got a wife and I don't think I should have to go out on the street, you know."

"I'm just tired, Gregory, that's all."

"Well, what about me?" He would fuss and fume and sometimes he got so jumpy he scared her.

"You're getting all evil, Gregory," she would say. And he would swear at her and stalk out of the house.

One day she just put it to him: "Why don't you go back to your mother?"

And he did. He packed his clothes and left.

Later, Jackie would reflect on those days and blame herself for what happened. She was still a child at the time — Runaway Child fit pretty well — and she would act like one. She was going through changes and she was too young to comprehend them. She figured, she was eighteen years old and she had made the scene and she was free. But she wasn't really free. She was a wife and a mother and she had obligations. It took a while for understanding to develop.

They separated in May, right after he heard from the police department. He went back to live with his parents, she stayed with her grandmother. It was a strange separation because he would come back to see her often, but he would not stay the night. He'd come home from work, change his clothes at his mother's, and go over to see Jackie. In some ways she felt the

135

separation was good because he was a police trainee and liked to study at night, and at least she was not tying him down. But after a while she didn't like it, she didn't like it at all. She wanted him back with her all the time.

One night she begged him to come back. "It'll be okay," she said. "We'll get a room or something away from my grandmother." It sounded good to him. In July his young brother Michael helped him move his things back in the grandmother's house. Later they did get a small apartment in the neighborhood.

They stayed together until November and then they separated again. This one went on, in its peculiar fashion, for ten months.

It was the same situation as before. Jackie still wasn't ready to assume responsibilities. She was working at a bookstore in Valley Stream at the time. They would both come home at the same hour, about five-thirty. Often they would go over to his parents for dinner. One day she came home tired, figuring that Gregory would go over to his mother's to eat. So she didn't cook anything. He came home tired because he had had to walk twenty blocks to bring Gregory home from the baby-sitter's house. He was hungry and there was nothing to eat.

They started arguing. He got angrier than she had ever seen him. He started shaking her. She became frightened. In the back of her mind was the thought that he still wasn't right from his Vietnam days. She worried that if he ever got too upset he might lose his mind. She was rationalizing, trying to excuse her own behavior. She left the house and went to her grandmother's.

They didn't see each other for a month. Then, one night, he came over to the grandmother's house. They had dinner together. His attitude had softened considerably.

"Will you come on back to me, Jackie?" he asked.

She said she would think about it.

That night when he left, her grandmother hopped on her. "Don't go back to him. That boy's not in his right mind." The grandmother cataloged a list of horrors, most of them imagined, running all of it into the granddaughter. Jackie didn't know what to do. They stayed apart.

But, as before, Greg came around often. The fact was, he really couldn't stay away from her. Around the first of the year, Jackie became pregnant. Gregory took good care of her. He made sure she saw the doctor regularly. He bought her maternity clothes. He was around most of the time. He knew they would come together again because, earlier in the year, he had made an application for a middle-income apartment in the Bronx.

The baby was born in August, a girl that Jackie named Tyhessia. In September of 1971 they ended the separation and the whole family moved into the new apartment.

Foster had received his notice to report to the police academy on April 29, 1970, to take a regulation medical examination and IQ test. If he passed he would be appointed a police trainee. When he walked into the room there were twenty-five men waiting, part of a group of a hundred and twenty-five who, if all went well, would receive appointments. One other, besides Foster, was black. His name was James Duffy.

The first thing Duffy noticed about Foster was the suit he was wearing. It was a green suit, double-breasted, with big lapels, very mod. Duffy went up to Foster.

"Where'd you get that suit, man?"

Foster grinned. "I had it made in Japan on the way back from Vietnam. I got a couple more like that."

They introduced themselves. Duffy's immediate impression was that Foster was a "cool guy." He was smaller than Duffy, a little stocky. Foster wore medium sideburns and a moustache and he had a full face. Another thing Duffy noticed about Foster was the way he talked. He spoke in a distinctive, rapid tone, yet as fast as he went he could still be understood. There was something unique about that speaking voice. Later, Duffy noticed a uniqueness in the way Foster walked. He once described Foster's walk as though "he was almost on a horse." Duffy liked Foster from the start.

They took their physical and IQ test and on May 8 both Duffy and Foster were assigned clerical duties at the police department's Bureau of Criminal Investigation on Broome Street, in downtown New York.

That day they met another black man, Darryl Anderson, who had been a trainee since he was seventeen. He would be twenty-one in December and then be eligible to go to the police academy. His job now was to break in eight new men, among them

Foster and Duffy (another one was George Mahoney, a white man, who later worked with Foster in the Ninth Precinct). The trainees were shown how to file fingerprints and various New York State reports. And it was Anderson who taught them how to do it. Trainees worked eight to four, no weekends, and earned four thousand dollars a year, which came to one hundred and thirteen dollars every two weeks in take-home money.

One of the first days he was on the job, Foster asked Anderson to help him cash a check from the post office. Later, when they became friends, he often borrowed money from Anderson. The trainees would get paid on a Thursday. By the following Monday Foster was on Anderson.

"You got two dollars to loan me to payday?" Foster would ask.

"You botherin' me again? Forget it. I'm not loanin' it to you." Anderson always loaned him the money.

At the beginning of their relationship, though, the three were feeling each other out. On their lunch hours they would sit outside the park across from 100 Center Street, which was the criminal courthouse. Sometimes they would go inside and listen to the cases. But most of the time they would just sit there and girl-watch. Anderson was the only black trainee down there until Duffy and Foster came along. He got along fine with the whites, but he felt it was always good to see another black face and pretty soon the three of them — Foster, Duffy, and Anderson (later, they were joined by a fourth brother, Larry Chiles) — were very tight.

They talked about everything.

"I tell you," Anderson said, "if I'd had my way, I'd a been a football player."

"Well, why did you become a cop?" Foster persisted.

"I don't know, it was a freak. Like — hey! — I just walked in and took the test. I don't know why. I figured it was a chance. I was in high school and there was a time when this police sergeant came over and told us about the opportunities. I said, 'Hey, this is a good opportunity.' So I took it. My father's a transit cop but before that sergeant came along I wasn't gonna bother about it."

"Almost the same way with me," Duffy said. "I didn't know what I wanted to do with my life. I was just walking on the street one day and there was a radio car by the sidewalk with brochures

138

set out on a table, right by the Woolworth store. A cop stopped me. 'Here,' he said, 'you look like the cop type. Take it and fill it out and mail it in.' So I did."

They laughed. "What about you, Greg? What'd you want to be?"

"A cop," Foster said simply. "I don't know why but since the time I was a kid I always wanted to be a cop; I *always* wanted to be one."

He was an able and conscientious trainee. Anderson would show him short cuts in the filing system but Foster would do it the hard way. He was well liked by police officers and the civilians who worked there. He was friendly and sociable and talked to everyone.

Still, the Musketeers were Foster, Anderson, and Duffy. Greg gave them all nicknames. In that way he was like Rocco Laurie; he was big about making up names. He called Duffy "Rabbit" (and, in turn, Duffy called Foster "Feather Head"). And Greg called Anderson "Gumps" because Darryl had a front row of false teeth.

Greg was the only one of the three who was married and he wasn't ashamed to tell them his troubles. "We're splittin' now," he admitted. "Oh, man, I'm not on good terms with her. I don't know what I should do. I think I should go ahead and get out on my own." He would express his fears to his friends and then she would call him up at lunchtime and after lunch Foster would be around smiling. The next day he would be back with a new story. "Oh, we made up," he'd say. Then he would confide in them, "All I really want out of life is my wife, a Dodge Charger or Challenger, and a co-op apartment in the Bronx. Then we'd make out fine.

"It's her grandmother. If we could get an apartment together things would be all right." But then he admitted that his parents didn't like Jackie, and that was a problem, too. Listening to Foster, Anderson felt sorry for him. He told Duffy, when Foster wasn't around, "He knows his family doesn't like his wife and her grandmother doesn't like him. How much pressure can a man live under before he starts to feel it?"

If there was pressure it didn't show up in his performance. He was a good trainee and he picked up fast. A police sergeant named Smith took a liking to Foster and told him war stories and taught him things about being a cop. He kept hammering home to Foster his philosophy. "Greg," he'd say, "the thing you must do, must *always* do, is go into something with a good attitude, because that way you can change, you can be flexible. Whereas if you go into things mad there's no way to change. Think the *best* things about your job and the people you're supposed to protect. Don't think bad things about them. You'll see how much easier it'll be to work with 'em." Foster never forgot what Sergeant Smith taught him.

As the time drew nearer for him to receive his appointment to the police academy, Foster became increasingly nervous. He was already in trouble because the police had found out that his father-in-law had a record. They also discovered that Greg had a heart murmur, possibly from rheumatic fever as a child, and he was fearful that he would not be accepted because of that.

Jim Duffy went to the academy in October. Greg Foster just waited.

He kept asking Darryl Anderson, "Do you think I'll get it? Do you think I'll get it?"

"Look," Anderson said, trying to be helpful, "I seen guys worse than you and they got it. That should be no problem."

"I really want it, Darryl."

"I know that."

He took one final physical and they called him to take another, also to take an electrocardiogram, to check his heart. It happened that at the time the chief police surgeon was the father of a marine who had been killed in Vietnam. He passed Foster.

He started at the academy on December 1, 1970. Jim Duffy was one class ahead of him. In Duffy's class was Rocco Laurie.

Foster and Laurie were never formally introduced to each other but they nodded and said hello when they met in the corridors or in the gym. Foster was the only black man in his class and Duffy was the only black man in Laurie's class and it was easy to pick them out. Beyond that, Foster and Laurie found out that each had been in Vietnam, and at about the same time. Already, there was mutual respect, an unspoken bond forming between them. But at the academy it never went beyond casual hellos.

Laurie was in Company M and he stood out because he was

the leader of the company. Duffy was in Company O. Foster was in Company Q, which Anderson soon named Company Quack. Early on, somebody in Foster's company arrested a man for carving his name on a park bench. So when Anderson or Duffy would see Foster in the hallways they would holler, "Quack, quack."

That never bothered Greg Foster. He would just Donald Duck back at them. He was doing his job, and he knew he was doing well. He was conscientious in academics and he excelled in the gym.

At the New York Police Academy, which is located on East Twentieth Street, the six-month curriculum for probationary patrolmen is divided into four fields — academic instruction, physical training, firearms instruction, and field training. It is an eight-to-four day and the recruits must be inside their homes by midnight every night. Any probationary policeman who gets in trouble after midnight is usually sacked from the force. Tough, explicit rules govern recruits' training and conduct at all times. "At the beginning," Darryl Anderson recalled, "they tell you the do's and the don't's, and there's more don't's than do's." Among the don't's were long hair, sideburns, and moustaches. Greg Foster shaved off his.

Foster had gone through it all in the marines, so he found the police routine almost like child's play. He had had plenty of experience with firearms, so he did well at the firing range. He had graduated from the street, so he was adept at boxing and judo and other forms of self-defense. The men had to run a half-mile almost every day and Foster always did it in around two minutes and twenty seconds. There were others who had trouble doing it in four minutes. To relieve the monotony, the apprentice cops would make bets on the races. They'd line up all the fast men in one group and the slow ones in another group and they would take bets on who would win in each group.

Foster's only weakness was swimming. But he faked it well enough to carry it off.

He was especially adept in the gym on straight physical exercises. Some of the recruits would cheat at push-ups or sit-ups, moving only their heads. Foster never cheated. Part of it was his marine training but part of it also was the feeling that he had to

141

prove himself. He was trying to show people that the heart murmur, or whatever it was, wouldn't affect him. Deep down inside, he was telling himself that if he let up, somebody might see him and say, "Yeah, Foster has a bad heart, let's get rid of him." He had seen it happen to others.

He did everything that was asked of him. He was a very serious person. Duffy, Anderson, Chiles — they knew that, of all of them, Foster wanted the job the most. "All Greg used to talk about was the job," Duffy remembered, "the job, the job, the job."

He was close only to his black friends, but he was friendly with most of the cops. He was shy and somewhat introverted among whites. Once he had to go for motor-scooter training to Randall's Island, which is just across a bridge from Manhattan. Everyone but Foster showed up on time. He came in late.

"What happened?" George Gibbons asked him.

"Aw, I took the bus and got off the wrong stop and had to walk over."

"Why didn't you tell us you needed a lift?"

"I didn't want to bother anyone." He got offers from a lot of his classmates to drive him home, but he refused. He said he'd take the bus back.

Some of that reserve melted away as Foster got to know the other men, and as he began to gain confidence in himself. The confidence came as he found he could perform academically and in every other way with the best of them.

He was happiest when he participated in actual police work in the precincts. He handled himself well in every job they asked him to do. The first notation in his memo book as a policeman was dated January 16, 1971. It read: "Best of luck. Know you'll be a good cop."

It was signed: "Lt. Reedy — William T. Reedy, 66th Precinct."

Things were looking better for Foster all the time. He was back with his wife, he had finally bought himself a new car (the Dodge Charger of his dreams), they would have their co-op apartment soon, and he was about to fulfill his boyhood dream. He was about to become a cop.

He graduated from the academy on May 19, 1971. Patrolman Gregory Foster, shield number 13737, was assigned to the Ninth Precinct.

142

There were moments, early in the first year of his marriage, when Rocco Laurie felt that it had all been a mistake. It was a turbulent period. He was appointed a police trainee in June of 1970. He entered the police academy September 1. Adelaide was working for the telephone company on Staten Island. They were living in a small apartment across the street from Silver Lake. There was tenderness and affection and passion between them, but much tension, too, the pendulum swinging erratically instead of in a smooth, rhythmic, safe arc. Adelaide Laurie was a product of tension. Rocco Laurie's life had been much more placid. He wanted peace and quiet and a certain amount of independence. That was the worst thing about his married life; he felt he was losing his independence.

As soon as they got back from their honeymoon, Adelaide's Uncle Matty came over and asked Rocco if he would like to join his softball team. "I'd love to," Rocco said, "but I have to ask my wife first." She gave her consent, so every Sunday morning he would go out and play softball. Sometimes Adelaide would go over to the uncle's house and do the laundry (they didn't have their own washing machine in the apartment) and wait with her Aunt Anne for the men to come home. And they would come in tired but happy and they would sit around and have coffee and talk. But the more Rocco went out and played softball, the more annoyed Adelaide became. The weekend was their only time together and now she was losing him then, too.

One day Rocco and Matty Iammatteo came into the house after a morning of softball and Adelaide said, "Let's go home now."

"I just want to talk with Uncle Matty awhile," Rocco said.

"Look," Dr. Iammatteo said, "why don't you stay here for dinner? Aunt Annie has some good steaks. Why go home and cook? You're not doing anything this afternoon, are you?"

"No," Rocco said, "we were just going to go home and hang around."

"Good. While the girls are cooking maybe you can help me

take the old model trains upstairs. We'll set 'em up there. It'll only take a half hour."

Adelaide had been silent up to then. Now she went into a rage. "Where does that leave me?" she screamed. "I'll be spending time here all alone."

"You'll be with my wife," Matty said hesitatingly.

"No, I want to go home." Before Rocco could say anything, she whacked him over the head with her pocketbook and ran out of the house.

"Ah, Rocco, look, don't have any more trouble." The uncle was embarrassed. "Just follow her out, go with her." And he did. After he left, the Iammatteos talked for a long time about the young couple.

"This was the way she was as a kid," Annie Iammatteo mused, "and she has a lot of growing up to do. If they love each other enough he'll put up with it and she'll outgrow it."

"I don't know." Matty paced the floor. "That niece of mine . . ."

"I feel Adelaide loves him very much," Annie broke in. "Sure, you can say that when a person loves you and dominates you so much that isn't love at all, but it depends on how you look at it. I think she feels in her heart that she loves him. Maybe that's the only way she knows how to love him."

The next time the uncle saw Rocco he said to him: "Be a little patient, Rocco, she'll grow up."

Rocco was silent. At the time he wasn't sure.

The strain was felt within his family, too. Rocco's brother and his wife saw a lot of the newlyweds, and they witnessed arguments. Rocco's parents felt the tension in all kinds of little ways. Adelaide was deathly afraid of Rocco's mother. The mother had such a commanding and overpowering personality that the daughter-in-law didn't know how to act in front of her. Rocco would tell his wife, "My mother thinks she's an expert on everything. Tell her off once in a while. Don't hold it in. Because if you tell her off you put her in her place and she won't bother you as much." But Adelaide could never do it. Never once in their marriage could she do it.

In the early days Adelaide would bring her laundry to her mother-in-law's house. And the mother-in-law would come on like a drill sergeant. "This goes with bleach," she commanded. "This goes here, this goes there." Timidly, Adelaide would let Mrs. Laurie do the work.

One night Adelaide was folding sheets and Mrs. Laurie marched over and took them right out of her hand. "I'll show you a fast way to do it," she said.

Rocco was watching. "Leave her alone, Ma. Let her do it herself."

"But I'm only trying to help. I want her to do it the fast way."

Adjustment was as difficult for Mrs. Laurie as it was for Adelaide. She found she was resenting Adelaide. Her daughter-in-law did a million little things to make her resent her, and they inflated in her mind. There were days when Adelaide and Rocco stayed away; the mother knew it was because of the daughter-in-law. She grew lonely. One day she called her son. "Gee, Rock," she said, full of self-pity, "I forgot how to cook. I got nobody to cook for around here."

A rift grew between them. The mother-in-law kept saying to herself, I've got to give her the benefit of the doubt. 'Cause she's my daughter-in-law. And she never had a mother or a father, and they all catered to her. But she would waver; she felt Adelaide was keeping mother and son apart.

The resentment was growing in Adelaide, too. She didn't want to share Rocco's love with anyone. She didn't want competition from sports or from his family. She wanted to be the main event in his life. Once she confessed to her husband, "The only person I like in your family is your father and the dog. Because the dog never says anything and your father never says anything."

One Sunday, just three months after they had taken their wedding vows, their marriage almost fell apart for good.

He had just come home from a long session of softball. Her resentment had turned to rage. As soon as he was in the house she was on him.

"I'm sick and tired of spending my time here cleaning up the house while you're out playing."

"Look, Adelaide, you know I like to play ball. It's the only thing I do without you."

She started to scream. He reddened. With her lung power

she could be heard all over the neighborhood. He put his hand over her mouth.

"Shut up," he ordered. "Shut up right now."

"Leave," she said abruptly, freeing his hand. "Go ahead, leave the house. I don't want you around."

He drew back, stunned. "Do you really want me to go?"

She was crying. "Yes, I really want you to go."

"Are you sure?"

"Yes, I'm sure."

He hesitated. "I'm asking you for the last time. Do you want me to go?"

"Get out," she screamed. "Get out! Get out! Get out!"

He stormed out of the house. Moments later she ran to the door, looking for him. He was gone. She went to the kitchen window that looked out into the street. His car was still there. He had left the car keys, his wallet, and his gun at home. She put on her housecoat and got into the car and went looking for him.

He had been picked up by a friend, who drove him to his parents' house. He came in, still in his sweat suit, his face pale. His mother knew immediately that there was trouble.

"Rocco, what happened?"

"It's all over, Ma."

"What are you talking about, Rocco?"

"I'm not going to be unhappy the rest of my life."

He told her about it. The mother tried to calm her son down. She talked soothingly to him. He tried to explain his side. "She knew when she married me that I liked sports, and I'm not giving up sports for her. All she's done since we were married is nag me."

Just then the phone rang. Mr. Laurie answered it. It was Adelaide. She wanted to know if Rocco was there. Anthony Laurie, Sr., looked at his wife. She nodded to him. "He's on his way home," he said.

Adelaide sat and waited. She was anxious. She planned to apologize as soon as he came in, run into his arms and give him a kiss and tell him how sorry she was for the way she acted. The doorbell rang. She rushed to open it. Mrs. Laurie stood in the doorway, her son just behind her.

She shot into the house, starting in on Adelaide without ceremony. "You're stupid, Adelaide," she said. "Don't you want this marriage to last? Well, my son is completely disgusted and right now he doesn't care whether he's married or not." As she talked she walked through the house. My God, it struck Adelaide, she's looking for dust. Mrs. Laurie went on and on like that while Adelaide stood there dumbfounded, unable to react. Rocco, too, said nothing. Finally, she left and the husband and wife looked at each other. Adelaide's hair was in curlers. She felt miserable. She began to cry.

"You had to bring your mother," she said bitterly.

"I didn't bring my mother, she wanted to come. What could I do?"

They sat down and talked. They talked it out. Adelaide told Rocco how unhappy she felt at being left alone every weekend. She said that it would be better if she could at least come and watch him play. He said he didn't think she was interested in sports. She told him she'd try to become interested. They reconciled.

He even tried to teach her how to play baseball. A couple of times he took her to the beach and he threw her baseballs and she tried to hit them with a bat, but she was hopeless. They had bought a dog, Buster, and on Saturday mornings Rocco would wake up Adelaide at six o'clock. "Come on, we're going to take the dog for a walk." They would go over to Silver Lake with the dog and try to jog. But the dog was tiny and Adelaide ended up carrying him and soon she gave up jogging.

When one got mad with the other, they tried to laugh it off. He would be watching television and she would call him in for dinner. He'd say, "Yeah, all right, I'll be right there."

And he would still be watching and she'd shout, "The food is on the table."

"All right, I'll be right in."

Finally, she would stomp into the living room. "If you don't come I'll take everything and throw it in the garbage." She was genuinely mad but he would start to laugh and say something funny and this helped dissolve her anger.

He enjoyed making fun of her, it got to be a game. Most of the time she didn't mind. She had a small, pert nose, but he always made comments about its gigantic size. "Don't turn your head this way, Boss, or you'll hit me in the head with your nose." Or, after she sneezed: "Watch out, you might blow out all the windows." She would start punching him and he would punch back. He decided to teach her to box. They moved around their small apartment recklessly, each one winging punches. Once she walked into a punch and her eye was discolored for a week. When she went to work the next day she told her friends that her husband had beaten her up.

She loved watching him shave. One day he said, "Adelaide, do it for me." She shaved him. Another time he was shaving and she was standing there watching him and he put some cream on her nose. She wiped it off and put some on his nose. Then he rubbed some in her hair. She took the can and squirted him with it. He got hold of the can and squirted her, and there was shaving cream all over the bathroom.

He would get up at five-thirty during the week to go to the police academy. She would get up with him. While he was in the bathroom she would press his gray uniform. She would lay it out on the bed. Then she would lay out his holster and she would put his gun in the holster, his shield next to it, and finally his handkerchief. He grew accustomed to that service. One morning she forgot to put the gun in the holster. He went out to the car and found he didn't have the gun.

"From now on," he said to her, "don't forget to do that." But she liked doing that for him. She hoped that someday he would teach her how to shoot guns. Later, when he was working nights, he told her, "Load the gun [he had another one by that time], keep it with you, and if anybody comes in this house that you don't know, you shoot first and then call me at the precinct and I'll come right home." She thought that was kind of a drastic course of action. If anybody broke in here, she said to herself, I'd faint. I'll never be able to use the gun. It frightened her a little to hear him talk that way. But by that time Rocco had seen much, and his views about crime and criminals had hardened.

From the moment he started his career as a cop, Rocco was meticulous about the profession. As far as he was concerned, everything had to be done by the book, and he never took a short cut. He was exactly like Gregory Foster in this respect.

Once he got to the academy he excelled in almost every phase of the training — marksmanship, physical conditioning, and academics. As a cop, there was no question he was going places.

He started in June as a trainee, doing clerical work at the police academy. The first day he was there another trainee came up and introduced himself.

"I'm Larry Perez. What's your name?"

"Rocco Laurie."

"That's Italian," Perez said.

"Yup, that's all Italian. That's my pedigree."

"I'm from Cuba even though I look as white as you." He and Laurie became close friends.

Perez was engaged to a pretty little Italian girl and when Rocco found out he told Perez, "Larry, don't get married. You'll be sorry."

They started to double-date, going to movies or on car drives. Perez would say, "Rock, this movie is playing at the Island, this one's at the Paramount. What do you want to go see?" And Rocco would say, "Let me ask the Boss first. I got to check with the Boss." It made Perez wonder about the wisdom of getting married.

They were in the same class at the academy but in different squads. Perez, who is a six-footer and weights over two hundred pounds, wrestled with Laurie in the gym. He found he couldn't handle him. Rocco would get him down and bite him and choke him and pretend that he was going to finish him off, the way the television wrestlers always operated. Perez would holler, "Hey, what are you doing?" And Laurie, laughing, would pin him almost immediately. Perez thought, Jeez, he's only playing with me. What happens if he ever gets serious?

After a while Perez asked the lieutenant in charge if he and Laurie could have the same lunch hour. He agreed. They went out and sat on a park bench and did just what Greg Foster and his friends were doing at about the same time — girl-watched. Like most cops, their conversation was filled with talk about sex. For a number of reasons, not the least being that because of the job and the uniform, the cop becomes a sex object to many women, sex does become a preoccupation with many cops. Shortly after Perez became a patrolman he went on a family dispute and a nineteen-year-old girl was in the room with her parents and she was talking in Spanish, not knowing that Perez understood perfectly. While Perez was putting down the information in his book the girl was saying, "Oh, he looks so good, if I could only fuck him. . . . I could really do a job on you, baby, and you wouldn't be able to walk for weeks. . . ." On and on she went — "if I could only do this to you, if I could only do that to you" — all the while looking innocently into Perez's face. He tried to control himself and he never said a word but he left the place shaking. Later he told Antoinette, who was now his wife, about it.

"I wonder," she said, "if ever the time came when you did have the occasion and someone like that kept after you, I wonder if you would give in."

Perez looked at her solemnly. "Listen, if she comes up to you, what can you do? You're the police, right? We got to please the public as much as we can."

As their academy life proceeded, Laurie and Perez talked about what they wanted to do as cops. They debated radio-car duty versus foot patrol.

"I'm thin-blooded," Larry said. "I can't stand the cold. I'll take the car."

"Not me," Rocco said. "I'd rather walk. You can see better what's going on, you get to know the people, you get to know the bad from the good."

Perez told Laurie that he would prefer to be assigned a quiet precinct. "I'd rather go to the One-two-three, Rock, right on Staten Island [he lived on Staten Island, too]. That's God's country. Or the Sixty-eight, which is in Bay Ridge and is mostly residential. That would be beautiful, too."

Laurie felt just the opposite. He told Perez he wanted an active precinct, he wanted to make a lot of collars.

(After graduation Perez was sent to a precinct in the Williamsburg section of Brooklyn, which is not a safe district at all. His first reaction was, oh, God, I'm going to quit the force. He was scared but after a while he found he was among brothers; he found out that in an active precinct the police are very close because they have no choice — everybody out there, the cops felt, was against them. Later Perez was transferred to a precinct in Queensboro that had the highest homicide rate in the city.)

One day Laurie was having trouble with his car. He had parked near the Staten Island ferry and Perez, who knew about cars, said he would walk back with him after work to look at it. Heading toward the ferry they passed Fifth Street, which is where the Ninth Precinct headquarters is located.

"I'd love working over here," Rocco said.

"Are you kidding? What do you want to work here for?"

"Well, look, it's close to the ferry. I can be home in no time."

"Yeah, but look at the way people live in the slums, Rock. You got everything down here — hippies, junkies, winos. You go into hallways, or onto roofs, or into those derelict buildings to see if there are junkies — anyone can take a run at you."

"This is the place to be," Rocco said. "Lots of action."

"Who needs it?" Larry said.

"I want to make the bureau," Rocco said. "I'm going for detective."

"The bureau?" Larry said derisively. "What good is the bureau going to do you if you get wiped out down here."

"I'm not gonna be wiped out," Rocco laughed. "I survived Nam, I'll survive anywhere."

The six months at the academy were one of the most pleasant interludes of Rocco Laurie's life. He found he could compete easily with the other men, that, in fact, he was a cut above them in most cases. He scored high in everything except long-distance running; he just didn't have the speed. But his academic grades were high, mostly in the nineties, his marksmanship was excellent, and he was No. 1 in the gym.

On the day of his graduation the Laurie family all went to the academy together. Adelaide was with Rocco's mother and father, his brother Anthony and Anthony's wife, Kathy. Before the ceremonies began, Mrs. Laurie scanned the audience. She seemed restless. Suddenly, she leaned over and whispered to Adelaide, "Well, you didn't let him get away from you, did you?"

Adelaide was stunned. "What do you mean by that?" she said. The implication was clear to her, that she had been out to get him right from the start. Perhaps it was true, she thought, though for most of the time she had been the passive partner in the courtship. But why bring it up now, at that moment, at a time when all of them should have been sharing their pride in the accomplishments of her husband and their son?

Rocco's father stepped in at once. "What's meant to be is meant to be," he said. "What happened, happened. Only the future counts now."

The bitterness cut into Adelaide until the ceremonies began and she saw Rocco marching down the aisle, handsome in his blue uniform, handsomer than she ever remembered seeing him. She felt a surge of love for her husband. They were all overwhelmed when the honors were announced. He was awarded a .38-caliber Smith and Wesson revolver for being the most physically fit man in his graduating class. That wasn't all. The academy's highest honor, the Bloomingdale trophy, for the student who attains the highest general average in the school, was also given to Probationary Patrolman Rocco W. Laurie, shield number 11019.

PART FOUR

The
Partners

When there's nothing betwixt a man and
the world but his partners, it don't make
a damn bit of diff'rence the color
of his hide.

— JOHN SEELYE, *The Kid*

Well, the job was getting to him. He couldn't stand the way those people were living down there in the East Village. It's something else. He had said, "Jackie, you don't know how lucky you are. You ought to see what a lot of people go through, how these kids go without food, half-dressed, things like that." I had told him, "Gregory, before all this is over with, you're going to hate that job. You're going to want to leave." He told me he found out I was right. He just couldn't take it. It was getting to him.

Rocco, after he had been there awhile, began to compare it to Vietnam. In Vietnam, he said to me, you know who your enemies are, the ones with the slanty eyes. But the East Village is a jungle, and you don't know, you just don't know who your enemies are.

I parked nervously on the street, between Avenues B and C. I had brought the old Olds, with the dent in the front fender. I was wearing my youngest son's dungarees and an old denim shirt, hoping to blend in. Still, I felt conspicuous. The street throbbed. Little children, not more than five or six years old, were pounding rocks on caps on the stoops. Puerto Rican men and women stood in clusters on the street, talking. White men and black men — junkies — walked vacantly along the street. A white girl, dressed in a halter and skirt, was standing in a doorway, drinking out of a wine bottle. She may have been sixteen. Men came out of the door, brushing by her, ignoring her as she ignored them, her head thrust back, her lips gripped on the bottle, sucking.

The street was speckled with garbage. Buddy, who was a building super down there, had once told me: "There's always a guy taking a shit out the window." Trash cans stood sentry in front of every stoop but they were overflowing, mostly with bottles. It was a tropical night and whatever air circulated through the street was thick with the smell of musk and the smell of fear. Dogs barked — the barks of mongrels and German shepherds — and you could hear the *bap* from the exploding caps. And there was music from radios flowing out of open windows and the rapid chatter of Spanish coming from all over the street. The street throbbed and I wondered for a moment that even given its sinister aspects — for it was, after all, New York's lowermost depths — might this not be the new vital center of American life today? Might it not be down here, among this polyglot of races and raw, basic emotions, down here where survival techniques were best learned — might not the meaning of American life be flowing down here rather than uptown and upcountry, where it was smooth and sterile and the menace was still an undercurrent? Might it not be down here that Americans would find themselves again? Nevertheless, knowing that life, for all its survival instincts, was very cheap in the East Village, in the heart of the Ninth Precinct, I was afraid.

I knocked on the door, which was padded, lead-thick, like the side of a Brink's truck. I could hear music inside. I knocked again, and waited, pawing, feeling furtive. Finally, someone heard the knock and Marie opened the door. She smiled and invited me in, offered me a drink, and excused the disorder. She was wearing a light mini-dress and her legs stood out; she was the only pale horse in the race. Her stringy brown hair tumbled about loosely. Her eyes were tired, harried.

The door was shut and I saw six locks of assorted sizes running down the front. The windows, which were at street level, were barred. A big stand-up electric fan whirled away in the small living room, stirring the curtains. There was a large enclosed stereo system, a liquor cabinet, a couch, one easy chair. It was crowded. A black woman was sitting on the couch drinking. Two small children sat beside her, eating peanuts. A black man in a goatee was lying on the floor drinking. Another black man was sitting on a trunk drinking. They were, all of them, rocking in some way to the music — either head rocks, body rocks, or leg rocks.

In the back of the small apartment, beyond the kitchenette, was a small bedroom, just big enough for the mattress on the floor. The walls were painted deep blue. Buddy Williams, a handsome man with a becoming Afro and a small black moustache, was resting on the mattress. He was wearing slacks, a white

T-shirt, and sandals. He looked tired, too. There were bags under his brown eyes, but his eyes were alert and wary and expressive. He rose to greet me and shook hands. He was very tall, but he let his shoulders droop. To be too tall meant he would be too visible. Buddy Williams, I learned soon enough, preferred to remain an invisible man.

He was born and raised in Harlem, 135th Street and Eighth Avenue. He played basketball in high school and went to a black college in the West. He was in the army for two years. He worked in the post office a year before he went into the service, and a year after he came out. "After that," he said, "I just went out trying to make it."

"By doing a lot of different things?" I asked.

"Everything," Buddy said. "Mostly illegal. Not too much, though. Like, I'm not into it because I enjoy it. I'm into it because it's the only way I can make the type of money that I need to live for the type of mentality I have, the type of things I like to do. I'm not qualified to make twenty to thirty thousand dollars a year. So what can I do? This is my only thing."

"You mean like after-hour clubs?" I knew that Buddy had owned a little bar in the neighborhood where he served drinks for fifty cents a shot, where you could socialize without being hassled.

"Right. You know, different things. Like, I've been in the policy, you know, taking numbers, stuff like that. So many people, when you're into something illegal, right away they think you're a criminal or something. And yet now — like when I started out eight or nine years ago in the policy and stuff, it was a bad thing. Like, you'd go to jail for five years if they caught you. But now, what do we have? We have off-track betting. They're getting ready to legalize gambling in the state. It's really a funny thing. It's just like years ago if you were selling marijuana, you'd get ten years. Now they're getting ready to legalize that, I think. You see, like to me everything is relative. So I don't really feel myself as a bad guy.

"I'm not really a criminal or a hustler or anything. It's the only way I know of going out and making some money. Period. Like if I go out right now, get a job for a hundred and fifty dollars a week, how do I live off it? It's not for me, because I've seen too many beautiful things in life and I enjoy nice things. I like to take my girl out. I want to be able to not worry about the check, how much it's going to be and so forth."

His voice was deep and authoritative, but he spoke low and it was hard to pick up his words because of the din coming from the living room. Marie suggested that maybe Buddy should tell them to go home. He rose, went into the living room, whispered softly to each of them, and they all stood up silently and left. "He's like an adviser to these people," Marie whispered to me, "a father confessor. They all love him. He should have been a priest." He and Marie moved in the living room. They drank slowly.

"When I first came to the East Village six or seven years ago, it was a whole different thing. I sorta liked the relaxed way that people were. I used to sleep out in Tompkins Park all night. The flower people were down there and there was love. It was really beautiful. We used to sit down and I used to talk to the fellows and girls — white, black, pink; it didn't matter. It was such a relaxed thing. And when it changed was in 1965 when these two kids who were tripping on acid were killed. Soon after that the whole thing changed. Now the only white kids down here are either people that are on drugs — hard stuff, I'm talking about, heroin, stuff like that — or they're runaways, rebelling against the Establishment, or some bullshit. Now things are very uptight. There's a fear down here that people have. Right now it's very uncomfortable at all times, unless I'm in the house."

"Why do people still live here?" I asked, knowing it was a stupid question.

"They got to live somewhere. Most of them are on welfare and pretty uptight and they're into whatever type of hustle they can do, whatever they can get into to supplement their little welfare. Because no one can live off welfare, not really. And most of the people around here, they're doing something illegally: prostitution or selling some type of drugs, because this is definitely the drug center. And the police down here, they turn their backs on things."

For the first time Marie spoke up. "This is when I first came to New York. I was coming to live with my girl friend. We were riding on bicycles, a bright day two or three years ago. And three cops were standing on the corner in front of Tenth

158

Street, Avenue B. And we were coming down Tenth Street and four guys came out of the park and took our purses and split. Those cops, who had watched the whole thing, slowly turned around. We were all bloody. They came up and said: 'What happened to you?' Fucking pigs," she said coldly. "They saw the whole thing and did nothing."

"This is true," Buddy said. "Actually, they're frustrated in a way themselves. It's just like they can't do too much. It's not their fault. They can't do too much because the lieutenants and the captains, they tie them down. Like, I know when I was in Harlem working in this policy place, we used to pay off the whole precinct. I don't mean every policeman in the precinct. But the money would go to the captain and he would pass it on. I was just a little spoke in the wheel. I was nothing. There were big people up there. But I knew what was going on. They'd come around to the back door and we'd give them four or five hundred dollars.

"Now down here, there's two or three policemen coming here. They ride around. They come in here to drink booze. They ride around drunk half the night. Now how can they be effective on their jobs? This one guy hits the booze. He tells me all the time — all he wants to do is retire.

"I had a narcotics policeman, plainclothes — undercover, I guess you call him — working with me selling drugs out the door. That's right. In fact I saw him yesterday. He came by, he wanted to get some business. He was sitting right there" — Buddy pointed to me — "badge, gun, everything — and selling drugs out the door. So, you see, what can you do?"

I wondered about Foster and Laurie. I knew that Buddy had met both of them.

"This friend of mine, Nate, he brought Foster in. He said, 'This is a friend of mine.' He introduced him. He wasn't in uniform then. Then he told me he was a policeman. And after that I'd see him on the beat. He seemed like a very nice fellow. He was quiet but he was also very efficient. He did his job. He would arrest you in a minute if he caught you doing something wrong. One day he took these two fellows in the hallway and he found the works, but no drugs — needles and stuff. That's something he could have taken them to jail for. But he talked to them and let them go.

"Laurie was the same way. He would never bother you unless you got out of place. That's the kind of a cat he was. He was a cool cat. And the word was getting around that these two fellows were, really, for policemen around here — because everyone has a thing against policemen around here — they were really getting to people. Like, they could be trusted. When I say trusted I mean like, a junkie, he would feel he could talk to them if anything went wrong or anything.

"I think some cops really start out dedicated on the thing. But it ends up where you cannot buck the graft. If, in other words, Foster and Laurie had gone against the higher-ups, they'd probably be working out of Canarsie.

"Foster and Laurie were on what they call Neighborhood Police Teams. But that's bullshit. I found a little paper one day asking, 'Do you know the names of the policemen on your beat?' This is all political bullshit. They had two or three people coming around talking to people who they really had contempt for. But they had to do it because the sergeant said go out and do it. Maybe not Foster and Laurie, because they came along at a time when you know they were going to try to change situations. The rest of it; they were just trying to keep everyone cool, especially during the summertime because the police know in the summertime all the niggers and Puerto Ricans start rioting. 'Cause it's warm out."

Buddy talked cynically about politicians coming into the area with two hundred thousand dollars to keep things cool, giving people sandwiches, and pocketing one hundred and fifty thousand dollars for themselves. The fan kept the air circulating but sweat glistened on everyone's face.

He talked about drugs, how the best dope comes from uptown but the best market is in the East Village. "Right now," he said, "you could walk out there and buy anything you wanted to buy. At first, you couldn't buy it from me because if I saw you I'd panic. Because, you see, I'm cautious. Like I say, I'm in a business thing and I have a fear of going to jail and I've never been to jail. The thing is, like there are a lot of kids out there right now. They'd say, all right, I'll go get you something *if* you give me something for it. I don't mean money. I mean drugs. And they're so uptight or sick or something they'll take it and get it, even though they may know it's possible you may be a policeman."

I asked, "How do all the different ethnic groups live together around here?"

"By necessity." Buddy laughed. "In my two buildings there are a lot of white people. You never see them 'cause they totally live in fear. Remember the fellow we found dead over there?"

"Talk about cops," Marie said. "One night Buddy was super down there, we were scrubbing the halls, cleaning 'em up. And I smelled a terrible odor. We started knocking on doors and nobody would come out. It was ridiculous. And we called the cops and they found this guy. This old man had been dead for about a week, and they made jokes about it, about his genitals and all. He was lying in there naked and one of the cops said, 'Come on inside and look at his balls.' And that's their attitude."

"We have quite a few old people living in the building but these people are there because they have nowhere else to go. They're paying forty or fifty dollars a month, where are they gonna go? But they never come out. They hide. Like that door where this old man was found dead. He had a table up against the door." Buddy was silent for a moment, tinkling his glass. "Worse than Vietnam down here. I wouldn't be a policeman down here, not in uniform.

"You see, there's another thing about the policemen down here that's bad for the community. They'll do things down here that they wouldn't do on Fifth or Park Avenue. Like one day two or three of 'em ran in here. Remember that time?" he said, looking at Marie. She nodded. "They said they had a call that someone was coming out of the apartment and they wanted to catch him by running out my window. The point is, they just came in. That's illegal. They had no place to come in here. And that's why they usually don't mess with me. They know, number one, I'm no junkie. I don't have any police record and I've never been in jail and the only way they could do anything to me is to get me dead to right. If they do anything stupid — 'cause I'm not stupid — I'm going over there to find out who, what, and why it happened. But they take advantage of people down here because these people are not in a position to get lawyers. They don't have any political minds. The people down here are just uptight and afraid. It's just a helluva situation. I know one thing — I'm going to get out of here as soon as I can."

"Why do you stay down here, Marie?" I asked. She smiled, looking at Buddy, preferring not to answer the question, or not knowing how.

"That's a good question," Buddy said. "Marie is young, she's got her future ahead of her, she's got a lot of things going for her. I think it's a good experience for her as long as she doesn't get harmed. But I think that Marie will get out. I hope so.

"I think personally that Marie, her head is into getting close to people. Marie has no fear. I've taken her uptown with me and she fritters about totally free many times. You can't do that. She doesn't realize that people — some people, not everybody — are treacherous, they're ready to do harm to you. That's how bad things are today, especially when you get into the minority groups. You know, I'll take her uptown. I've had her in places where she's the only white person in the whole place and I don't want her to go. If I'm taking her places where I know people, naturally I don't mind taking her because I know they gonna look out for her. But there's certain places I don't want her to go because there are people in Harlem today who'll hurt her only because she's white.

"I had that happen. This friend of mine, this black friend of mine, took this white girl up to Harlem, to Club Baron. They were coming out, walked over to the car, and he went over to the driver's side to open the door. Some fellow walked right over and stabbed the girl. She died right there on the street, right on the ground. That type of thing. Now all he knew was that she was white. You see, this is the type of mind that's out here today. The only thing to do is look out for yourself. That's the way I feel. I just look out for myself and have people around me that's gonna help me. I don't like the people a lot of times that I'm involved with."

Marie moved over and sat on the arm of Buddy's chair. She leaned down and brushed her lips against his forehead. He smiled gently.

"I want to get out. I've been in it too long. I can't be in there fighting and all this kind of stuff. I had these gates put on the window for Marie and she said to me, she said, 'Well, I've never been robbed.' See, but you can't think in those terms. I'm gonna put some gates on the back window. Now the gates will all come together with a crowbar in a minute, but at least it gives you time to get yourself together — *if* you're in the house. If they come in and nobody's here and they steal everything, that means nothing. Oh, it means something — material things. But you can get more. But if you're in this house sleeping or something, and they come in, it's a startling thing and you could get killed or something."

"Is there any way it can get better around here?"

"I can't say. If it does get better it will have to change. People don't want to change things. Like, my landlord came around today raising hell with me. I can't stand him. I talked to him like I feel about him — like he's shit to me. But you see, I'm not uptight for the job. I have the job for a reason. The reason is cover. It's a legitimate job, you know, those supers' jobs. If anything happens, you say, well, I'm a super, I work. I can talk to them because I'm not uptight. In other words, I don't need the fifty dollars a week I get for two buildings. I don't really need it. But I need the legitimacy. I've paid fifteen to twenty dollars to be on the books as a bartender even though I wasn't working, just to be legal. The point is, the man cares nothing if I ask him for two gallons of disinfectant to wash the hall. He tells me, I'm not in the disinfectant business. All these people exploit the people. Slumlords and politicians do the same thing.

"Even with welfare," Buddy went on, "they say — here's a woman who has maybe two or three kids, why is she on welfare? So she goes out. She may make a hundred and twenty dollars a week. She's got to pay twenty dollars per kid a week for a babysitter. By the time they take everything out she may have cleared fifty dollars a week. Now, she gets more than that on welfare, so why should she work? They force these people on welfare and even though a lot of them are triflin' people and they don't want to work, there are a lot of them — most of them are women — who would like to work because when you work you have a better mind and you feel you're doing something. You have something moving, instead of sitting around on the stoop all day like these people waiting every two weeks for the check to come."

The sounds of the street rose above the steady hum of the fan: The squeal of brakes from a bus out on the avenue. . . . Dogs yelping at each other and at people. . . . Adult voices now beginning to rise in passion. . . . Children playing loudly just outside the window. Every time the fan blew the curtains apart, a knot of kids, bent over, would look into the room. They spoke a mixture of English and Spanish.

"Kiss her and we'll go away," one of them said. He might have been eight years old. At first Marie and Buddy smiled. "Hey, mister, kiss her. Not the coon — you." Soon the kids were chattering loudly, their voices becoming more combative. Mostly it was Spanish but the word "fuck" kept being repeated. Finally, Buddy bolted for the door, ran out on the street, and cleared them out of there.

"They don't mean anything," he said apologetically when he came back. "They're looking for things to do, you know. Street kids. They start young around here. Soon as they're able to walk they're out on the street, alone."

It was quiet for a while. Buddy's brief departure seemed to have broken a spell. But he apparently wanted to restore the connection. "I think the best question you asked me tonight," he said to me, "was why is Marie down here."

"Because you're down here," Marie said finally. "I got to stay with Buddy."

The doorbell rang. "Who's there!" Buddy barked. He listened at the door, then opened it. It was Nate, the big, heavyset ex-marine who had left most of one hand in Saigon the day he stepped on a mine. Nate now works for Buddy as a janitor, and in some of Buddy's other enterprises. He talked about Gregory Foster.

"I met him through a friend who was a narco cop. I brought Greg upstairs to the club once to say hello. He always had a smile. He'd have a drink and say, 'Got to get home to my wife before she kills me.' Laurie's a cool cat, too. He would never bother you unless you got out of place."

They talked about Buddy's club. "I got it going because there are a lot of Spanish clubs around here. Actually, it was just a place for neighborhood friends to go. See, most of these people can't afford to go to a bar and hang out, so we charged 'em fifty cents for a little drink, even though it was illegal. We tried to get a membership thing going. Only reason it didn't work is because the people, they'd come in, break up the place, get drunk, want to fight. It wasn't worth it. I put about a thousand dollars in it — more than that — trying to get it nice. It was really a beautiful place. But it couldn't work. People around here are just too frustrated. They're really uptight."

"Foster would come in every now and then," Nate remembered. "He would say things like, 'You fellows don't have a license, try not to have any trouble.' Little things like that."

"Usually," Buddy said, "when two men get together, either they're talking about some woman who we can lay — you know how men are — or something. We never talked anything about that. Foster would come in, 'How are ya, how's the club going?' He'd say something like that. I'd say fine. 'Well, you fellows make sure you keep it cool.' And he would never stay more than ten or fifteen minutes."

"In other words," Nate said, "if he said something he meant it. He told you to do something, you realized you had to do it because he wasn't fucking around."

The talk got around to cops again. "We had a friend of ours get shot down here and we never saw a policeman. Like, one day we had a little party in the club. I'm sitting out there in a car in front of the club with some friends of mine from uptown. Some fellows went out from the bar and got into a little argument in the car parked right behind the car where I was sitting with my friends. And the fellow back there said, 'I'll show you what I'm going to do.' He snatched open the door and fired three shots, shot the fellow three times in the chest. He staggered across the street. I got across the street, the fellow who shot him is gone, the other one is dying. We couldn't find a policeman. We didn't even see a policeman. They don't care about people down here.

"I've known in the past four or five months four or five people that's gotten shot, people that I personally know. Like Henry the other night, he was shot in the leg. Mousey, Kenny — I call him Gunsmoke. They were shot. Around here we have four or five fellows, we work together, it's the only way to make it. It has nothing to do with how bad you are, how tough you handle yourself physically. Anyone can get shot, killed."

"I'm going to Iowa," Nate said. "Got to find a little home. I think I'd go anywhere to get away from here."

"Would you go south?" I asked.

"Go south? I wouldn't even go to the southern part of this room."

It was late now. Buddy and Marie were yawning, Nate had left, saying he had a few things to attend to. I prepared to leave. "What do you want to do with yourself?" I asked Buddy.

"I don't know. I often ask myself, what can I do? And that's nothing. I could go on a job and learn something, I'm not talking about that. I'm trying to get me enough money together to buy me a home, pay for it, buy a small car. . . . Then I won't mind going out making a hundred and twenty-five dollars a week if I don't have those bills."

"The American dream?" Buddy laughed.

"When I was working at the post office, and that was years ago, this white fellow sat down and we had a conversation. This was in the Kennedy era and everything was sweet and beautiful and we were all complimenting each other and he said to me, 'Well, we're doing the same job and making the same amount of money.' Which was true. He was a temp sub and I was a temp sub. But he lived on Washington Avenue, up near Queens Boulevard, and he was paying maybe a hundred and twenty-five dollars a month rent. Now, I was living down on Ninety-first and Amsterdam and I was paying a hundred and fifty dollars a month rent. And the only reason I was paying it was because I was black. The point is, he could do more with his money than I could do with mine. I know it. Right now you can go in certain stores around here and every welfare day everything goes up a penny or two. And we get inferior food and meats down here.

"You know what I mean? And people don't realize it but it's true. And so many people try to do something about it, but they're up against it. It's just bullshit."

Buddy flung out his hands. I couldn't tell if it was a gesture of hopelessness or if it was just meant to emphasize his thoughts. His hands moved rhythmically, almost as if they were timed to the weariness in his voice. Outside, the dogs were still barking and the buses were squealing down the avenue and the noise was, in its totality, a roar, the crush of whitewater careening down-river.

"Like, I don't know when I ever sat and talked like this. Because it's futile, it's *futile*. There's nothing to say. Only thing you can do is just go on out, do the best you can, make as much as you can, and just, like I say, be impersonal." He turned to Marie and began stroking her arm, a tender look on his face, a pained look, too. "Don't get involved with people's problems. Because if you do you just fail. . . . You can't help everybody. You can't do it. Not down here, you can't."

D *on't get involved with people's problems. . . . You can't help everybody.* Foster and Laurie didn't believe that for a minute. Either they were too young, too idealistic, or too new to the miseries of the East Village. Whatever the reasons, they cared.

In his first months in the Ninth Precinct Gregory Foster befriended street kids he met on his beat, young Puerto Rican boys who had always hated cops, who had been beaten down by cops, who had never known a "good" cop in their lives. These kids came to idealize Foster. To them he was "the best cop we ever had around here."

Rocco Laurie was the same way. Immediately, he made friends with shopkeepers down there, and he even tried to help addicts he felt were still capable of being helped. One of them, whose life he literally saved, said about the young cop: "Rock was my cure. There's some of him walking around inside me."

Alone and together Foster and Laurie were involved with the people.

They came to the Ninth Precinct six weeks apart. A line in Rocco Laurie's memo book reads: "April 2, 1971 P.A. Graduation." Then, three lines down: "April 5, 1971 9th Pct. 0800-1600." Gregory Foster got out of the police academy on May 19 and was assigned immediately to the Ninth Precinct.

Their first six or seven months in the precinct they mostly

worked separately. But they did get to talk to each other and to learn something about each other. Laurie remembered Foster from the police academy and he had heard about his Vietnam reputation, so he went out of his way to talk to him. They made small talk at first because Laurie was wary of black men and uncomfortable with them, even when they were police officers, and Foster was wary of white men and uncomfortable with them, for reasons founded in history.

On June 11, Laurie was on security at the station house and was assigned a prisoner of Foster's. On July 2 and 3, because of the Independence Day holidays, the precinct was short of men. Foster and Laurie were assigned to ride in a radio car. They worked midnight to eight both nights and it was mostly quiet — one maternity case, a reported street fight that turned out to be unfounded, a robbery case in which the victim had been kicked in the side and had to be rushed to the hospital, a robbery in progress that the partners came upon too late (it was already being handled by the Anti-Crime Unit), and some random investigations that came to nothing. They worked one more day together, July 6 — an eight-to-four — and that was all until they became partners.

But it was those sessions that formed the idea in each man's head that maybe someday Foster and Laurie could team up. One day Foster came home and told his wife, "Laurie's the only white fella I can trust. Most of the other guys are chicken."

"What do you mean, chicken?" Jackie asked.

"Chicken, Jackie, chicken. I don't want any part of 'em. Laurie's not chicken."

Laurie was beginning to feel the same way about Foster. One summer night Rocco and the man he was then working with were parked in a squad car when a man ran out of a bar.

"There's a guy inside," he said, "pointing a gun at another guy."

Later Laurie told Adelaide what had happened. "My partner went in there behind me with his gun drawn, which is fine, but he had it cocked. Now if he tripped he would have killed me. This is something you don't do." Laurie thought a moment. "Foster would never have done that. His gun would have been on its way out, but he's smart. He uses his head. I wouldn't mind working with him, Adelaide. I don't think it would be unsafe. He's not a stupid cop. A lot of cops do stupid things. They don't think. Foster's been around. He thinks."

Working those two nights together in early July gave Foster and Laurie a chance to get to know each other a little. They talked about their home lives and their ambitions. They noted that each had been married about the same length of time, and that they had married as soon as they got out of the marines. But neither one opened up to the other about the problems in his marriage. They talked more about their ambitions. Laurie told Foster he wanted to make detective. Foster said he planned to go to John Jay College part-time and that maybe someday he could become a probationary officer or even a lawyer. They talked about Vietnam. They told each other about their experiences in Nam. Neither one held back. Again, they noted that each had sustained similar shocks. Each had been brushed by death. Each, for some reason, had survived when they could just as easily not have survived. They came out of those two nights with a feeling of respect for each other. They weren't friends by any means — it was not like Laurie and Larry Perez or Foster and Darryl Anderson, each making friends quickly with men of their "own kind." The gulf of race still spread wide between them. But each sensed in the other a bond that might possibly transcend race. They didn't talk about becoming partners then, but it was an unspoken thought on both men's minds.

The first night Gregory Foster showed up for duty at the Ninth Precinct, fresh from the academy, it was very warm. Most of the police in the station house were in short sleeves. Foster kept his jacket on. A black cop, Andy Glover, came over to him.

"It's kind of warm in here," Glover said. "What are you doing with your jacket on?"

"I'd just as soon keep it on," Foster said. "I feel comfortable."

The older cop just sighed. "I'm Andy Glover."

"Greg Foster."

Glover asked Foster about himself, where he came from, what he was up to, whether he was married. He was trying to loosen up the rookie. A few days later they gave him Foster as a partner.

They were quite different in disposition. Glover who was then thirty, had already been on the force for five years. He had seen all kinds of action and been to a number of different precincts including the Forty-first, which is better known as Fort Apache. He had come to be a rather cautious policeman. Foster was different altogether. As soon as he hit the streets he was flying. He never wanted to go in or take a blow. He was looking for action. He was ready to climb any stairs on a family dispute, poke his head into any back alley, roam on top of any roof if there was a report of trouble. Glover was more inclined to avoid trouble if he could. Not that he wasn't a good cop. He did his duty. He was tough, he was reliable. But he didn't go out of his way to find trouble.

Glover found that, in the early days, Foster would sometimes become excitable, and Andy would just say, "Cool it. Hey, listen, you know, this job can drive you crazy out here in this street. Take it easy."

"But, Andy, we got to do this."

"Listen," Glover said patiently, "you've got a long way to go on the job here and there's no use trying to do it in one day, or even in the first year you're out on the street."

One Saturday morning they were working together and they saw a car coming up Tenth Street the wrong way. Cars were coming down the other side and the offending car jumped the sidewalk to avoid hitting anyone. Foster and Glover rushed over to the car. Greg reached the man first and asked him for his license and registration. Glover stood there, watching. Suddenly, he saw Foster become livid, grab the man, throw him up against the side of the car, and holler, "Up with your hands." Glover rushed over, not knowing what was happening.

"Hey, man what's going on? You're busting like you been bit."

"Look at this," Foster said. Tucked in between the driver's license and registration was a ten-dollar bill. "This guy offered me a bribe," Foster sputtered. "He's trying to bribe me."

"Just give the guy a ticket and forget about it," Glover said wearily. "You'd have trouble proving it. I see the money but he ain't said anything to you. Just let him know you didn't ask to be bribed."

Another Saturday morning they were walking at a time when cars had to be moved from one side of the street to allow for sanitation trucks to clean the curbs. Foster saw that none of the cars on the block had moved.

"Man, I want to tag those cars," he said.

"Forget it." Glover went on down the street and stood on the corner talking to someone. When he came back he found that Foster had tagged the whole block.

People were hollering indignantly out the windows: "Where do you want us to park?"

"Hey, man," Glover said, "what in hell are you doing?"

"I don't care," Foster said. "This is a violation."

Glover mumbled, "Jeez, you're too much. You see anything that looks like a violation, you got to straighten it out. Man, nobody likes to get summoned for little things like that."

But that was Foster's way in his early months on the force. He was hard, unyielding. As they got to know each other better, Glover would try to talk to him, try to convince him to let up. "Greg, you can create enemies out here on the streets so easily. Let's not create enemies out here if we don't have to. You know, people figure you're a police officer and you're going to take advantage of them simply because it's us that's got the law on our side. So if you don't have to rile 'em, don't, there's no need to."

They would talk in the station house while they waited to go on duty. Often, George Mahoney, who had worked with Greg as a trainee, was with him at the academy, and had come to the precinct a month after Greg, joined the conversation.

"Greg," Andy would say, "some guys never learn. There are police officers who have never learned. They go out there and they're going to correct the whole situation, the whole world. You can't do it. Otherwise, you're going to have ulcers before you retire, or something."

Mahoney would join in. "You can't do it alone, Greg. It's too big a job. No one person, no number of people, can handle it. It's too big, man. For every junkie you lock up down there, there's fifteen to take his place. You're better off getting the big people if you can."

Foster listened, but he found it hard to follow their reasoning. He was a police officer. His job was to uphold the law. He had *sworn* to uphold the law. He had come out of an experience

171

where he had witnessed death because people hadn't done their jobs, or hadn't taken precautions, or had eased up. He had come out alive because he had never eased up. It didn't make sense, what they were saying.

One day, early in his career as a police officer, the complexities of his job did become clearer to him.

He arrested a black man who had threatened passersby on the street with a knife. The man was drunk and abusive. He began to call Foster names. He struck out at Foster. He got so nasty that Foster blew up. He punched the drunk, hitting him three or four times.

He brought him into the station house. Patrolman Richie O'Neill was there at the time. O'Neill, the Ninth Precinct's PBA delegate, noted Foster's rage. He introduced himself.

"Look, Foster," he said, "don't ever let those people get under your skin. Because it doesn't matter. It just doesn't matter what they say."

Foster was sweating. His face was still tight with anger. "You hear the names the mother called me?"

"Let him call you anything. He's sitting there, he's handcuffed. He can't cause you any physical hurt. Just ignore him, let it go. Don't even listen to him. Just do what you have to do, fill out the card."

Foster was calm now. "Yeah, you're right," he said. "I shouldn't have done it." Later, when O'Neill got to know Foster better and observed him, he found Foster to be a "real good cop"; he noted that Foster had developed self-discipline on the job.

That incident helped inspire the self-discipline. The next day, Foster's prisoner died in his cell. Foster came to the precinct and when he heard the news he was inconsolable. "Maybe it was my fault, maybe I did it."

"It wasn't your fault," said a fellow cop, Bobby Cruz. "The guy was a wino. He was probably in bad shape all along."

"I dunno," Foster said. "Maybe I killed him."

"It *wasn't* your fault." Cruz started to lecture Foster. "On this job, Greg, you can't take anything personal. You can't let what a prisoner says get to you, and you can't let what happens to a prisoner get to you. You got to be impersonal."

The trouble with Gregory Foster, his brothers in the Ninth

soon learned, was that Foster did tend to take things personally. He couldn't be indifferent to people. "He cared about people out in the street whether they were bad guys or good guys," Bobby Cruz recalled. "To him, people were human beings and he wanted to treat everybody the same. His whole thing was going out on the street and making friends with the people, trying to do the right thing, trying to help out as best he could."

There was a police department investigation of the prisoner's death. It was found he had died from natural causes and Foster was completely absolved. But he had learned something, and after that he became a more careful police officer, a more compassionate police officer and, in effect, a more complete police officer.

Before he and Rocco Laurie became partners officially, Foster was out on the street making friends. Kids, especially, began to trust him because, they found, he was treating them fair. If he saw a youngster doing something wrong he would say, "Next time I catch you doing that I'm really going to put you away." He tried to talk to junkies, too, tried to convince them to get off the stuff. He rarely bothered junkies unless he caught them shooting up. He tried preventive police work, which wasn't always that easy in the Ninth Precinct.

Once, on a call for a family dispute, Foster ran up three flights of stairs, straight into a man who put a gun to his head. The man pulled the trigger three times. Each time there was a click, but no explosion. Luckily, Foster was able to subdue his assailant before the gun started working. Another time he was attacked by a knife-wielder. Somehow, he was able to make the collar without being hurt.

He showed his newfound maturity in many ways. One night at about eleven-thirty two men got into an argument on the corner of Eleventh Street and Avenue B. One of the men pulled out a gun and fired two shots at the other one. Three policemen, Foster among them, were a half block away. One of the cops, who was an expert marksman, whipped out his gun and took aim at the gunman's head. Before he could fire, Foster, gun out, sprinted up to the gunman and commanded: "Drop the gun." The man did as he was told but as Foster tried to handcuff him he began to fight. Foster pulled out his gun again and laid it against his prisoner's head.

"I just saved your life, man, but I'll blow your head off if you don't stop moving."

Foster made the arrest and brought the man in for attempted murder.

In the meantime, Laurie was into his own things, too. He was learning how to be a cop and, like Foster, some of the learning came the hard way.

One day early in May Laurie was on station-house security. A prisoner was brought in. While he was being booked upstairs the prisoner's brother swept into the station house.

"Where's my brother? I want to see him."

"You can't see him now," Laurie said. "He's being booked."

The man became loud and abusive, demanding to see his brother. Laurie tried to reason with him. "Go home and wait for him to call you. You'd be better off getting him a lawyer."

"I ain't going home until I see him."

The desk officer became exasperated. "Laurie, for Chrissakes, just get rid of him. I don't care how you do it but get rid of him."

Laurie gripped him by the arm. The brother swore, uttering an unkind reference to Laurie's wife, and took a swing at Laurie. Laurie reddened. He grabbed the brother and took him upstairs and, as he later told his wife, bounced him off every wall. The boy came out of it unmarked but Laurie's knuckles were swollen and bleeding and he was sent to the hospital for repairs. In his memo book Laurie wrote his own interpretation of the incident: "Told by desk officers to remove one male Negro from station house. After escorting same outside he became loud and abusive and when told to desist he did shove, kick and knock me to the ground causing injury to both hands. . . . Was treated myself at Bellevue — Diagnosis: contusions, abrasions both hands." Laurie's explanation, which had been suggested to him by other veteran cops, was accepted.

That was the only time Laurie ever laid hands on a prisoner. He was really very placid and self-controlled. As time went on, he began to get a reputation as being soft on prisoners. Once, when a black man who had been arrested asked Laurie for a cigarette, Laurie, who didn't smoke, went out and bought the prisoner a pack of cigarettes. Another time, a prisoner of Laurie's wrote him apologizing for behaving badly toward him. A cop who worked the closest with Laurie in those early months, George Gibbons, characterized Rocco as a good cop. "He was good to the people, he kept his cool. He never got too excited and he was never too harsh."

When they rode together Laurie and Gibbons (who was also new on the force) would ask each other questions — is this right, is that right? They were trying always to go by the book.

Laurie's duty was fairly mundane at the beginning. Once he was called to an apartment where an obese woman was stuck in the bathtub. Exercising as much tact as possible he lifted the woman out of the tub.

The one thing that bothered him down in the Ninth was the junkies. He had seen the effect of drugs on marines in Vietnam and it had left a deep impression on him. He was filled with revulsion for kids he came across in the East Village who were hooked. He would come home and tell Adelaide different things about junkies he had seen.

"My God," she said, "how can they live like that?"

"They're not living, they're dying. They are dying a little bit each day. They disgust me."

Rather than arrest them he would take their equipment and smash it. One time he found two teen-age junkies huddled in an abandoned building with all their paraphernalia around them. Laurie broke the needles and crunched them on the floor. He made the two take off their shoes and socks and walk on the broken glass. "You want to be junkies," he said with loathing, "go ahead, be junkies. That's all you're good for."

He was offered a seat in a radio car but he turned it down. He didn't like car duty. He felt most cops became lazy in the car. He also didn't like the partner they offered him because he was a fat man who had a reputation for abusing his prisoners.

What he wanted was to get on the Neighborhood Police Team. The opportunity arose when one of the men in the team was switched to Anti-Crime. He was accepted and he requested Gregory Foster as his partner.

At the time, Laurie had ambivalent feelings about blacks. His family's attitude toward blacks was, at best, reserved. Growing up on Staten Island, he had no black friends, and the performance

175

and attitudes of some black marines in Vietnam had disturbed him. And now he was working at a hazardous job in an area where black and Puerto Ricans seemed to be committing the majority of crimes.

On the other hand, he liked the black cops he had met in the Ninth Precinct. He and Frank Dudley, a black police officer, discussed the subject one day when they drew duty together. Laurie told Dudley that it didn't matter whether you were black or white, that people were people and that there was good and bad in everybody. What bothered him the most, he said, what disgusted him, was seeing the way people lived down there. He thought he could help by being on the Neighborhood Police Team.

"A good cop," he told Dudley, "is supposed to go out on the street and establish rapport with the people, the civilians he's working for, and one hand washes the other."

"What do you mean?" Dudley asked.

"Any cop who walks out there and says to himself, well, I'm not going to be friendly with these people because they're Puerto Rican or black or what have you, he's dead. He's useless. As far as a cop is concerned you can't do it that way. You have to go out there and get friendly with these people, drink their coffee, listen to their bitching, and try to develop as best you can."

It was Foster who came to Laurie and suggested they get together.

"You think the sarge will let us?" Laurie asked.

"Why don't you try and ask him. Maybe you can tell him that we were in Vietnam together? He might go for that."

Rocco told Andy Glover that he wanted to work with Foster and he asked Glover if he would mind. "Hey, listen," Glover said, "I don't care. It's fine with me to put you guys together. If you guys get along, I think that's all Sergeant Reddy will want to know."

One day Laurie went up to Sergeant Reddy, who ran the Neighborhood Police Team. "I'd like to bring my buddy, Greg Foster into the Neighborhood Police Team as my partner."

"How come?"

"Well, we were in the Marine Corps together and we understand how each other feels about things, about people, and I think we can work as a team."

"Let me check out Foster," Sergeant Reddy said. It occurred to Reddy that it would be desirable to have a black cop and a white cop together out there. He knew that situations developed in the street where the presence of a black officer could help smooth over possible inflammatory situations. He knew, too, that Foster was street-wise and could help Laurie in some ways because Laurie's background had been different. Best of all, they seemed to relate to each other as individuals. He called them both in one day and questioned them closely.

"I know why you joined the Neighborhood Police Team, Laurie. What about you, Foster, why'd you want to join?"

"I like the hours."

Everybody laughed but there was truth to it. The Neighborhood Police Team worked only two shifts — eight-to-four and four-to-twelve. No midnight-to-eights required. And they had a definite beat; they weren't moved around as most street patrolmen are. Foster turned serious, trying to collect his thoughts. "I feel I can do more for the people here as part of the Neighborhood Police Team concept than if I was just on a beat. I enjoy going in and rapping with people, you know, not only storekeepers and that, but kids and stuff. I can find out more, too. You make friends with a super or something and you learn things — is something going on? Is there a pusher living in the building? Is someone using one of those apartments for a shooting gallery? So it's a combination of things. You've got more flexibility," Foster said, concluding one of the longest speeches he had ever been known to make.

"There's another thing," Laurie added. "We've both been in Nam, we've both seen a lot of things. We've gotten our asses shot at and we survived. You'd have to say, I guess, we've got luck going with us. Come right down to it, we trust each other. And it's not like a marriage. If we don't think it's working we'll end it. But I think it will work."

"We may be young," Foster said, "but you got to say we've been around. We're old hands at this kind of a job."

Laurie was twenty-three years old. Foster was twenty-two years old. They had been police officers for less than a year. Both of them figured they could conquer the world.

The partners were standing on the corner of the avenue, when they heard a shout: "Officer! Officer!"

Down the block a man stood in the middle of the street, waving his arms. Foster and Laurie trotted down the avenue. As they ran, each one kept a hand on his back pocket, to keep his gun from jiggling against his buttocks and to be ready to pull it if necessary.

The man had on a white frock. He was the elderly Jewish barber they often talked to on their beat.

"What's wrong?" Laurie asked.

"I cut the hair. I cut her the whiskers and she stand up and say I don't have money to pay. I wash her hair, I cut the whiskers, the whiskers, and the hair. . . ."

"She didn't pay you nothing?" Foster said.

"Nothing."

"Well, how much does it come to?" Laurie wanted to know.

"Four dollars."

"Okay, we'll see what we can do, okay? Did you hear that, Greg? He cut her the whiskers."

They went into the barbershop and the woman was standing there defiantly. She had a butch haircut, and, indeed, there were bristles under her chin. She was a middle-aged white woman. A set of false teeth swam in her mouth. Her lower lip was huge, hovering over her chin, a pink, rubbery landing pad. She wore a shapeless dirty dress under a plain brown coat. Her eyes seemed focused on different planets.

"I paid for the haircut twice," she said angrily.

"Who paid for it?" Foster asked.

"My husband. He's the head of the Atomic Commission."

"Oh, he's the head of the Atomic Commission." Laurie looked at Foster, a wry grin spreading on his face.

"This is a waste of time," Foster said.

"Where's your husband now?" Laurie asked, amused by the situation.

"Getting a haircut someplace in the neighborhood."

"And your name's what?" Laurie was writing in his memo book.

"My real name's Laura. I'm from Michigan. My uncle is a police chief in Michigan. He was head of the detective force in New York. Head of the Canadian Mounties, too." She worked her lower lip, moving it up and down like a window shade.

"We have to take you to the hospital, dear," Foster said. "How old are you, Laura?"

"Thirty-eight. I'll be thirty-nine my next birthday and that's next month. I'm a navy nurse."

Foster left the shop and walked to the corner and called the precinct. "Got a psycho here to go to Bellevue." He explained it briefly and walked back to the shop to wait for the patrol car. Laurie was trying to keep her calm.

"You just relax, Laura," he said, "and we'll get this all straightened out."

"How many in the hell times do you have to pay for something?"

"Sit tight, Laura," Foster said. He looked out the shop window, waiting impatiently for the car to come.

"I had a brother the Nazis murdered. He was a government geologist."

"We're going to bring you to a doctor who will help you out, Laura," Laurie said.

"Help me how?"

"Well," Foster said, "maybe he can give you a few dollars and you can pay for your haircut."

"It's been paid twice. This is getting to be a damn joke, like the Nazis."

"There are a lot of Nazis still around, you know," Laurie said, looking out the window, waiting for the car to come. They were both getting itchy now, wanting to be through with it. The woman was beginning to make them uneasy.

"The bombers are all around," she said.

"Well, we're not going to take you in no bombers," Laurie said. "You don't have to worry about that."

"They're there wherever I am, whether you like it or not." The woman began to quiver. "They tried to kidnap me and put me in a hospital twice."

"No, that's not going to happen now."

"Afraid they'll kill me."

"No," Foster said softly.

The car came up and Foster and Laurie brought her outside and put her in the back seat and Laurie got into the back with her. As they started off for the hospital the woman was talking about all people in her country being twenty feet high. "Because they're on the right diet all their lives." Foster went back on the avenue alone, walking the beat by himself until his partner returned from Bellevue.

Psycho cases abound in the Ninth Precinct, where minds unhinge through neglect, through drugs, through poverty, or through a general loss of humanity. One day Foster and Laurie ran into the celebrated Ray Man of the East Village. The first time Foster looked at the man's eyes they seemed burned out. They were bright red — no white showed at all — and they seemed to be focusing in fourteen different directions at the same time. The Ray Man told the two young cops that a secret organization was sending waves into his apartment. "You can't convince me there aren't any rays coming at me," he insisted. "They're coming at me right now." He was sent to Bellevue and, afterward, Laurie said to Foster, "Someday we might find out that the psychos are normal and we're the ones that are crazy."

"I've thought that all along," Foster said drily.

One night they heard a call come over the radio, a ten–fifty-six — "ambulance may be needed." It was just off the avenue in their sector and they hustled to the site. They reached it at the same time as a patrol car. Two well-dressed women were standing outside and a policeman was already talking with one of them, who identified herself as a director of social services.

"We fear for his life," she said. "I'm afraid that he might take — "

"He's the only one in the apartment?" the officer asked. She said yes.

"You think he'll open the door for us?"

"No, I don't think so. We have no way to communicate," she said. "There's no way to break through to him."

The cops clustered together, trying to figure out what to do. Police detest psycho cases because of their unpredictability. The smallest person, when under stress, can gain great strength. Police get hurt that way.

The six policemen, including Foster and Laurie, moved in. One of them, hand on his gun, kicked open the door. An emaciated young white man was sitting at the kitchen table, oblivious to their entrance. He was wearing dungarees. His feet were bare. A copy of an article on B. F. Skinner was on the table. So was a large kitchen knife. A cat was perched atop the stove, licking at a dirty plate.

"Just relax, Bill," one of the officers said softly. "No problems. You just relax, okay?" They moved closer, slowly, surrounding the young man, who had not uttered a sound. One cop took the knife. There was money on the table. An officer began to count it.

"You got seventy-nine dollars there, Bill," he said to the boy.

"Is there change?" The young man could hardly be heard.

"Yeah, we'll give you that, too. We'll give you your cigarettes, we'll give you your house key and everything else you want."

"We'll leave the light on," another officer said, "so that you don't get robbed, you know."

Cautiously they talked to him, trying to keep him calm. As one of the officers went to put on handcuffs, the young man suddenly roused himself. He began to thrash around wildly. Foster and Laurie grabbed him from behind. They pulled him out of the chair and each with an arm on him, walked him out the door.

"Speed," one of the officers said after the car had left for Bellevue. "He might go looney up there in half an hour. You can't bring those guys out of it."

"Yeah, and when they come out of their trip they go right back on it."

Foster and Laurie walked back to the avenue. Neither one spoke for a while.

They were still not used to psychos, to junkies, to prostitutes, to the horrors they were seeing now, all the time, that were making them equate the Ninth Precinct with Vietnam at its worst. In an article for *New York* magazine Julie Baumgold wrote: "Cops see people with the civilization peeling and shredding off them till they are bleeding, sweating, violent bundles of naked instincts, desperate beasts of swamps and sumps of humanity. A kind of Cop-Warp comes over them. They get these quivering crime sensors and come to see a world of potential perpetrators, a motive to every action, the feeling that something mean is about to happen." But Foster and Laurie were still too new to feel that way. They still felt there was a humanity in people, that not everyone was lost and desperate, not everyone was an animal, that as bad as it was down there it could get better and they — the two of them — would help it get better.

Still, they were tough cops. They were understanding to people who, they felt, returned their understanding. They didn't push kids who committed minor transgressions. But they did lean hard on criminals. They kept hitting pushers and prostitutes and disorderly persons who might have a knife or a gun on them, ready to use. They made arrests; they were making more arrests than any of the other foot men in the precinct.

They were an odd couple in some ways. Laurie was more reserved, more sure of himself. When he made a collar he never raised his voice. He always moved and spoke with quiet authority. He commanded instant respect. He was a rookie cop but it didn't seem that way. Foster was more excitable. Although he was quieter among his fellow cops — and less relaxed — than Laurie, it was easier for him to relate to the people down there than it was for Laurie. So he was looser on the street. But he had one quirk. He was always tougher on black offenders than on white ones. He got mad at them, called them niggers and raised hell with them. Possibly it was because he felt he had to convince the white cops that he wasn't soft on his own kind. Or that he hated black criminals for making it hard for other black men. In many ways, Gregory Foster was a moralist. He wanted things to improve for black people and when black people in the Ninth Precinct committed crimes, he felt it was hurting the cause of blacks everywhere.

They were in no way the ideal cop couple. There is a great mystique about cop partners, that it is in some cases an even more intense relationship than between marriage partners. Darryl Anderson once described it this way: "When you start working together in the police jobs, you start hitting it off. You could be white or black, black or white, whatever. You start a relationship. The more you work with each other the more it becomes like platonic love. I'm not talking about homosexuals or nothing," Anderson took pains to point out, "I'm talking about platonic love, you know, where his family is your family and so on and so forth. You know, the longer you're together this is how it is."

Anderson's idealization of the relationship between cops is exaggerated. The one thing they all share in common is the danger of the job, and that unites them more than anything. Otherwise, except in certain long-run attachments, one cop treats another cop just as any businessman or worker treats a fellow worker. For eight hours a day the partnership flourishes. Then, except for casual socializing, it's over.

It hadn't even reached that stage yet between Foster and Laurie.

Rocco once complained to his mother that Foster was cold and hard to reach but then he said, "Ma, he's a good cop and he doesn't show favoritism. I respect him as a worker." Another time he told Larry Perez, "Foster's a very good cop and he thinks the way I do. He was in the marines and he's not like pussy whatever. He'll back you up."

That was the thing about partners: would your partner back you up? Foster once told his friend Jim Duffy, "There's a lot of guys I wouldn't work with. You know — hey, where did your partner go? Where you look behind you and your partner ain't behind you. I know Laurie's gonna be behind me when I need him."

Foster was not afraid of anything and he once told Jackie that Laurie was the same way. "He tries to keep people out of trouble," Gregory said one day, "just like me. And he believes in the law, too. He has a very strong head for the law."

There was one time when Captain Rogers, who headed the Ninth Precinct, called Foster in and offered him a seat in a radio car. Foster said, "Sir, I'd like to talk it over with my partner."

Foster told Laurie about it. "I like it better on foot, Greg. You get to talk to more people on foot."

"Yeah, I see what you mean."

"Besides, if we have someplace we want to watch, we can watch it better on foot because you can go in and up on the roof. You can go up on the second floor and watch a rear building or a rear yard. With the radio you can set up something with the car. But

183

you can't hide the car, you see. You can't put the car anyplace. On foot you just stand on the corner and you can drift into the building if you're following somebody."

"Yeah," Foster said, "but it's warmer in the car."

"Hell with that. Keep moving, you keep warm."

So Foster told Captain Rogers that he would just as soon stay a foot patrolman and the Foster-Laurie team remained together. And they kept moving.

They were particularly good at a special sport of some of the officers of the Ninth Precinct — lurking. A fellow cop, Peter Wocial, was always lurking around. He would say, "Come on, Rock, come on, Greg, let's lurk." And in their spare time, and out of uniform, they would go into alleys, looking around in dark spots or on roofs, observing, lurking.

One night that way Rocco and Greg came upon two kids fighting. A knife fell out of one of the boy's pockets. The other one opened it and lunged at the boy, the blade just missing the boy's throat. Foster and Laurie saw what was happening and ran up to the boy. He turned and fled into a building. They followed him up the stairs. They finally cornered him on the roof and he surrendered. They took him back to the station house and because he was a juvenile the boy was later put in a home.

For the most part, Foster and Laurie established good relations with the kids of the area. Especially Foster. One day in the early summer, when he was still working with Andy Glover, he was approached by a couple of Puerto Rican boys.

"Hey, Cool," one of them said, "what's your name?"

"You said it." Foster grinned. After that he was always "Mr. Cool" to the boys.

There were a dozen or so Puerto Rican boys, ages eleven to sixteen, who were organized into a loose gang. They played baseball and basketball in a small park on Twelfth Street. And there were times when Foster would go over and play with them. He would borrow one of the boys' gloves and pitch to them and after a while he became even closer to them.

He helped them keep out of trouble. There were boys who had been on the street all their lives, boys from poverty backgrounds who found the next meal at a fruit stand or a bakery shop or a candy counter. They were always stealing. They stole apples, bananas, cookies, cakes. They stole boxes of ice cream. They would run in, grab what they could, and take off. After Foster came around and talked to them they stopped, although one of the kids did admit to Foster that "sometimes a group of guys would take a bite of ice cream and then put it back inside. That's not a big thing." Foster just glared at the boy.

They were untamed kids. Some of them had a habit of throwing bottles out their windows. Foster said stop it and they stopped. The same thing happened when he saw them clinging to the back of buses, taking free rides down the avenue. He told them to get off. "You're gonna get hurt," he said. "If you get hurt, they're going to blame it on the cops." Whenever there was serious trouble on the block Foster would check out the kids first, making sure they were not involved. "Where's the guys?" he would ask one of them. The boys got used to him calling them "guys."

Soon the "guys" were calling Foster "the best cop we ever had around here." When they saw him with his partner — whom they liked, too, but didn't know as well — it was "Shaft and his friend." But all other times Foster was "Mr. Cool" to them.

The kids couldn't get over his attitude, which was strange to them, something they had never before witnessed in policemen. One of the boys, Ruben Colon, a thin, handsome, delicate-featured youngster of thirteen, once explained, "He was the first cop we got to like around here. Being cool made him friendly and made him be friendly with us. I think he really believed that a cop should help people and not just arrest people. He'd rather make you his friend than make an arrest."

Without preaching, Foster began to reach them, began to get them to understand the distinction between right and wrong. At the same time they were telling him their troubles, too. "All cops ain't sweet," little José Figuero told Foster one day. "We was in a group walking and there were these two cops and a cop pokes his head out the window and says, 'Look at all those fucking Puerto Ricans.'"

"Yeah," George Rivera interrupted, "I went to sit on top of a car one day. A cop was already sitting on it. I was just doing it for fun. The cop said, 'Is this your car? Then get the hell off

185

it.' If we was white," Rivera told Foster, "he wouldn't say anything."

Foster listened to them patiently and told them to cool it, that things were changing for the better and that by the time they grew up it would really be different, they would see.

Foster helped tame the boys and helped make them aware of themselves as human beings. He did it in the simplest of ways, by respecting them as individuals. One day just before Christmas a delegation of the boys — who were now banded together into an organization called, appropriately, the "Cool Ones" (initiation was three lashes across the back) — came to the station house and presented to Gregory Foster a plaque they had made themselves. It had his name and shield number on it and it was signed, "From the boys of the neighborhood." Nobody in the Ninth Precinct could ever remember anything like that being done for one of them before.

The word began to spread in the neighborhood that Foster and Laurie were good ones. They began getting tips from people in the neighborhood who had come to trust them. People even showed up at the station house asking for them — people with information on dope pushers and other illegal operations. Foster and Laurie began to get a reputation. One member of the Ninth Precinct, seeing them in action, called them "two dynamite cops." But they were also relentless cops. Because of their relentlessness not everyone in the precinct loved them. Some people, the wrong people, hated them.

At the time there was a conflict in philosophy in the police department. The policy was for street-level police officers not to become involved in drugs. The feeling among the police brass was that these cops should stick to burglaries and robberies and let the special narcotics units handle drugs. But in the Ninth Precinct, at least, the people who were committing burglaries and robberies were the same people who were involved in drugs. It got to be a dilemma for Sergeant Reddy. At community meetings he would listen to complaints: "Why aren't you doing something about drugs? They're selling drugs right on the street corner here. . . . They're selling them in my building or on my block. Why aren't the police doing something about it?" The inference was that the cops were either condoning the drug business or, worse, that they were being paid off for not cracking down. So Sergeant Reddy walked a tightrope. If he received information he felt was good information, that involved not the street junkie but the man dealing with drugs, he would turn his men loose.

One day, acting on a tip, Foster and Laurie raided an apartment in the area. They arrested six people for using hard drugs. As they were being led out, one of them, Mike Lerro, went up to Laurie, "I want out," he said, "help me."

Laurie looked closely at the young man. He was thin to the point of emaciation. His eyes were glassy and watery, his cheeks were sunken. He had the classic look of a heroin addict.

They talked later. Lerro told Laurie he had been in the marines, that he had started using drugs in the service.

"Why did you do it?" Laurie asked angrily. "You know, I could have taken it, too. It's plentiful over there. But I didn't take it. Why the hell did you take it?"

Lerro started to cry. Laurie said, "You know it's wrong, you don't do it."

"Help me get off the stuff," Lerro said. "I'll die if I don't get help."

"How long you been hooked?"

"Five years."

"How much of a habit you got?"

"Fifty dollars a day, maybe a hundred."

"How do you get the money?"

"You know, hustling, stealing."

Laurie thought for a moment. "Okay, Lerro, here's what I'm gonna do. I saw your record. You spent thirteen months at Dannemora. You go back there you ain't gonna make it. When your case comes to trial I'll tell the judge we were in Vietnam together. I'll try to get you on a methadone program. But this is the thing," Laurie said, "you got to help me, too."

"How?" Lerro asked, instantly coming to attention.

"I'm looking for a big arrest. If you help me make a big arrest I'll speak in your favor to the judge and I'll get you started on the methadone."

"I'll do it," Lerro said, sniffling, "I'm desperate."

187

Laurie went to Sergeant Reddy, asking permission to pursue the operation. "If you want to do it on your own time," Reddy said, "you have my permission to do it. But you're on your own, remember that."

Greg Foster had gone off on vacation, so Laurie asked Pete Wocial to work with him and Wocial was eager to do it. But it was slow going. Laurie kept on top of Lerro. He would go to Lerro's apartment and Lerro, if he was home, would say he was setting it up. If he wasn't at home he would leave a note: "I had to go out, I'll be right back." After a while Rocco began to feel he was getting the runaround. One day he caught up with Lerro and said, "Look, you have one more chance to set up this meeting. If not, forget it. I'm not going to do anything more to help you."

Two days later Lerro made the contact. Laurie was to meet the dealer at a certain street corner. Mike would go with him. When he got there he was kept waiting for ten minutes. Then he saw a young, well-dressed young white man approaching him. The dealer looked closely at Laurie. Rocco was wearing dungarees and a pale blue work shirt. He had on an old marine field jacket. His hair was untrimmed and he needed a shave.

"My name's Rocco Laurie," he said, shaking hands. "I go to Wagner College (Wagner is on Staten Island). I deal there but I'm running out of places to make a buy. Mike here told me you could help."

The young dealer studied Laurie. "All right," he said at last, "you come over to my place this Saturday. Mike says you're okay. If you can get the cash up, I'll have it for you."

"How much?"

"Probably be three thousand dollars' worth."

"I'll be there."

He went right back to Sergeant Reddy and told him about the meeting and that he would need money. Reddy said it was impossible, only narcotics detectives could take funds from the department. So Laurie and Pete Wocial went to their own banks and each withdrew two hundred dollars in small bills.

That night Rocco went home and told Adelaide all about it. She was upset. "Rocco, don't do it, it's not worth it. Sure, you'll make the good arrest, but you can't fight the whole city."

"It's all right, Boss," he said soothingly. "I got it set up where nothing can happen."

Later he told his parents and they were worried, too. Rocco's brother Anthony blurted out, "Don't play cops and robbers, Rock. Where's it going to get you?"

"It's my job," he said simply. "I'm doing my job."

That Saturday as he got ready to leave for the East Village, his wife started to cry. "God forbid," she said, "what if something ever happened?"

"Don't worry, Adelaide," he said. "You know I'm careful. You know I don't take chances."

"All right," she said finally, "but call me the minute it's over." They kissed and she was sick all day.

Laurie met Mike Lerro and the two of them went up to the dealer's apartment at St. Mark's Place. It was a plush pad, with thick rugs and fancy furniture and a color TV set, and Rocco thought bitterly, he's got all of this by selling pills and marijuana to the kids who come to the Village.

The dealer was not alone. His girl friend, who looked like she might have been eighteen, was with him. The TV was on and they were watching a college football game. Rocco tried to act casual. He had his jacket on. He didn't want to take it off because he had his gun in his jacket pocket.

"Why don't you take the jacket off, Rocco?" the dealer kept saying. "It's warm in here, baby, you don't want to catch cold when you go out." Gingerly, Rocco removed the jacket and laid it across his lap so that he would have easy access to his gun. He had the PPK with him, a small automatic, not his police gun.

The dealer kept getting calls from a man in a hotel uptown. He told Rocco the man was from Colorado and he had all the stuff. Rocco thought how he would love to put the collar on that guy.

They watched the game and the dealer made no move to do anything. Laurie watched with him, under some tension. The dealer lit up a joint. He passed it to the girl, she passed it to Laurie. Laurie took a couple of tokes and passed it on to Mike. He didn't notice that it had any effect on him.

Suddenly, the dealer got up. "I don't have it here," he said

189

abruptly. "I'm going to go get the stuff. You stay here and be comfortable."

"Here's taxi money," Rocco said, throwing a ten-dollar bill at him. The dealer grinned and took the money.

Pete Wocial was staked outside. As soon as Mike Lerro came out the door he was supposed to go in. Wocial saw the dealer go out and he was puzzled. He wondered what was going on.

Minutes later a tall, husky black man came in. He took off his coat, the girl introduced him all around, and he sat down to watch the football game. He was obviously another customer and Laurie thought, one guy I can handle, but two? He didn't know what he was going to do.

During the afternoon others came in and out of the apartment, but none stayed. It was only the girl, the black man, Mike and Laurie. An hour and a half after he left, the dealer returned. He was carrying a guitar case.

He opened the case and it was full of plastic bags, and the bags were full of marijuana. Rocco didn't know what to do. The dealer was there, the black man was there, and Rocco was alone and he was wondering how he was going to pull it off. He knew Pete was outside, but he was in the apartment by himself.

"Okay," the dealer said, "let's have your green."

Laurie pulled a wad of bills from his pocket. "You count the money," the pusher said.

"No," Rocco said, "you count it."

The dealer came over and started to go through the bills. At that moment the other man went out of the room. As the dealer got into the count, the pile got lower and lower. It was immediately apparent to him that there was no three thousand dollars in the pile. He was about to say something when Rocco drew his gun and held it at the side of the man's head.

"Don't make a sound," he said softly. Quickly, he handcuffed him.

Then it got hairy. The black man returned to the room and Mike Lerro bolted for the door, hollering, "It's happening, it's happening, come quick!" The door closed behind him and locked. Laurie turned cold. He was alone in the room. Holding the dealer in front of him he trained the gun on the black man. He told the girl to sit there quietly.

In seconds Pete Wocial was at the door. He kicked it in and covered them with his gun.

"Take it, take it," the dealer said, "just don't kill me. Take everything." He figured the two men were thieves, not cops.

There were four pounds of grass in the haul. As soon as the men were booked in the station house the narcotics detectives were brought in and Rocco handed over the case to them. A reporter from the *Daily News* was there, and a photographer. Rocco absolutely refused to have his picture taken. "I don't want any praise for this," he said. "I was doing my job, what I got paid for, and if this gets in the paper it will break my guy's cover. I don't want them to find out that he set it up."

Adelaide Laurie's tears were tears of happiness this time when Rocco returned. He sat down and told her all about it. The only thing he was sorry about, he said, laughing, was that he and the dealer had talked a lot about football and he had begun to like the guy.

"When will the case be coming up?" Adelaide asked.

"Late January, I guess," he said. "I'm sure I'll have to testify but first I got to take care of Mike."

The next day Laurie met Lerro in the East Village and took him to the Mary Scranton Foundation, a nonprofit agency that treated heroin addicts for twenty dollars a week. Laurie, in uniform, gave the receptionist the twenty dollars, for Lerro's first treatment. The receptionist recalled thinking later that it was the first time she had ever seen a cop pay for an addict.

Right after that, Laurie and Gregory Foster were back on the beat again, working the avenue together as partners. A new year was almost upon them and they were both, in their own way and for their own reasons, looking forward to 1972.

After the first year the state of marriage for Gregory Foster and Rocco Laurie was still not suspended in perfect grace but it was getting better. Both men were settling down to the rites of marriage, they were adapting, becoming housebroken;

both were beginning to accept their wives' turns of mind. At the same time, the wives were moving toward their husbands, too, modifying their positions, compromising, meeting their men now if not on a field of daisies at least not on a pitted battlefield. At least Gregory and Jackie were now living together. And Adelaide had seemed to have curbed her extreme possessiveness so that Rocco could now go out and play ball and do some things on his own. And when they saw members of his family it was not quite the strain it had been at the beginning.

It helped that both the Fosters and the Lauries had found their own love nests. The Fosters moved into their apartment in the Bronx in September. A month earlier the Lauries had moved into a small house on Staten Island.

All along Rocco had told his wife, "The things that I want in this life are a wife, a house, a dog and children." He was ready for children but Adelaide wasn't yet. Otherwise he had it all.

When they found the house they wanted to buy, Rocco and Adelaide asked Uncle Matty to look at it, not his parents. Adelaide explained to Rocco that she would rather not have his mother along any more because she would criticize every house they looked at, and, though she would probably be right in her criticism, they would never buy a house that way. "Okay," he said, "when we buy the house we'll ask her to come over *after* it's bought."

So Dr. Iammatteo looked at the house — a small Cape Cod with a living room, sun porch, kitchen and dining room down-stairs, and two small bedrooms upstairs — and told Rocco and Adelaide that the money seemed right and if they liked it that was all that mattered. They put down the binder and Adelaide immediately called her mother-in-law. Instead of congratulating her, Mrs. Laurie said, "I hope you kids know what you're doing. Where is this house? What does it look like? Do you get water in the basement? Are there cracks in the ceiling?"

She and her husband came over to look at the house and they weren't very enthused. Mr. Laurie noticed that there was a brook behind the house that might overflow and he saw that the house needed a lot of work and he knew that Rocco wasn't very handy.

"And why would you buy a house with only two bedrooms?" he said. "You can't raise a family that way."

192

"We've got time for that," Rocco said. "We don't have to stay here forever."

The house was bought and they loved it. Soon the criticisms were forgotten and on October 31, on Rocco's twenty-third birthday, Adelaide held her first party at the house. Everything sparkled and Adelaide had prepared all the food. Mrs. Laurie was impressed that the house looked so clean and she was proud of her daughter-in-law that day and, she admitted to herself grudgingly, she had never seen her son looking so well.

Gregory Foster's twenty-second birthday was on November 6 but since he worked that night, Jackie decided against giving him a party. Besides, their money was low. Financially, it was hard going for both men. Laurie had been able to afford the house, which cost thirty-seven thousand five hundred dollars, because he had put money away while in Vietnam, there was still wedding-gift money left, and Adelaide had some money saved that her father had left her. Also, Adelaide was working, and they didn't have children to worry about.

Foster would have liked to have bought a house, too. When Jackie first met him he was saving pictures of model homes. He had a whole book of them, with different homes that he wanted. But now, with two small children, he was just barely making it. At this time, his salary was four hundred dollars every two weeks but his take-home pay was only three hundred and twenty-one dollars. The rent was two hundred and eight dollars a month and he had just bought a 1969 Dodge Charger — his dream car — and so after the rent and the food and all the other bills, he had just about enough money to buy gas for the car and lunch for himself.

He always turned over his paycheck to Jackie. He didn't drink much and he didn't smoke and he didn't gamble and he didn't care about clothing for himself. He would walk around the apartment in his dungarees and every once in a while he would take them out to his mother and have her resew them. He was gaining weight and busting out of his clothes, which were wearing out, anyway. Jackie would say to him, "Gregory, please go out and get yourself some dungarees." He wouldn't want to spend the money. If his shoes got holes in them he would take them to the shoemaker rather than buy a new pair. The only way he got something he needed was when Jackie would go out and buy it for him. "His problem," his mother once told Jackie, "is that he's giving you too much." She knew it was true.

He was, really, a model husband at home. He worked hard; he was now going to John Jay College two nights a week, taking a course in psychology and law, hoping that he might someday become a court officer or even a lawyer. If the children got sick he would see that they got immediate medical attention. When he made a promise to his wife he always kept it. Jackie, who was tougher than her husband, sometimes thought that Gregory was too good.

They lived simply. They would listen to records and watch TV and go to the movies. They saw *The French Connection* (the Lauries saw it too and Rocco laughed at the police work depicted) and Greg immediately associated himself with Popeye Doyle. After every detective story he saw that he liked, he became the leading character. When the first Negro detective movie came out, *Cotton Comes to Harlem*, Greg identified with the black detective, Crawford. Then came *Shaft* and it didn't hurt that the kids in the Ninth Precinct started calling him Shaft. He took to dressing like Shaft, wearing a turtleneck sweater, short leather jacket, and a trench coat. After Shaft it was *Dirty Harry*; Clint Eastwood became his man and Greg became Dirty Harry.

He loved his children, especially Tyhessia. He was more attached to Tyhessia than his son because she had been born when he was home and he felt that little Gregory was closer to his mother. Tyhessia was his. When he had the eight-to-four duty he would get up early to play with Tyhessia. He told Jackie that after he made an arrest and he felt it was okay, that he was out of it all right, the first thing he would think about was Tyhessia.

"You forget you've got a wife and son, right?" Jackie asked.

"Yeah," Gregory said, unabashed, "but you know how it is."

The truth was that both Foster and Laurie felt more at ease on the job than they did at home. It wasn't that domestic life was so bad — it *was* getting better for both of them — it was a kind of "cop-warp" of their own. They were both obsessed with the job. They found fulfillment as police officers that they could not yet find as husbands. Both Foster and Laurie liked the job — *loved* the job — and that sense of satisfaction offers, to any man, the sternest kind of competition to the uncertainties of domestic life.

One element that may have hindered the domesticity of Foster and Laurie was the family wildlife they often encountered in the Ninth Precinct. Family disputes — a ten–fifty-two — occurred all the time in that area; and it was always bad news for cops. It usually meant climbing flights of stairs where you were an easy setup for an ambush. And, once at the door, the husband might be waiting with a gun in his hand, or a butcher's knife. So many times, too, by the time they got to the door the cops would find that the abused woman would refuse to press charges. Cops hate to get involved in family disputes but it is an everyday event for them, especially among the members of the Neighborhood Police Team in the East Village.

One night, working the four-to-twelve, Foster and Laurie heard the ten–fifty-two come over the radio, a family dispute on Tenth Street just off Avenue B. They rushed over to the apartment house. People were standing around outside, staring at the bluecoats. Foster and Laurie walked up four flights of stairs. On each landing a knot of people stood around, chattering in Spanish, staring with unsmiling faces at the cops. They reached the apartment. The door was made of steel and it was closed. Laurie knocked on the door. Immediately, a man opened it, identifying himself as a friend. The cops stepped gingerly into the apartment. A round fluorescent ceiling light lit up the kitchen. There was a refrigerator and an old stove and a small battered table. Next to the kitchen was a small bedroom. A man stood straddled between the kitchen and the bedroom. His face was streaked by red lines, from a woman's fingernails, the lines running down his face like a series of ski slopes seen from the air, only embedded in red, not white. A stout, middle-aged woman was sitting on the bed whispering. She began talking in Spanish.

"Tell them," she said to the friend, who acted as interpreter, "that I came all right from the job. And he started with the dirty words. Then, Pedrine, he kicked me. Look, he kicked me here." She held out a leg. The stocking was torn and there were visible bruises. "Then I tried to defend myself and I scratched

195

him with my nails. Look at the bottle, that bottle he broke over me."

The interpreter explained, "What she said is that they were fighting, they got into an argument and he tried to hit her with the bottle in the head and she scratched."

"That's fair," Foster said.

"With the nails I hit him," the woman said in Spanish. "But, Pedrine, you know that he always hits me. Look in the head, the head . . ."

"You shouldn't mess around," Laurie said to the husband. "She's bigger than you."

"All the time she is very angry," the husband said in broken English. "I don't know for what. She's very angry, angry, angry."

"What are you going to do?" Foster said sternly. "Are you going to keep fighting with her or are you going to knock it off?"

"No, forget it," the husband said. "No, forget it."

"We don't want to keep coming back," Laurie said.

"Always he has beaten me," the woman said. "All the life. It's the first time I have defended myself."

"Do you love your wife?" Laurie asked.

"Sure," the husband said.

"She loves you?"

"Sure, sure."

"I want you to take him," the woman said vehemently, a gleam of hard, bright awareness on her face. "And I want him to leave. Tell him to leave, leave!"

"She loves you? Do you love your husband? Ask her?"

"Si or non," the friend said.

"He's saying if you love me, Mamita," the husband spoke in a beseeching tone.

"Yes or no," Foster said.

"Tell him to leave," was all the woman would say. "Let him leave, leave, leave so I can live my life in peace."

"Let's take a walk until she calms down," Laurie said, coming to a decision.

"Let her calm down," Foster said.

"Tell him to go," the woman cried hysterically. "Tell him to go. I don't want no problem. Tell him the whole life he has beaten me and I have never done anything to him, because I feel

196

sorry that he was drinking. But now he is beating me and not drinking."

"Why don't you take a walk?" Foster said, moving in and nudging her husband. "Come on, you'll only get in trouble if you stay. Go outside and keep cool."

"No," the husband said.

"I'm not saying get out of your house. I'm saying go take a walk and cool down. 'Cause you're not going to settle anything fighting with her here. Right?"

"Listen, my friend," Laurie said. "I think we better go take a walk."

"We'll go out for a little while," Foster said, "until Mama cools off and then you come back and talk it over, okay? Otherwise you're going to keep fighting with her."

"I'm not angry," the husband said eagerly. But he put on his coat.

"Tell her," Laurie said to the friend who was interpreting, "that he's going to go outside until they cool down and if they can't talk after that, she goes to family court and gets a summons against him."

They walked down the stairs, the husband and the friend with the two police officers. There were still grave-faced people, men and women and small children, huddled in the hallways. In the street the friend and the husband went one way, Foster and Laurie the other.

They talked about it. "It's all we could do," Foster said to Laurie. "She'd have never let us lock the guy up, regardless of what he did."

"Yeah, and you have to try and let him look like he's still the man in the family. . . ."

"Machismo, Rock, that's what they call it."

"How's your machismo lately?" Laurie asked.

"Hanging loose," Greg laughed.

Early in November Larry Perez talked with Rocco over the phone. Larry and Antoinette Perez were the only couple the Lauries saw. Otherwise, except for an occasional date with Rocco's brother Anthony and his wife, Kathy, they stayed by themselves. That was the way they wanted it.

197

"Hey, Rock," Perez said, "they just opened up Walt Disney in Florida. Why don't you take some time off and we'll all go there?"

"That's a good idea," Rocco said. "Let me talk it over with my wife."

"You always have to talk everything over with your wife. It's just the other way around here."

Rocco laughed. "Let me speak to the Boss. The Boss says yes, we'll go."

Adelaide liked the idea, too, so the week before Thanksgiving the Lauries drove to Florida with the Perezes. They went to Disneyland in Orlando and drove to Miami. Rocco bought his wife a chess set there. "I'm going to teach you the game," he said to Adelaide. "When you start beating me I'll quit."

The Lauries came back from Florida broke but refreshed and Rocco worked on the house, painting it and trying to make kitchen cabinets with the help of an older and more experienced cousin, Billy O'Brien. Adelaide began to get ready for the Christmas holidays.

While Rocco was on vacation Foster worked with different partners, none steady. And he kept busy. He made a robbery collar one day where he had to give chase. Another time he was just coming to work when he saw a man snatch a woman's pocketbook. He ran after the man, his gun out. Just then, some police from the Tactical Police Force came along and saw the black man running on the street with his gun out. They pulled out their guns, ready to shoot Foster.

"Hold it," Greg hollered breathlessly as he caught up with the purse snatcher. "I'm on the job." He let them have the arrest.

In this period he also made a felony narcotics bust. He hated narcotics peddlers as much as Laurie and he seemed to have the ones in the neighborhood on the run. Andy Glover remarked on it to his new partner in Anti-Crime, George Mahoney. "That Foster," Glover said, "he ain't playing no games out there."

Glover and Foster were still good friends even though they no longer worked together. He liked to kid Greg about his weight. Once Glover saw him at the station house. "Hey, man," Glover said, "your blouse is getting tighter on you."

"Clothes shrunk," Foster grinned.

Greg and Jackie couldn't afford to take a vacation. They stayed home mostly and Greg played his *Shaft* record when he felt like being Shaft, and Jackie listened to her records, too. She told Greg she didn't mind being in the house. "As long as I have records and I can jump around, I'm okay."

He told her little about his work. He would have told her more but she didn't want to hear about it. She told him once, "When you leave your job, leave your job, don't bring it home." He did mention the prostitutes down there and his distaste for them. "It's a terrible thing for a woman to go out there and do her thing on the street."

"That's her life, you know," Jackie said.

"That's no life," Greg said, "that's a living death. Bad as being a junkie."

One evening they went to Times Square to a movie. Greg was trying to park his car when a black prostitute came over and said hello. Jackie slid out of the front seat and stared at the woman. The prostitute stared right back. "What the fuck are you looking at?" she said.

Gregory said, "What did you say to my wife?" He pulled out his badge. The woman took one look and ran for her life.

"Look how fast she got the wind," Jackie said.

"I'll go after her."

"Let her go, Gregory. I want to go to the movies."

Adelaide and Rocco spent their second New Year's Eve together as man and wife in a much happier state than their first. That year they were supposed to go to a party given by Billy and Marie O'Brien. On the way they had a fight in the car and Rocco got mad and punched the dashboard so hard it cracked. He took her home and went to the party himself and watched a football game on television with a friend. This time, at the O'Briens' again, Adelaide was in a very good mood. She had a little to drink and she and Rocco were very sociable and pleasant and they mingled with everybody. This was a surprise because they usually stayed off by themselves at parties, and it prompted Rocco's brother to say to himself, hey, it's improving between them. Maybe their marriage will work out after all.

New Year's Eve was just another night for Jackie and Greg Foster. They stayed home alone. Jackie wanted to go to a family reunion a cousin was holding but Greg didn't want to have anything to do with her family and he absolutely refused to go. "You're gonna walk if you want to go," he said. She stayed.

He wanted pigs' feet for dinner on New Year's Eve but the pigs' feet he bought were too salty and he couldn't eat them. So the night was kind of a washout and Jackie and Greg went to bed early, not bothering to stay up and ring in 1972.

Into January the partners worked together. They were getting along well, respecting each other, building up a trust in each other. Theirs was still a limited partnership, which ended when they took off their uniforms. The social barrier was much too wide yet for either of them to cross. But on the job they worked in harmony. Both were totally honest, and each one knew it, and that was a strong basis for the success of their partnership.

On January 15 the two men were working the four-to-twelve. They were standing on a corner. Suddenly, a car pulled up and a man rushed out.

"Someone just pointed a gun at us and pulled the trigger," he screamed in broken English, "but the gun didn't go off."

He gave the cops the address. Foster and Laurie jumped into the car and, in a matter of seconds, were let out in front of a grocery store. They told the occupants of the car not to move.

Foster ran into the store, Laurie right behind him. They saw a swarthy, black-haired man holding a gun. When he saw the policemen he wheeled and ran toward the back of the store. The store was crowded but people backed off and Foster and Laurie chased him. When they caught up with him the gun was gone.

"Where is it?" Laurie asked.

"What you talking about?"

"The gun, man, the gun," Foster barked.

"No gun."

They searched the back room. Foster found it wedged between the back of the freezer and the wall. Rocco put the cuffs on the man.

At the station house, while they fingerprinted and booked the suspect, Rocco asked, "What kind of a gun is it?"

"It wasn't such a good gun," the suspect said, "because it didn't work too well."

He was locked up for possession of an unlicensed weapon and attempted murder. Rocco took the arrest and was put in for an EPD citation — "excellent police duty."

One night, Anthony and Kathy Laurie took Adelaide and Rocco to dinner and the theater. They were more friendly now than they had been for a long while, mainly because Adelaide had loosened up so. They went to a Spanish restaurant, the Seville, and they took a cab uptown to see the Broadway play *Marigolds*. Rocco fell asleep during the show but Adelaide enjoyed it. Afterward they went back for the car and Rocco said, "I'll show you where I work." He drove around the East Village. They came to the women's detention home and he told them about the riots they had had there.

"You really have to feel sorry for these girls," Anthony said. "They're probably all screwed up, they've been tossed around so much."

Rocco got mad. "Feel sorry for them? They have it good there. They have three meals a day. They have a place to stay. What more could they want? They have it a lot better than a lot of people in this world." Rocco Laurie was a conservative; he believed that mercy should be saved for those who most deserved it.

He showed them the apartment on St. Mark's Place where he had made the collar on the drug dealer. "You better watch yourself," Anthony blurted out, "or you're going to get yourself killed."

Rocco just sat back in the car placidly. "Not me," he said. "I'll never get myself killed. I'm too careful."

A few days later Adelaide and Rocco got a call from Brooks Matyi. He had come to see them in New York twice. Once Adelaide had cooked an Italian meal for him. The other time they all went to Chinatown. "When the weather gets nice," Brooks said, "I'd love to have you and Adelaide come to my house. Bucks County is beautiful in the spring."

"Sounds great," Rocco said. "We'll do it. I'll give you a call as soon as I know when I have a free weekend."

He didn't work on Tuesday night, January 24, and he and Adelaide went to his mother's for dinner. He looked very pale to

Mrs. Laurie, but she was pleased that they ate well. She was especially pleased to see her daughter-in-law seem to enjoy her food. She thought, for once she's making me feel like she likes something. Oh, holy God, she said to herself, maybe she's getting used to us.

She talked to Rocco about Vietnam and about his police work. "Rock," she said, "if you had to do it all over again, with the way the people are acting toward cops and all, would you do it all over again?"

Rocco smiled. "Oh, yeah, Ma," he said, "I would, I sure would."

The next day his mother called him to see how he was. She was worried about him. "Gee, Rock," she said, "I hope I didn't wake you up."

"No, Ma. I just got up."

"Are you walking a beat tonight?"

"No, I'm going to be in a patrol car."

"That's good because it's very windy."

"Yeah, but I don't like the car. I like walking."

He stayed on the phone with her for a long time. He didn't seem to want to stop talking. She liked that but, finally, she had to break it off because she was at work.

"I'll talk to you in a couple of days," he said.

"Yeah. And Rock," she said before hanging up, "take care of yourself, willya?"

Greg Foster heard from his mother that week, too. For some reason she phoned him to tell him how proud she was of him, how he was achieving things by going to school while working at his job. Greg was stunned because he had never heard his mother speak quite so warmly to him before, never heard her tell him that she was *proud* of him.

There was one night early in the week that Greg did talk about his job with Jackie. He was tired and discouraged and he admitted to her for the first time his doubts. "You wouldn't believe how people live out there, Jackie," he said. "You don't know how lucky we are. People out there are bad."

"Do you want to give up the police," she asked.

"I'm thinking about it." He broke it off and put Marvin Gaye on the record player.

He had started his four-to-twelver on Monday the twenty-third. He was off Tuesday and Wednesday (the night Rocco worked in a car). That last night off he and Larry Chiles, his old friend from the academy, talked. Greg told Larry about the people in the Ninth Precinct, how a lot of them respected him but a lot hated him because of the work he was doing. "I'm stepping on a lot of toes down there," he told Larry, "and I know it."

Larry Chiles said to him, half joking, "You better slow down, Greg, or one day I'm going to be reading about you."

"Nothing's going to happen to me," Foster said. "I can take care of myself."

I can take care of myself. . . . I'm very careful. The litany was repeated constantly by both Foster and Laurie. Way back when Rocco first told Adelaide he was going to the Ninth Precinct she had been so frightened. "Oh, my God," she said to him, "of all places to go." He told her that that was what he wanted, that he didn't want to spend his twenty years on Staten Island. And she told him, "Please be careful. I worry." And he told her, "Don't worry, you know I'm always careful."

They shared a common philosophy. It came partly from their Vietnam background and partly from their own instincts, their own sure knowledge that what they were doing was right and that, God willing, they could indeed take care of themselves. Theirs was the total dedication of young policemen, idealistic, sure of themselves, untainted by corruption, ready to do what had to be done, at whatever the cost. And there was no way they could die because they had been through the fire and lived, and they had learned from the experience. No, they could not be touched. The thought never occurred to either of them that life *was* sometimes unfair and that there would come a time when they would each be as naked and as alone as a baby kicking in his mother's womb.

Foster and Laurie hooked up again on Thursday, the twenty-sixth day of January.

Sometimes we'd walk from Forty-second Street down to Rocke-feller Center, and walk through Central Park to get the train. And I always begged him to take me up to St. Patrick's. We used to walk by it. I wanted to see what it looked like, I always wanted to see what the church looked like. I would always beg him and get so mad because he was Catholic and he knew what to do in there. But he would never take me, he didn't want to go. And then, when I did go, I didn't see nothing but his casket.

PART FIVE

Victims
and
Survivors

God is hard on men, and
especially on women.
— GEORGE SAND

Staten Island, the most sheltered of the boroughs, the most suburban, nevertheless shared the heat with the rest of New York City. In the orange and gray twilight, the dust and haze and smog and pollution clung to the New York skyline, stretching its smoky tentacles to the small single-family house on the small treelined dead-end street where Rocco Laurie had grown to manhood.

I paused at the doorway, reading the decal pasted on one of the small windowpanes in the door: "My Son Is a United States Marine." The motto encircled the *semper fidelis* marine eagle, which was perched atop the world, a fragile globe that clung to the marine anchor for support. "My Son Is a United States Marine." The words enveloped the eagle like the humidity in the summer air.

The father, Anthony Laurie, Sr., pulled himself off the stoop where he had been chatting with a neighbor and walked toward his own house. He was small and shriveled, a thin man wearing khaki pants and an open-necked short-sleeved sports shirt. His face was as tan as his pants but dark circles girded the eyes and played off of his prominent hawk nose. He shook hands tentatively and walked me into the house.

The mother was waiting, a large woman, large in body and in face. She was wearing a black and white dress. Her hair was a conbination of brown and fading red. She wore glasses that did not soften her features. Her face was sallow, the grief marks visible under the eyes. She had a gruff, deep voice, a commanding voice. Annie Laurie her name, Italian not Irish, but immaterial. Call her the American mother.

The round kitchen table was covered with green linoleum. Two ceramic pieces hung on the wall, pieces that had been executed by the daughter-in-law, Adelaide Laurie.

Mrs. Laurie lit a cigarette and pulled up one of the boxes that were strewn on the floor at her feet. "The cellar's full," she said, puffing on the cigarette. "I don't want to part with anything here, like the marine clothes and things." She thought of the night she had taken her second son down to the cellar to the steel closet that was full of his marine uniforms. "Rock," she had said, "get these things out of here. What are you going to do with them, anyway?"

"Ma," he had told her, "I can sell them to the hippies, you know."

But he never had a chance to and so Mrs. Laurie had given most of his clothes to the church. "But I got his boots down there yet. I got his ice skates down there, I got his weights down there. I've got a trunk full of books back there. There's still junk spread around this house yet."

She opened up one of the photo albums. The father was impatient. "Where's that book from the police academy that you said he had? I thought you said he had it."

She sat over the album, smoking, and turned to the first page, hearing the father but not hearing. "I've got it someplace." She showed me a card. "He made it in kindergarten." The salutation read: "I love you mother."

She looked tired. "We don't sleep so well any more. We never sleep late any more, do we? When the kids were home I used to love to sleep late. You know what happens to me now? I fall asleep in that chair, then I say, let me go to bed, I'm so tired. Then when I get in bed I can't sleep. So many things go through your mind. You go back and back. You go back to all the things that the kids went through. You think of so many things." She gestured with her arms, waving through the cigarette smoke, and it was like the years moving aside, like she was opening a path for herself so that she could see clearer to her roots and to the elements that had formed her life when she was young.

"Let's see, Rocco was going to be twenty-four and I'm going to be fifty-eight. I got married in forty-six. So I was thirty-two when he was born." She looked at the father. "That means you're going to be seventy."

The father worked for Con Edison on Staten Island as a trouble shooter for forty-seven years. He retired in 1967 on a modest pension.

The father said, "I got married when I was forty-six years old. Why I did that, I was waiting until my mother and father. . . .

208

Well, my mother died first. Then I lived with my father and my sister."

"I knew him a long time, though. I didn't want to marry him when he was younger. He was too old for me."

The father interrupted. "You didn't realize how good I was."

She laughed. "When I married you you were a little guinea. My mother died when I was fourteen and there were ten of us living in Elizabeth, New Jersey. I had a sister who was eight, a brother who was ten, my sister Margaret was twelve. I was fourteen and the others were older. I was just finishing my first year of high school and the others were working so I stayed home and took care of the family. We had a vegetable business and a grocery store at the time but times weren't good like they are now. I stayed home for seventeen years.

"So I came to Staten Island one week to visit my cousin and he" — she pointed at the father — "came one night and I didn't even look at him. I was only eighteen years old. To me, he was an old man already.

"My father was very strict, and that was another thing."

"I would never have married. If my father were alive today," the father said, "I wouldn't have married."

She stopped him with a look. "He wanted to get married when I was younger and I didn't. He wanted to run off and get married. I couldn't do that."

"Like I said, I wanted to make sure my father was taken care of."

"You were too interested in playing the horses."

Color rose in the father's face. "She brought up playing the horses. I've been playing horses at least forty years, I'll say. It didn't hurt me any. I'm not a winner, let's put it that way. But I won and I lost. It was a pastime for me."

The mother's voice softened. "He never took anything from us. He used to get maybe eight dollars spending money. If he played on that, that was his problem."

"If I went broke, I went broke. She's got a brother who always tried to get anything from his wife to play the horses. Not me."

"HOW DID YOU HEAR ABOUT IT?" Her raspy voice rose to a pitch. "Now who would tell you that?"

"You."

She started through the photographs. "Look at him when he was a baby. You know, that kid wouldn't sleep the whole night through until he was almost nine months old. He'd stay up all night long."

"He was allergic to the milk," the father remembered. "We had to give him goat's milk."

"Here he is when he was three months old. He's wearing the suit Anthony had as a baby. Anthony outgrew it so fast." She lit a cigarette, placed it on the ashtray, and bent over the album. She had trouble seeing, she had cataracts in both eyes.

"Here's when he must have been seventeen months old. He was blond when he was small. I remember, I used to walk him and I used to be light, too, and everybody used to turn around and look at him and ask his name and when I said Rocco I guess they couldn't understand that. You see, everybody knows that's an Italian name. 'This little blond baby a Rocco?' "

She moved to another page. "These are oldies, believe me." The picture showed the brothers together, by the seashore in New Jersey, with an aunt and uncle. "We went away with them kids for ten years."

The father said, "We never did much during the year. I wasn't making much of a salary, but it was enough. We were getting by."

The mother said, "Just as long as we paid our bills. We always ate good."

"We always ate good is right."

The father used to go to New York when he was single, to Yankee Stadium. "I didn't miss a week going up there to see the Yankees play. I saw Babe Ruth, all of them. We'd make a day of it, four or five of us. Go up there, go to the game, eat, then go to Radio City or some other place to the show. We'd come here one or two in the morning. After I got married we'd go up there maybe once a year."

"Like, Anthony used to love to go to New York, I'd say, no, Anthony, thank you, I'll stay home. I hate New York."

The father said, "Now you can have it with all the colored people and Puerto Ricans there. You can't hear yourself talk."

But the seashore was something else, clean, pure, quiet, ethnically right. "From the time when the kids were small," she said, "we saved to go away for two weeks. It was the only way we could go. Take a cottage, eat our meals there. It was a nice area and Rocco and Anthony loved it.

"This one time," the mother remembered, "we took this one place. It was cheap but it was a mess when we got there. There was blood all over the walls from mosquitoes and things. Rocco was upset. I said to all of them, 'Go down to the beach while I clean up the place.' So I did. And Rocco came back and lay on the bed and said, 'Well, now I feel better, Ma.' That woman would have liked us back every year because I was cleaning her walls down."

There were more pictures of the boys by the sea. "That's where Rocco and Anthony learned to swim so good." For the first time, the father seemed interested in studying the old pictures. He got up from his chair to look closer. "Rocco was a beautiful swimmer and diver and everything. I don't want to have you believe that I'm bragging about him, but I know he was good in almost everything."

The mother said, "He always wanted to get somewhere."

There was a picture of Rocco with a shot put in his hand. "One day, I remember, he came home and he said, 'Ma, I threw that shot put today and I threw it pretty far.' I said, 'What the devil's a shot put?' "

"That all started because of the guy who was the champ of this city Y. He could really throw the shot and one day he watched Rocco throw it and he laughed at him. And Rocco said to me, 'Daddy,' he said, 'if there's one thing I'm going to do, I'm going to beat this fella.'

"I said, 'All right, Rocco, that means a lot of practice.' We went back of the house, where there was a field, now there are all new homes. We cut down all the brush and cleared a nice space and he was out there every night after school. On Saturdays, too. I'm telling you, on Saturday morning he'd go out there and practice for a couple of hours. He'd get almost exhausted. Then he lifted weights and did push-ups. There's a guy down here who could tell you some of the stories when Rocco was a marine. This guy was an Indian, I think he said. And he thought he was good at this wrestling thing and Rocco would get him down right away. And that man respected Rocco so much that he used to go to see if Rocco was in his bunk and stuff like that. And he loved Rocco after that."

She stopped at a picture of Rocco in his white Communion suit. She lit a cigarette. "He was sick, he had his suit all ready but he had a very high temperature and a sore throat so the doctors said no, he couldn't go. I cried.

"My Anthony was so religious. He wanted to be a priest at one time. I said, 'But, Anthony, you're too young. If, when you get older and you still feel that way, then it's up to you, but right now I don't think you should. Then he started going out with girls and that was the end of it.

"Rocco was religious, too. He told me he went to church all the time he was in Vietnam, all the time he was in the marines. But when he got back he stopped. That Tuesday night before it happened, when he came over, I said, 'Gee, Rocco, that's not right, you always went to church. All of a sudden now that you're married, you don't.' He said, 'Yeah, Ma, I got to start going again.' I used to get annoyed with both of them, he and Adelaide, because they didn't go to church. But Rocco said, 'Hey, Ma, you don't lose your religion. I still say my prayers before I go to bed at night.' And he did, too.

"Even Anthony, he got so that church didn't mean anything to him any more. But when this happened Anthony changed some of his ideas a lot. He said, 'Ma, to me Rocco was indestructible. There has to be somebody or you wouldn't be able to live through it.' And that's true. I used to say to Rocco, 'If dying is like sleeping I don't have to worry.' He'd get a little annoyed because I used to worry. He'd say to me, 'What's the use of worrying? You could go out and get hit by a car.' But you always worry. All the time he was in Vietnam, I worried. See, all the girl friend worries is whether he's writing. But a mother says, please, God, just let him take care of himself."

The father thought he should change the direction of the conversation. "I remember the time I took Rocco to the racetrack at Monmouth Park. I won a race big, sixty-two dollars. When the race ended I said to Rocco, 'What horse went past here first, Rocco?' He said, 'Three.' I said, 'Good, good, I got him. Now on the way home we'll eat a nice big dinner. You can eat to your heart's content.' "

The mother said, "But he never believed in gambling. He was the type of kid who would always have a dollar because he was very thrifty."

"If he had to spend money," the father said, "he'd spend it on her."

"He had seven or eight thousand dollars when he got married."

"It's funny how they switched," the mother said. "When they were small Anthony was the one who knew how to take care of money. And Rocco, I figured it didn't faze him. All of a sudden, I don't know what changed him. He was the one who never paid any attention to anything. I always thought Anthony was going to be the goody-goody. And it turned out the opposite way. So, you don't know."

The boys were always different, she said. Anthony was studious, Rocco was athletic. "One day they both rushed home from school with their report cards. Anthony did better. 'Oh, Ma,' Rocco said, 'I'll never be smart like Anthony.' 'Shut up,' I said. 'Your brother envies you because you can play ball, you can do anything you want.' 'But, Ma,' he said, 'I'll never be smart like Anthony.' I said, 'Hey, Rock, everybody's different in the world.'"

"He was a very good ballplayer," the father said. "If he'd stuck to baseball he'd probably been a star. But once he threw the shot he was no good for baseball. His arm went on him." They were looking at a picture of a Little League team.

"Oh, I can't believe it, I'm telling you. You know, he was the kind of a boy, you looked at him you just couldn't believe he was in the baseball. I used to go nuts with the baseball thing, running up there to see him play, because he had to work," she said, nodding at her husband, "and someone had to go watch Rocco. I remember the very first time I went there, I said, 'Rocco, I'm the only woman up here.'"

"Rocco was some hitter," the father said. "When he socked a home run it was a home run. I gave Anthony the ball that he had."

"His first home run," the mother said.

"I put the date on it. I said to Anthony, 'Save it, someday . . .'"
He let drop whatever it was he was going to say. Suddenly, he seemed embarrassed talking about the son the way he had, all the praise and all the pride he felt for the one son. He pulled away

213

from the photo albums and reached down and picked up the newspapers they had saved. The mother took the papers.

"All I seem to have is Friday, Friday, Friday. What happened to the other ones?"

"You seem to have a lot of Fridays." The Friday papers carried the first story of the shootings.

"Here's one from the *Advance*. This was right on the front page." She reached for a pair of dark glasses and clipped them to her regular glasses. She could see better with the dark glasses on. There seemed to be a closeness in the room. Cigarette smoke hung over the table. There was a stillness that hadn't been there before. The mother started reading from the paper.

"He was very fair and straightforward. He was always very reluctant to push people around. Maybe he was too straight, a good student, an outstanding athlete." She began to paraphrase. And she began to cry.

"He graduated with highest honors from the police academy in April and received the commissioner's trophy. The shot-put records Laurie set are still among the top five. . . . He won both the PSAL and Eastern States shot put championship and also won a complete athletic scholarship to Iona College. After two years at Iona he left and became a police trainee and in 1968 he enlisted in the marines for two years." She pulled out a yellow tissue and dabbed at her eyes. "They only have corporal there," she said. "He made sergeant."

She began to read again. "Patrolman David Bauberger, staff member at the academy, said that Laurie, his company sergeant, was a very conscientious fellow. He was a good worker, very cooperative and very friendly. Following his graduation he was assigned to the Ninth Precinct with his partner, Foster." She stopped reading word for word. It was too difficult because she was crying harder. "Then they tell about his being married and survived by his parents and a brother." She read once more: "Most of those who knew Laurie refused to believe what had happened, or realized it with great difficulty. He was the kind of guy you would point to and say, 'I want my son to be like that.' "

She threw the paper aside. She lifted the dark glasses. Her eyes were filled with pain and, for the first time, there was bitterness, too. She said, "I just wonder if they were out to get them or if it was just two cops."

The father said, "It was planned. I imagine so."

The mother said, "No, I don't know. I don't know who to believe any more."

The father said, "They say they shot him in the back and everything else. I think it was planned."

The mother said, "How did they stop and take that watch off his wrist? They said there were four, but I don't know. Now if they get them they don't give them the chair. It's a federal law. No executions."

The father said, "I told the commissioner, 'You tried it without capital punishment and it didn't work. Why don't you bring it back again?' They don't answer you."

The mother said, "All I hear is how cruel it is to kill another person. What about what they're doing to us? Isn't this cruel? My son, a good boy like him, had to die for some kooks that they're going to let walk the streets again in seven years. When I saw those pictures. . . . Well, like one of the cops said to me, 'I'm beginning to really hate the niggers.' I'm really beginning to hate them, too." Forgotten for the moment was Rocco's partner, Gregory Foster, dead, too, dead alongside their son. Grief twists souls. The survivors suffer the most.

The mother said, "Do they know, do they know what we go through in a thing like this? Isn't this cruel what they're doing to us? For no reason? Here's a boy who had so much to live for, so many plans in his life, everything he was going to do. For what? Better they should be dead than my son. At least he would have been useful to society."

The father said, "Wasn't it cruel for those four guys to kill two cops? Kill and shoot them in the back?"

The mother looked up to the ceiling. "Oh, God, I don't understand people, I don't understand people. You kill somebody, you should pay for it. When they deliberately kill people, why shouldn't they pay for it? What's so cruel about that? Isn't it just as cruel for us to think what we have to go through for the rest of our lives?"

She dropped the papers to the floor and lit a cigarette, trying to compose herself. She sniffed quietly as she turned to the album again. "You can see how blond Rocco is here. This was when he was in cub scouts. Gee, we went through a lot of trouble for all this junk."

Again, she slid back to the past. "Rocco was always going, this kid. He'd never sit still for a minute. Always he used to sit on the floor and play with those army men. He had so many of them. He'd talk to them and play with his army. And then he started with the Indians. You know, they had an Indian village in Atlantic City. Well, my sister-in-law bought him the ax, the wagon wheels, and they were expensive things. And he used to sit on that floor, he'd talk to himself playing with these things. And when it came to the baseball cards! We had baseball cards until they were coming out of our ears. I made him give them all away then. I said, 'Rock, oh, come on. There's so much junk in this house.' I'm still trying to get rid of it. Look at these short pants here. The kids laugh at these now."

It was a lovely picture of Rocco as a cub scout. I stared at it a long time. "He's a cute kid," the mother said. "He doesn't look Italian, does he? As a matter of fact, when they brought him down on that stretcher, I looked at him and said, 'Oh, God, look at how dark his hair is.' 'cause I'd always pictured him as blond in my mind. It's a funny thing but it stayed with me. When they brought him down on the stretcher after they had told us he was dead I looked at him and said, 'Oh, my God, he looks just like he was sleeping.' He had such light skin, I could see the beard."

She put the dark clip-ons back over her glasses. The tears moved freely. She wiped her eyes. She kept staring at that picture of her son as a cub scout, standing in a parade, an angelic look on his face, kids all around him with American flags in their hands, a parade in the early fifties when innocence was still desirable in America. She looked at the picture and the past and the present — the present being that moment when it stopped for the mother and the father, that early morning when they were told their son was dead — the past and the present flooded together.

"I remember I used to say, 'Oh God, please let me live to see my boys grow up.' Because I was old and I figured I'd never live long enough. At the wake I told Adelaide I never thought I would ever say in my own words that I wouldn't live to see him grow up. I thought I would never say, *if only I could change places with him.* 'Cause I never figured I would ever have to stand over my own son. I figured he would stand over me.

"I kept hoping before the stretcher came, I kept saying, 'Oh, God,' I even said, 'Oh, Rock, I prayed you out of Vietnam. I'll pray you out of anything.' And I kept saying, 'Oh, God, he's such a strong boy. You know it's not going to be. You know what I mean, you know it.' But he had a bullet in the neck. When he was laid out you could see; after all, he didn't have a big neck, my son. And every time I'd go to the funeral home I'd cover it because it didn't look like him over there, because his neck wasn't like that. And toward the end, at the wake, it started to ooze."

She dabbed at her eyes. The father sat at the table, mute, staring into space.

"When they brought him out in the stretcher they had a white sheet over him. But they left his face open. His hair was, oh so dark. And his skin was so light, his beard showed. I used to say, 'Oh, Rocco, how come you're so light and your beard shows so much?' And I touched him and I said, 'Oh, my God, he's still warm.' He looked like he was sleeping."

Her eyes were closed now. She was rocking, being transported back in time to that awful night.

They had Gregory Foster up on the table and they were pumping away, but there was nothing that could be done for him. He had come to Bellevue dead and his death was pronounced officially in the emergency room while he was still being worked on.

There was hardly a head left. One of the eight bullets that struck him went right through him and came out of his mouth. A policeman on the scene described Foster's head as being "like a marshmallow. There was nothing left back there but fat." They had shot both his eyes out, and torn a hole in the back of his head, and part of his brain fluid had been left back on Avenue B — a puddle of blood mixed with the mind-giving elixir, just a viscous wet spot stretching three feet in length and a foot across. And then the snow came and the clean white nuggets spread over the sidewalk, purifying and providing penitence over the blood.

Jackie Foster's brother-in-law, who rode with her in the radio car to the hospital, knew that Gregory was dead, but he told her nothing. The police officers had shut off their radio so that nothing about the death would come through their receiver. They said nothing to her. They had been ordered to tell her that Gregory Foster had been in an accident. They had done that. They said no more.

So when she got out of the car in front of the emergency entrance at the great hospital she still felt her husband was alive. She was frightened by the sight of so many police around, of lights flashing, of newspaper photographers snapping pictures. There was bewilderment in her eyes, in the set of her mouth, and apprehension. She walked through the emergency door and was guided into a small room.

She was there alone for only a few seconds and then the police chaplain, Monsignor Joseph Dunne, came in, followed by a policewoman. Monsignor Dunne bent over the wife and whispered gently.

"Mrs. Foster, your husband has had an accident and he is dead. I'm so sorry."

I don't know what went on after that. I kept my feelings inside me because it was just as if somebody had stuck a knife in me, and I couldn't feel. That's the way I felt. I couldn't believe that Gregory was dead. He was so happy that day. Everything was so . . . it was just so hard to believe. He was shot up so bad that nobody in the family could see him. They just shot both his eyes out, and he had such pretty eyes. He had long eyelashes. And the undertaker said at first there was nothing he could do with him, that I would have to have a closed casket. So then they worked on him and they told me I could have an open casket but that he would have to have a net over him, and that his face couldn't be touched. You could see that they had put his eyes back together up there. The way they shot him, it was so clean because they didn't touch his eyebrows at all. His eyebrows were still the way they were. He had very thick eyebrows. From the cheekbone on down he looked like Gregory. They didn't touch his body at all. He was still husky like he was. Just in the back of the head — that's the only way they could have gotten Gregory.

Gregory Foster's mother and father and their youngest son, Michael, came in. Jackie Foster went over to the mother and they embraced. "I'm sorry," she said and she backed away and was by herself.

"Oh, God, my son," Gregory's father wailed. And Gregory's brother, who was sixteen, took it the worst of all and had to have sedation.

After a while a patrol car took Jackie home to her children and she didn't sleep for a month.

In another room down the corridor, Adelaide Laurie could hear the screams. She knew it was Mrs. Foster and she felt terrible and it was like a nightmare. But at least her Rocco was still alive.

He could not talk but he was still alive. He had been shot six times. Twice he was shot in the groin after he had fallen. (A witness said later he heard one of the murderers say, "Shoot them in the balls.") A bullet had pierced his penis. All of the bullets had passed completely through him, each making entrance and exit wounds. One of the bullets had rebounded up off the pavement and entered his body a second time. One bullet had struck his neck. Blood was oozing through the hole. The preliminary indications for Rocco Laurie were hopeful because most of the bullets had not struck vital organs. But doctors worried about the neck wound.

A couple of patrolmen from the Ninth Precinct went into the operating room with Rocco until they were told to get out. They went outside and watched through a window. They saw four doctors working on Rocco. Patrolman Jim Liedy was one of those looking in. Before Laurie was wheeled into the operating room he asked a doctor, "What are his chances?"

"He's going to make it," the doctor said. He was wearing a green uniform and rubber gloves. He seemed to reconsider his statement. "He's got a fifty-fifty chance, I think. But we have to find where the bullets are."

Rocco was in surgery when Dr. Iammatteo got to the hospital. "What happened?" he asked one of the doctors.

219

"He's been hit in the extremities," the doctor said.

The chiropractor flushed. "Look, I'm a doctor in my own right. You don't have to tell me about extremities. How serious is it?"

"He's been badly shot up. We don't know the extent of it."

Matty went in to console his niece. She seemed very bad. She was sobbing bitterly. "Adelaide," he said gently, "what about his parents? Shouldn't they be told?"

"I'd rather not disturb them," Adelaide said.

"I should call her," Matty said.

It was Mrs. Laurie who called the hospital. Her brother had phoned her from New Jersey and told her about the shooting. Now she had Dr. Iammatteo on the phone.

"Is it true?" she asked.

"It is, Mrs. Laurie."

"Goddamn it," she said, "can't you people tell me anything about what's going on?"

Dr. Iammatteo told her what the doctors had said to him. "It's snowing out," he said. "The roads are bad. Stay home and I'll keep you posted."

"Like hell I will," she said. "I'll come if I have to crawl on my hand and knees." About an hour and a half later she and her husband and Rocco's brother and his wife Kathy arrived.

Anthony Laurie, Jr., had gotten the call at about two in the morning. He had received calls like that late at night before and had always thought — correctly, it turned out — that "it was some crazy wrong number." But this time when the phone rang he knew immediately that it was something bad. He crawled over his sleeping wife to answer the phone.

It was his mother. She was crying. Then she said, "Oh, my God, it's him, it's really him." All Anthony could think of was that it was his father, that something had happened to his father. Then his mother said, "Rocco. He was shot."

Anthony and Kathy rushed over to his parents' home. Then he drove with them to Bellevue. "He can't die," Kathy said to her husband, "not Rocco. He's too tough. It's impossible."

Anthony didn't answer at once, for he felt the same; that Rocco couldn't die. His mother had told him that Foster was dead and he said, "We'll have to send flowers." But he couldn't conceive — could not conceive — his brother dying.

As they walked in the emergency entrance, Anthony saw a man standing there, blood dripping from his head. He hardly paid attention, not sure whether he had seen right or whether it was all part of a dream. The whole thing was like a dream to him. He seemed to be sleepwalking in hell and the sight of the bleeding man only intensified the feeling.

They went down a corridor to where there were three offices. They went into the middle office, through another door, into a small room. Adelaide was sitting in a chair. Her face and hair were disheveled. One tear was running down the cheek. A policewoman was standing beside her, on one side. Her Uncle Matty stood on the other side.

Kathy went over and kneeled down in front of Adelaide. "Are you all right?" she whispered. Aldelaide nodded her head and said nothing.

The mother was furious that she had not been called. She said to one of the police officers, "Why didn't somebody get in touch with us? I hope you never do that to another mother."

Anthony told her to shut up. "That doesn't do any good now," he said. He asked one of the policemen from Staten Island who had driven Adelaide to the hospital about his brother.

"Oh, he only got it in the leg," the cop said.

"Then why is his condition listed as critical?"

Moments later a doctor came in. His surgical mask hung loosely around his neck. "We can't be optimistic at this point," the doctor said. The mother fainted. They opened her dress in the back and they gave her a needle. When she came to she was calm. She took out her rosary beads and suggested that everyone pray.

The doctors had traced the course of the bullet in the neck. It had severed the carotid artery and the internal jugular vein.

Just then a friend of Rocco's from the police academy, Angel Cruz, came in the room. He walked over to Anthony Laurie. "Are you Rocco's brother?" Anthony nodded. "I'd like to speak to you outside."

They went into the corridor. "He's not going to make it." Cruz began to cry.

"Are you sure?" Anthony said frantically. "How do you know?"

"There's no hope. He's too shot up."

"Are you telling me that he's already dead?"

"No, not yet."

Anthony went back inside and asked Kathy to come out with him. He told her and she cried, "No, it can't be, it can't be."

It was four-forty in the morning when Captain Edward Rogers, the commanding officer of the Ninth Precinct, walked in the room. "I'd like to have everybody together," he said.

Captain Rogers had come in earlier in the evening, after the police surgeon had told him that it didn't look good for Rocco Laurie, that the young police officer wasn't responding well at all. Rogers tried to comfort Adelaide and Mr. and Mrs. Laurie. Monsignor Dunne was saying the rosary at the time and Rogers left the room quietly. And now he was back because the surgeon had just told him, "Laurie has passed away." Rogers knew he now had the most difficult job in the world to perform. No matter how gentle or how kind you try to be in telling someone that his loved one is dead, eventually you have to come out with the words — "he's dead." No matter how you try to cut the cake, Rogers thought to himself, anguished by what he had to do, you still have to come out and say those words — "he's dead."

The family was spread around. Kathy and Anthony were standing by the doorway. Dr. Iammatteo stood behind Adelaide's chair. Mr. Laurie, frail, his face drained of color, rose from his chair. He stood there, waiting. Adelaide and Mrs. Laurie remained seated.

Captain Rogers said the words he hated to say and Anthony rushed over to hug his father and Kathy moved toward the mother. "My son, my son," she wailed and passed out. Adelaide began to scream. They tried to put their arms around her and she was screaming, "No, no, I can't believe it. It can't be." And she began running from one side of the room to the other, like a caged animal. And with her fists she banged on the wall until they removed her and sat her back on a chair. The father slumped in the seat, sitting there with his head in his hands, moaning softly, "My pride and joy, my pride and joy."

And then a calmness settled over the room and Adelaide in a controlled voice demanded to see her husband. Captain Rogers didn't think it was a good idea but the hospital authorities said it would be all right once they cleaned up the body.

In about fifteen minutes they were led down a corridor to another room. Rocco Laurie was lying on a portable stretcher. A sheet was pulled up around his neck. The mother and father threw themselves on top of the body; both were crying uncontrollably. Adelaide started running her fingers through his hair and began kissing him. The police finally had to move in and separate them all from the body.

Mrs. Laurie was put in a wheelchair. A policeman wheeled her out of the room. Adelaide had gone limp and was half carried from the room. Anthony, alone, stood there for a moment, chilled as he had never before been in his life. His brother looked like he was asleep. His face was white, pure white, and his lips were blue. His hair was wet. Anthony went over and silently touched his face. He noticed that his chin was cold but the rest of his face was still warm. He still could not believe that his brother was dead.

Captain Rogers drove the widow back to Staten Island, where she would be staying with her in-laws. She was calmer now. In the car she kept repeating, "He promised to fix the door next week on his day off, he promised to fix that door. He's never going to fix that door now." And she sobbed silently to herself.

The day before the funeral, the Cool Ones took the subway to the Bronx, traveling in a group to the funeral home where Gregory Foster was laid out. When they got there they all kneeled down and prayed and some of the boys began to cry. One of them cried so hard that he had to leave the room. A short time later he returned and he sat down and cried again. He told Jackie Foster, "There are no more Mr. Cools around and there won't be another one like him, either." He said that he had cut out her husband's picture and he was going to save it. A lot of the other boys also had cut out pictures of Foster from the newspapers and put them in their wallets. Before they left the funeral home they dropped a letter next to the guest register. A few days later it was picked up and reprinted in all the New York newspapers. The letter read:

223

In Memory Of Gregory Foster — "Mr. Cool" to Us!

Mr. Cool, if I ever have the temptation of getting into trouble, I'll close my eyes and I'll believe I see you walking down the Ave., cool as always, going into our clubhouse and asking us — "Are you keeping Cool, kids?"

I will always remember when we play basketball with you and when we play baseball in the summer in 12th St. Park. I still have my glove and I remember the last time you use it to pitch part of one game.

Every time you hear about some kids in trouble, you used to look for us and make sure we didn't have any part of it. I will always remember your last words to us — "Keep out of trouble, hey guys, stay Cool."

We know that you are still with us walking down the Ave. and keeping us cool. We'll miss you but we won't ever forget about you because we are sure you'll be beside us.

From now on, all the other cops will be "Mr. Cool" to us, but none as cool as you.

It was signed by José Figuero, David Carrion, Ruben Colon, Raul Rosaro, George Rivera, José León, Eggie Torres, Johnny Perez, Eddie Bora, Carlos Rivera and Miguel Blasco.

The shock, the rage, the sorrow of Foster and Laurie's death was not confined to the tight boundaries of the Ninth Precinct. There was an extraordinary reaction from people all over the country. A letter Jackie Foster received from a doctor and his wife seemed to sum up the public's attitude toward the two men: "Even those of us who never met your husband will miss him — we will miss him as we miss all the great men who have been the victims of the society they were trying to help. Please keep faith and know that you are in all of our prayers."

Suddenly, through a combination of circumstances, Foster and Laurie had become symbols for all the forgotten virtues of American life. For one thing, the terror of it, the wanton killings in cold blood, enraged people everywhere, thus drawing them together. It seemed to be a killing without reason except that these young men wore the blue. Also, the news reports immediately romanticized the relationship between Foster and Laurie. Their superiors in the Ninth Precinct, knowing only what they had been told, gave the press the information that Foster and Laurie had been buddies in Vietnam, that Laurie had been Foster's sergeant and that they had been friends ever since. At a time when black and white relations in the United States were rubbing raw once again, it seemed comforting to middle-class Americans to know that there were still instances when black and white could live together and work together and even die together in perfect harmony. The fact that Foster, a black man, was killed by a black man also helped blur an emerging stereotype of the black man as an outlaw in America. Beyond that, there were the basic links between the two men. They were young and idealistic. They had served bravely in a war where bravery didn't seem to matter very much. Each had recently been married and the one had young children. And they were, just like everyone else, groping for the American dream. That their dreams had been shattered for them while they were doing duty in a national crisis spot — urban America — made them even larger than life.

Tributes began to pour in to both widows. President Nixon sent them each a letter, with flowers. There were condolence letters from other public officials all over the country but both widows heard from the ordinary people, too — mass cards, envelopes containing money (the Patrolmen's Benevolent Association supervised a fund for the widows that eventually went over the forty-thousand-dollar mark), and personal notes. Mrs. Diane Piagentini, whose husband, Patrolman Joseph Piagentini, was killed along with his black partner, Waverly Jones, in the same way eight months earlier (possibly by some of the same men) wrote Jackie Foster and Adelaide Laurie: "It was not long ago that your grief was also mine and still is. I know this is very hard for you to believe, as it was for me, but I got through it." To Jackie she said: "I also have two children, ages two and three, and now you will have to live and breathe for them. If there should come a time when you would like to speak with someone who has been through this terrible nightmare, please do not hesitate to call me."

And Jackie heard from Waverly Jones's sister. "I hope my card and letter will give you some comfort. I know it will never bring Gregory back. How well I know, when my brother, Waverly Jones, was murdered in May. I go to his grave every weekend and still ask why. There is no sense to this killing. I hope they find these guys. God, I hope they do."

Outrage over the murders mingled with sorrow for the dead men. A woman in Darien, Connecticut, wrote Adelaide saying: "I've cut out the *Times*'s pictures of Mr. Laurie and Mr. Foster and it is pinned to the Bulletin Board in the kitchen where we — my husband, my four children — will always be reminded of the sacrifices these men made and so that we will never forget."

Grief was widespread but felt most deeply by those who were closest to the two men. Brooks Matyi was away on a skiing trip in northern New York. That whole weekend he didn't see a newspaper, watch television, or listen to the radio. He got back about one-thirty on Monday morning and was surprised to see that his father and mother were waiting for him. They both looked at him strangely. Brooks's mother immediately ran to him and put her arms around him.

"I have something to tell you," she said, suddenly trembling. "Rocco's dead. He was killed up in New York."

At first Brooks didn't understand. He had a friend from Pennsylvania named Rocco Grande. He thought, Rocco's dead? What's he doing up in New York? And then it hit him and he went to pieces and he cried for three days. ("I don't think it's any crime for a man to cry," he said much later. "And I was more than close to Rocco. I loved the guy.")

Out in California Sergeant Ray Riepe, Greg Foster's platoon leader, saw it on the television news and recognized Foster's name and his face. "He was a good man," he mumbled dully to his wife. "That's why he got killed, probably. They always kill the good ones."

Many of the people who lived in the East Village, in that squalid enclave of thieves, whores, pimps, junkies, and poor people trying to survive, the people who knew Foster and Laurie or saw them on the beat, were stunned and saddened by the deaths. On the street they were saying to each other, "Hey, man, that real cool cop got shot."

The day after it happened, two plainclothesmen jumped out of a car on Avenue B and started searching two suspicious-looking men. A young junkie came by and derided them, saying, "Look at those two mean cops." A black woman was standing there watching it all and she yelled at the junkie, "What do you expect? They shot two of the nicest cops in the neighborhood."

The police in the Ninth were uptight. Eugene Lewis, a black cop, a member of the Ninth Precinct's Neighborhood Police Team, didn't know what had happened until he was on his way to work early that Friday morning. He got off the subway train at Astor Place, picked up a *Daily News*, looked briefly at the headline, put the newspaper under his arm, and walked toward Fifth Street. Then he pulled out the paper and looked again. Suddenly, his legs felt weak. He saw a patrol car parked at the corner of Fifth Street and Second Avenue, and a patrolman he did not recognize standing by the car. He walked toward the cop, hoping he could get more information, hoping maybe that the cop would tell him it was all a mistake. As he came near the cop and started to speak, the cop, who was in the Ninth Precinct but who did not recognize Lewis, pulled out a gun and pushed Lewis against the car.

"Hey," Lewis said, "I'm on the job."

The cop sitting in the car looked out and recognized Lewis. Lewis grinned, unconcerned. "How you doin'?" he said. The outside cop put his gun back and said he was sorry. Then they told him what had happened.

Afterward, Lewis reflected that maybe he would have done the same thing considering the circumstances. He rationalized, "I'm pretty nervous sitting in a radio car when it's not moving because you can't see what's behind you and people have a tendency to walk behind the car. There's always a blind spot and you can't see anyone until you turn around." And, Lewis thought, "I don't like people walking behind me in the street when I'm wearing the uniform — especially when I'm by myself." Only in the back of his mind would he permit himself to think that the real reason the cop had backed him up against the car and drawn his gun was because Lewis was a black man.

Some of the bitterness and mistrust and hatred between the races — even pitting black men against black men — did seep

227

through the grief in the days immediately following the deaths. Frank Dudley, a black cop from the Ninth, was standing duty beside the coffin at the funeral home when a group of black teen-age boys came in. They walked by the body slowly and then one of them said in a deliberate voice, loud enough for Dudley to hear, "Good for the pig." And he came up to Dudley and spat out the words, "You might be next."

But most black people were outraged by the murders. One man wrote Adelaide Laurie and told her to try and not condemn black people as a whole for the actions of "a cowardly few." And Jackie Foster received a letter from a man who tried to articulate the personal shame he felt over the killings:

> I along with other people, especially other Black people, really feel and regret the loss of your husband Gregory. I feel it in a special way because your husband and I are the same age and I once wanted to be a policeman. . . .
>
> You see, when I learned of your husband's death along with Patrolman Laurie's I felt that it could have been me lying there in the street killed by our "so-called brothers." And there is no doubt in my mind that your husband was a beautiful and together brother, a real asset in today's Black struggle.
>
> Mrs. Foster, please, please don't feel that you — our people — aren't worth a damn because I and other Black people mourn with you the loss of your husband and feel, honestly feel, that his death along with Patrolman Laurie's was nothing but a waste. I will always relate Gregory's death to Malcolm X's, if you can dig where it's coming from.
>
> May God be with you and your family now and forever. I will continue to pray for you and Gregory now and always.
>
> Love, Peace, Happiness, and Understanding. . . .

Love, Peace, Happiness, and Understanding. The lost values in American life. People sensed that Foster and Laurie believed in those values and shared them with each other. That was why the national response was so remarkable. Their deaths, of course, were without reason, but their lives seemed to have been filled with reason. Because of the circumstances of their lives — because of what they had experienced and what they had seen — they may have come to understand a little better than most people the meaning of "the good life." They had been ordinary human beings, thrust into roles that had made them just a little more extraordinary than most other people.

Police honor guards stood at the head and feet of both men's caskets, rotating at fifteen-minute intervals during the three-day wake. Larry Cummings was one of those who was a member of Rocco Laurie's honor guard in the Staten Island funeral home. Afterward he said, "I'd face a guy with a gun before I go through one like this again." He listened in anguish as Adelaide talked to her husband, he watched while she lifted, *lifted* Rocco up so that she could embrace the now marble-hard figure. Cummings had not been a smoker up to that time. He has smoked ever since.

It was Anthony Laurie who wound up making most of the arrangements. The day they returned from the hospital Anthony kept asking Adelaide, "Where do you want Rocco to be laid out?" She just shook her head violently and covered her ears. She was dazed and still crying. At one point when she was sobbing loudly the mother said, "Let's try to be calm. Rocco would want it that way. He's right above us saying, 'Ma, what good is it going to do you? What good is it going to do you?'"

"Don't tell me what he would have wanted," Adelaide shrieked. "How do you know what he would have wanted?" And she put her hands to her ears and sobbed in anguish.

It went on that way continuously. The father or the brother would make a suggestion and Adelaide would refuse to listen, clamping her ears with her hands. Her Aunt Anne, suggested later, "I think she had given herself to him completely, in the sense where she felt he was taking the place of her mother, her father, everything she never had. I feel that he was everything to her. When he died, I think a part of her died."

She did make one decision that day. When they asked her if her husband should be laid out in his police uniform she refused. It was the uniform that killed him, she felt, that was the symbol of his blood sacrifice. So Anthony went out and bought a shirt and tie for his brother, and he bought fresh shirts and black ties for his father and himself, and he helped pick out the black clothes Adelaide and his mother would wear.

The immediate family went to the funeral home on Saturday afternoon to view the body for the first time, before the public would be admitted. Anthony went over and touched his brother's face, which was now covered with makeup. He felt it was like touching a statue. He noticed that Rocco's hair was combed straight back. "That's not the way my brother combed his hair," he said. The undertaker gave him a comb and the brother combed his hair the correct way.

Those three days until they closed the coffin on Tuesday morning, Adelaide never left Rocco's side. Cummings and the other guards found it almost unbearable because she kept talking to her husband. *My baby, my baby, why did they take you? Why did they do this to me? You told me you would never leave me again. . . .* She stood at the head of the coffin, refusing to sit. When Police Commissioner Murphy came in she said to him, "Please catch the men who did it."

There were such moments of lucidity. When Brooks Matyi came in he was so shaken he didn't want to approach the coffin. Adelaide took him by the hand. "Look, don't be afraid," she whispered, "don't be afraid of him." A complete stranger came over to her at one point and said, "He has the face of a saint and you have the face of an angel."

She listened like that at times, but mostly it was the litany: *Rocco, we have to go home now. Rocco, finish up the cellar, let's finish up the kitchen. . . . Let's go home and see the dog.* The tears flowed as she would touch his hair or stroke his face or lean down and kiss him and, always, the monologue: *My poor Rocco. Why did they do this terrible thing to you? You promised me you'd never leave me again when you came back from Vietnam and now you have left me again. . . . How could you do this to me? Why did you leave me? How much I love you. . . . Tell me you love me. . . .* On and on, as the people flowed by, sorrowing, silent, filled with pity for the wife and the parents; the people, unable to understand the absurdity of the young man's death, fearful now for themselves and for the violence that had come to America and seemed to be touching all their lives.

The day before the funeral two of Gregory Foster's brothers came to the Staten Island funeral home to pay their respects to Rocco Laurie. Anthony Laurie was touched by their gesture. The two brothers stood in a small room with members of the police honor guard who were not then on duty. Anthony Laurie went over to them.

"Come sit with us," he said.

They did and the oldest brother met Rocco's wife and parents, and he kept repeating, "They were so young, they were so young."

Before they left, Anthony said to them, "Tell your sister-in-law that we would like to come and see her after the funeral." They said they would.

Gregory Foster was laid out in a funeral home in the Bronx, in a ghetto area. His parents had wanted him in St. Albans but Jacqueline Foster insisted on the Bronx because it would be closer to her apartment. "That's the only time I'll have to be with him," she told them, "until he goes in the ground."

The PBA flew in an expert from California to work on Gregory's face. His father very much wanted an open casket but no one was sure whether the face could be put together. The police expert worked for nine hours straight, through the night. On Saturday morning Jackie Foster went to the funeral home. It would be up to her to decide on an open or closed casket. She was dazed, almost uncomprehending, when she looked down at her husband. Except for the eyes, she thought, it did look like him. So it would be an open coffin.

To George Mahoney, who was one of those from the Ninth in the honor guard, Greg Foster looked like a fifty-year-old man. They had a veil over Foster's face and nobody could touch it. Jackie Foster hungered to. She sat there and thought, I want to kiss him so badly, touch his face. All she could do was lay her head on his arm and hold his hand. But there was one moment that first day when she forgot herself. George Mahoney and another officer, Ray Murphy, were standing guard and Jackie Foster knocked down the veil and tried to touch his face. They thought the whole face was going to come off. They pulled her away. She became hysterical. They carried her to a car and drove her to a hospital and she was put under sedation. The funeral home was closed until the police expert could come over and doctor the face again.

It was better on Monday but now the people were asking why

the widow had not allowed little Gregory and Tyhessia to come to the funeral home to see their father. They told her that Jacqueline Kennedy and Coretta King had done it. "I'm not Jacqueline Kennedy and I'm not Mrs. King," she said. "It's bad enough for me to remember my husband this way."

"But," they argued, "your son would remember him sleeping."

"No, he wouldn't. My son doesn't forget things. He would never have forgotten if he had seen Gregory like that." It happened that Jackie Foster's little sister, who was only two months older than little Gregory, was allowed to see the body. She came by and hollered for Gregory to wake up. Jackie Foster felt her son would have done the same because at home Gregory had a habit of jumping on his father in bed to wake him up. And he wouldn't have understood. He was a sensitive child. Whenever she cried at home in those days, little Gregory would come up to his mother and ask her why she was crying. Once she was lying on the couch and he went and got a pillow off the bed and dragged out the quilt and put it on her. Little Gregory knew there was something wrong. Jackie didn't want her son to see how bad it was.

So the children stayed home and Jackie bore the burden by herself, though his parents and his brothers and sisters were there through it all. Gregory's mother carried herself with immense dignity. George Mahoney was very impressed by the mother. She had told him, "Black, white, or indifferent — you're all cops. You're all blue to me. You all have to be careful."

Bobby Cruz, another member of the honor guard, talked to Mrs. Foster about her son. "He was a damn good cop, Mrs. Foster, a dedicated cop. He was dedicated because it was in him. It has to be in you," he explained. "You have to have a certain feeling for the job, a certain respect for the uniform that you're wearing. And you have to go and put up with this nonsense day in and day out. Your son was that type of cop."

Mrs. Foster told him that the only thing Gregory ever talked about when he came home to dinner was the type of people he worked with. "He had a great love for all of you," she said. "He felt the Ninth was his home and the cops were his brothers."

One of his brothers on duty beside the coffin was Frank Dudley, and it tore him up being there. "If you can imagine," he explained later, "standing at the head of the coffin, looking at a guy you know and had some feeling for as a cop. The first thing you feel is that it could have been you. The second thing is that it's ridiculous to take a man's life. The third thing, I guess, is that you pray to God it doesn't happen to you."

Because of the outpouring of emotion generated by the death of the two young cops, the overwhelming feeling of sympathy toward the two men so many Americans seemed to want to identify with, ranking members of the police department thought it would be a good idea if Foster and Laurie could be buried together. Both were Catholics. Why not one great funeral at St. Patrick's, a showcase funeral that would not only demonstrate the solidarity of the police, no matter their color, but create massive public support for police everywhere? Monsignor Dunne, the police chaplain, was designated as the emissary to try and arrange the joint funeral.

He went to see Jacqueline Foster first and she gave her consent. She wanted her husband buried in St. Patrick's. Even though he had never taken her inside the great cathedral, she felt it was something Gregory would have wanted.

It was not so easy when Monsignor Dunne went to Staten Island. Adelaide Laurie would not consent to a joint funeral. She wanted her husband buried in the church where they had been married. The monsignor appealed to Rocco's parents and his brother. They said no, too. They felt Adelaide was right, that Rocco should be buried where he was born, raised, and married.

So it was decided to have Foster's funeral first in New York, and Laurie's later in the afternoon on Staten Island.

Tuesday morning the Foster family went to the funeral home for the last time. They were going to seal the casket, and everybody broke down. Jacqueline Foster could not believe that she would never see her husband again. She fought once more to get close to the body. Two of the policemen took her under the arms and walked her outside. And, just as they were closing the casket, George Mahoney gave Foster's sixteen-year-old brother Michael the blue patrolman's hat, the hat that Gregory Foster had worn for only a year and a half. The boy broke into tears and grabbed

Mahoney's arm: "Why did my brother die?" he cried. Mahoney choked back tears and could not answer.

Shortly after ten on the morning of the first day of February, a clear, bitter-cold winter morning, the funeral procession for Gregory Foster moved down Fifth Avenue toward the cathedral. Ahead of the hearse was car 1899 from the Ninth Precinct, moving slowly down the avenue, a symbol of the fellowship between Foster and his fellow officers of the precinct. Waiting on the street, stretched out along four blocks of Fifth Avenue, were over four thousand policemen. They had come from as far away as Boston and Washington; all had covered the lower part of their shield with a black band. They watched in silence, at attention, as the limousines moved toward the cathedral, a long line of men in blue, their somber faces filled once more with recognition of the risks they all took as police officers. Behind the rows of police stood the people, waiting, watching, silent.

The flag-draped coffin was lifted out of the hearse and eight pallbearers — eight policemen from different precincts in the city — began their slow walk up the steps of the cathedral. An honor guard of marines, with rifles and flags at attention, stood by. Someone shouted, "Present arms!" and four blocks of police officers saluted.

The coffin passed Mayor Lindsay, who had his cossack hat held to his heart. Beside the mayor stood Commissioner Murphy, looking bent and drained, his hat at his heart. A special assistant from the White House stood with them, too, Marine Colonel John V. Brennan, saluting stiffly. Behind the coffin came the widow. She was half-dragged into the church by her brother-in-law and a husky New York detective. Behind her walked the mother and the father, and then the brothers and the sisters of Gregory Foster, Michael still clutching his brother's blue cap. Then came the relatives and friends, almost a hundred black people, "all those working people," wrote *New York Post* columnist Pete Hamill, "who are never seen on TV except when someone dies. Their faces were ruined and baffled." They moved into the church past a cordon of police, heading down the aisle to the altar, where Terence Cardinal Cooke sat robed in scarlet. Behind them came the cops, filling every seat, as large a funeral, someone later estimated, as the one they had in St. Patrick's for Robert Kennedy.

234

Organ music boomed from the choir loft as Cardinal Cooke walked up the aisle and sprinkled holy water on the coffin. Then he turned and slowly the procession moved toward the altar. High above, the stained-glass windows gleamed in the light, telling, Hamill wrote, "the old sweet promise of Christianity; death as redemption, the necessity for love, the grace and splendor of human beings."

The eulogy was delivered by Monsignor Dunne. "Policemen may die," he intoned, "and widows will weep for their fatherless children, as the city decays — unless and until God's laws are seen as the basis of any civil laws, and the officer enforcing the law regains the dignity and the respect which his authority deserves." There was a stirring among the uniformed men. Many leaned forward to hear better.

"Gregory Foster and Rocco Laurie evidently loved New York and its people, having gone to school here, having associated as New Yorkers with the marines while in Vietnam, and then deciding to do their thing as police officers, working with people who needed them most — in the ghetto — the East Village. They decided to work together, black and white, on the Neighborhood Police Team. They were anxious to work to see the ills of society, the injustice, hardships, and the inhumanity of one man to another. Warfare taught them the value of human life. They knew that in serving and helping people, they also served Christ, whose image is in all men. The best place to find Christ, they thought, was in the ghetto. . . . Their deaths will not have been in vain if all of us survivors who still love New York will turn to God for the courage and determination to avenge these deaths, not with convictions and not with executions, as the laws require, but by doing what these men did.

"Finish their work with an effort to overcome hate, dealing with conflict, eliminating injustice in employment, housing, and education, and freeing the youths from the slavery of addiction, which in turn fosters inhumanity and crime in our society. These are the goals for which these men died."

Monsignor Dunne paused and looked around the huge cathedral staring into the sea of faces. "They had found the crucified Christ in the ghetto," he cried, "and now they rest in His arms."

Then the monsignor offered the mass. Jacqueline Foster walked the few steps to the Communion rail, accepted the host, turned, and was helped back to the pew. The congregation stood as Cardinal Cooke, in miter and cope, led the farewell prayers: *Through Him, with Him, in Him.* . . . . They all stood: Jacqueline's older sister, erect and solemn; an elderly white man beside her, his hands clasped together; the mother, listening, absorbing it all; the father, the sisters, the brothers; Michael, holding tight to the cap; the police officers and everyone else who had crowded into the cathedral, standing silently. But Jacqueline Foster could not stand. She sat there, a white handkerchief at her face, while her brother-in-law sat with her, trying to comfort her. And then the organ tolled and the words went out: *Agnus Dei qui peccata mundi.* . . . Our father who art in heaven . . ." And the procession began to leave the church.

The coffin was carried down the steps between two honor lines of police and marines. At the bottom of the steps, a priest and his white-robed altar boys, holding candles, offered a last prayer. A bugler played taps as they sprinkled holy water on the coffin. And the widow collapsed again and a group of men clustered around her to keep her from falling.

At eleven thirty-three Cardinal Cooke turned into Fiftieth Street, his robes blowing in the wind. It was over. The press moved toward the mayor and Commissioner Murphy before they stepped into their car. "Well, it's another day of terrible sadness," Murphy said, "to have buried such fine policemen. We must find some better way of ending this terrible violence. And when innocent police officers are struck down without a chance it tells us that there is terrible hatred and insanity that must be ended, it must be stopped."

"When is this going to stop? Mr. Mayor?" a reporter asked John Lindsay.

"When hatred ends." Lindsay, looking grieved and old, stepped into the car.

The funeral cortege moved to Farmingdale, Long Island, for the burial. In the car Jacqueline Foster revived enough to wonder why it was that they had given her husband such a splendid funeral. She looked out the window. The highway was open only to the funeral procession. As they passed every exit she saw a line of cars backed up waiting to go on the highway. She marveled at the power of people who could arrange such things. Eight motorcycle officers were in front of the hearse, two by two, leading the way to the gravesite.

When they reached the open land, the ground brown and hard from the winter cold, the marines were there. They gave Gregory a six-gun salute, and they blew taps again. Then they folded the flag and one of them presented it to the widow. Someone moved toward the casket and placed roses on top of it, and then Jacqueline Foster, who was nineteen years old and alone in her sorrow, lost consciousness.

The scene was repeated at 2 P.M. on a treelined street on Staten Island, the sun shining brightly, the air not as cold as it had been that morning on Fifth Avenue.

The family had stayed in the funeral home all morning, to the moment when they closed the casket and presented to the widow Rocco Laurie's blue cap. The family moved into limousines and waited for the casket to be put into the hearse.

When they reached the red-brick Church of the Blessed Sacrament they were all stunned by the sight. None of them had ever seen such a sea of policemen, an overwhelming wave of blue lining the streets. For hours these men had streamed through the Brooklyn-Battery tunnel, and as they did so, many of them turned on the sirens, and the tunnel echoed with the sound of wailing. Now they were lined up on the street, standing stiffly, while behind them massed the cameramen and ordinary spectators. Friends and neighbors of Rocco Laurie had been there for over an hour, waiting to pay their respects. Some held small children in their arms as they murmured to each other, "He was such a fine boy."

The mayor was waiting, too, and there were hisses from some of the policemen and random cries from the spectators, "Go home, Lindsay." To these people, who were bitter and afraid, John Lindsay was the symbol of official betrayal of law and order in their city. They were unforgiving toward him. Lindsay, however, stood there impassive, with the police commissioner and Colonel Brennan from the White House.

When Adelaide Laurie got out of the car, she looked around and trembled. It grew quiet. The only noise was the whir of a helicopter overhead. The widow wept anew and walked into the church, leaning heavily on the arm of her Uncle Matty, a lace mantilla covering her black hair.

The church was lit up for television cameras and the light hurt the family's eyes. Rocco's brother Anthony, who had been living on tranquilizers, felt his knees buckle when they had to stand for the mass. Adelaide did not stand. She could not. She sat, weeping to herself, sometimes glancing at the coffin, moving her hands back and forth from her forehead. The church held only seven hundred and fifty people and so most of the mourners stood outside, in the street, at respectful attention.

Monsignor Dunne spoke again, telling about how these men — Laurie and Foster — were "the best we have to offer. They are the scapegoats of society. Their lives are sacrificed so that you and I may live."

The Reverend Alvaro Arguello, who had officiated at the marriage of Adelaide and Rocco Laurie, celebrated the mass. In his eulogy he spoke of death as a beginning of another kind of life, a life with God. "There should be no bitterness in our souls," he said. "Through his death Rocco has reached the glory of Christ."

The service ended and the coffin was borne up the aisle. The policemen came to attention again, their faces full of bitterness, and Adelaide, in her ruin, moved out of the church. The pallbearers paused outside in the bright sunshine as taps was played. Many of the spectators wept while the cortege moved away, toward St. Peter's Cemetery for the burial services.

Adelaide Laurie sat next to his parents. She bit at her lips continuously but she could not fight back the tears. She watched the casket and heard the prayers and, in her numbness, she felt her life was over.

The next day she went, with her brother-in-law and his wife, to the Bronx to visit Jackie Foster. And they wept in each other's arms.

In the weeks that followed their husbands' deaths both widows knew despair and hopelessness and abandonment and a sense that life was not worth living. Each one's circumstances were different but each was experiencing shared emotions; each was going through the fire.

For Jackie Foster there were bitter arguments with Gregory's parents — over the way she had handled the funeral, how she was bringing up her children, matters concerning Gregory's estate. At one point her mother-in-law said to Jackie, "If you had been better to Gregory before you moved up here, God would have kept him alive." Soon she found herself and her children cut off altogether from his parents.

For Adelaide Laurie, the problem was Rocco's parents and his brother, and even her Uncle Matty, who had been so close to her through everything. She started out living with her in-laws. After bitter words she moved in with her uncle. That didn't work, either. She ended up alone in the house, her eighty-year-old grandmother cooking for her and coming to sleep with her.

And death was in Jackie Foster's mind, and death was in Adelaide Laurie's mind.

In February, Jackie was jumpy and she thought of suicide. "I wasn't thinking about my kids. I was really messed up. I couldn't stay in the house by myself. I couldn't stay in one place. I couldn't stay in my bed. I couldn't sleep. I couldn't do any of these things." Two months later it was still there, but now it had turned mystical. "I felt death on Gregory," she said, "and I feel it on myself. I feel somehow before the year is out that's where I'm gonna be at."

And what she felt about herself she felt about Adelaide Laurie. She could sense it the day after the funeral, when Adelaide came to visit her with Anthony Laurie and his wife.

It was in many ways an awkward visit. Anthony was struck that here she was in a big apartment in the Bronx, the living room was completely barren and there was no one there but a policewoman and little Gregory (Tyhessia was still being cared for by Jackie's

239

sister). Anthony Laurie couldn't help but feel sorry for her in comparison to his sister-in-law, who, he felt, had a million people waiting on her hand and foot, doing everything in the world for her, who wouldn't let her be alone.

He left with mixed feelings about the widow Foster. He was impressed by her honesty. She had told them about her first child being born out of wedlock. She said that her in-laws had never liked her, blaming it on the fact that she was an American Negro and they had come from the West Indies and regarded themselves as superior. But he was also annoyed by her naïveté. She would come out with statements like, "My husband never beat me up." Anthony couldn't understand that. Some husbands do beat up their wives but the wives don't go around talking about it one way or the other. He thought it nice the way she tried to console Adelaide, who was almost five years older than Jackie. He sensed a toughness in her, a core of reality that he felt was lacking in Adelaide. At one point Jackie told Adelaide, "Greg and Rocco were close, maybe we could be close now. When all this is over maybe we can take a trip together." What a time to think of that, Anthony thought, faintly disgusted, but admiring, too.

Through it all, Adelaide had very little to say. She was weary and somber and all she kept repeating to Jackie was, "You're lucky to have kids, so lucky to have kids." And after she left, Jackie thought, she's like me, she doesn't care whether she lives or dies.

During that visit Adelaide did tell Jackie how the police had taken away Rocco's gun, and how upset she was about that. Later Jackie told a friend in her apartment house, "That girl wants Rocco's gun and she wants it in a way that it can be fired. You can take it any way you want."

On the night of Rocco Laurie's death Captain Rogers had come to Laurie's home searching for the gun, the PPK. They found it in the attic and took it away and Adelaide protested when she found out. She talked to Richie O'Neill, the PBA delegate from the Ninth Precinct. "I bought the gun for him for his birthday," she said, "and I want it back. And I'll go to any lengths to get it back. Because it was his gun and I bought it for him. And I want it." She was shrill, almost hysterical. O'Neill told her that there was a law against automatic guns and that she would have to apply for a gun permit. And that it would take time. "That's really funny, isn't it?" Adelaide said bitterly. "I can't get a gun permit but everybody else seems to have a gun. Just anybody. I want the gun itself. I don't care whether you dismantle it or what you do with it. I want it. I can't have my husband's gun back but all these degenerates, how do they get these guns? Really, it's not fair."

O'Neill was gentle with her but he explained later that because of her state of mind "she was the last person I would want to see with a gun. Who the hell knows what she's going to do? You know, people who are distraught like that are capable of anything. And, if she does have it, perhaps her intention isn't to do away with herself. But if she does have it and on a particular night she becomes unusually depressed, who the hell knows?"

O'Neill had been through the business before. He had seen cop widows striving to come back to life. He knew that it was a struggle, a painful struggle. "When a wife suffers a loss of a husband it's a very sad thing," he said, "and people — anybody with a logical mind — can feel grief for them, and when they have children everybody says, 'Oh, what a shame.' Well, it is a shame financially and otherwise; however, in every other respect it's a good thing to have children. 'Cause it occupies the mind. Children keep them busy. They have to be busy. They can't, like Mrs. Laurie, throw their hands up in the air and do absolutely nothing. The only thing Mrs. Laurie did was feed herself. And that's not good. It's very harmful. Having children, the widow is forced to wake up, she has no choice. She can't let the child disintegrate. The child can't feed itself. So in that respect it's helpful to Mrs. Foster having two children. It keeps her busy."

Jacqueline Foster and Adelaide Laurie met again early in March. A benefit basketball game was played in Staten Island for a Rocco Laurie scholarship fund and Jackie was invited. She sat next to Adelaide and throughout the game she held Adelaide's hand. She felt the strain being there, a lone black face surrounded by white middle Americans. Adelaide's in-laws were at the game. They barely looked at Jacqueline and she got the feeling that when they did look at her they were thinking, if it wasn't for your husband our son would be alive today. Jackie still didn't know how Adelaide felt toward black people but she told her, "I've got a bigger apartment now with three bedrooms. Please, come and stay with me."

Adelaide smiled wanly. "If I ever get up and start doing things, I'd really like that." Jackie felt that Adelaide was still in a trance and, she thought, being around her puts me in one. I really feel sorry for her. I feel for what she feels but I still feel sorry for her.

It was mid-April when I drove to the Bronx to visit the widow Foster. She had moved. She couldn't stand the memories of the apartment where they had lived together briefly and she asked the police to find her another in the area. They did find her one in a new apartment building, a bigger apartment with three bedrooms that rented for three hundred dollars a month.

The living room floor had no rug on it and it was littered with gum wrappers, matchbooks, cigarette packages. Two pairs of women's shoes rested on a chair, a red jacket hung over the chair. The only furnishings in the living room were a long couch that was covered in a red plastic, and a big stereo set alongside one wall. The room was bare otherwise, except for a big yellow Easter bunny and a red fire truck. Off the L-shaped living room was a dining room table with four chairs. It adjoined the kitchen. Water was dripping in the kitchen sink from a leaky faucet. A half-empty glass of milk stood on a side table, and a dish of hard candy.

It was ten-fifteen and Jacqueline Foster was wearing a blue wrapper and slippers. There was a faint red tint to her hair, which was covered by a mantilla lace. She looked sleepy. Her eyes, almost oriental in cast, seemed half open and she did not focus directly on me. The first thing she showed me was a picture of her husband in a marine uniform.

She started by saying, "When they took my Gregory, they almost took me, too. We had our ups and downs, but that's still part of being married. We still loved each other."

A TV was going somewhere in the apartment. Otherwise, it was quiet. The children were still asleep. I thought she looked gaunt. "Oh, yes, I lost a lot of weight." She took out an album, a flower-covered album, and showed me pictures of herself and Gregory when they were in high school. The photos were soft, out of focus. He was wearing a white dinner jacket. She had on a long white gown. "I'm tall, about five-seven. I don't like being skinny. If Gregory could see me, he would laugh at me. I used to eat but since Gregory's death I can't bring myself to cook. I cook for little Gregory. I'm so used to cooking big meals, and things like that. I just can't bring myself to do it. If I try to cook, it comes down on me. I start missing Gregory. He's not there to eat."

She lit a cigarette. She said she was smoking two packs a day. "I been smoking a lot ever since the twenty-seventh of January." She inhaled deeply. "It's a funny thing, we got married on a snowy day; he got killed on a snowy day. I think about my Gregory lying down there in the snow. That cold weather. I know one thing" — she spoke in a low voice, almost a whisper, but with a command to it, as if she was showing slides to a class — "if I didn't have my kids I would have been right along with him. 'Cause they are the only reason that I have to live. I cared a lot for Gregory. We had our little ups and downs. But I miss him. He was always somebody to lean on when I had a problem. He always understood. I tell you, right now can't nothin' hurt me no more than my husband's death."

She sat at the dining room table, staring out into space. She squashed the cigarette and went to the refrigerator and got herself a can of fruit drink. She sat there talking about her husband, sucking from the can. Just then little Gregory came in. He was in his pajamas. He had rich brown skin, his brown eyes were big and full of questions. He looked at me grimly, almost afraid. He ran to his mother and flung his head in her lap.

"One morning, three mornings ago, I thought he came back. My son was hollering, pointing in that direction." She lifted her eyes toward the living room. " 'Mommy, Mommy, there goes Gregory.' I stood there for ten minutes. I found out he was pointing to this picture." She got up and came back with a large framed color photograph of her husband in police uniform, a head-and-shoulders shot, a jaunty smile on his face, his cap tilted at a slight, swaggering angle. He looked almost like a boulevardier. "It shook me up a little," she said, "but I don't mind seeing him. I just don't want to see him dead, the way his eyes were."

There was crying in the other room and Jackie went in and

brought back Tyhessia, a big bouncing baby with a full round face. "She has legs just like Gregory, baseball-bat legs. The same eyes, too." She put the baby on the floor and began to heat up a bottle. I noticed that both children had what looked like dark smudges under their eyes. When she came back with the bottle and had the baby on her lap and was feeding it to her she began to tell me about the voodoo and how she was trying to overcome it.

"They both got very sick. The doctor said she was all right, but there was something definitely wrong with her. My son, he had the black circles under his eyes. His eyes were just running steadily. They got sore. See, the voodoo starts as many days as they can get next to you. You don't even have to know anything about it."

"Do you really believe in that sort of thing?"

"I was raised in it. My grandmother believes in it. See, there's two different kinds. There's white magic and there's black magic. And the white magic is for good to keep the evil away. Black magic is when you're trying to hurt somebody, to get rid of them. And I went to this lady, she's a friend of my grandmother's. This lady is so good that even judges go to her. She sees these things. She sees visions. I would go to her house when I had problems and I would tell her the problems and she would give me religious candles, especially blessed."

She lit a cigarette. "And I went to this lady the first time when Gregory was in Vietnam. And that time the lady gave me some candles to burn and after they burned out she gave me St. Jude to burn; if you have problems or anything else you pray to St. Jude and he'll help you out. And I believe in St. Jude, I definitely believe in St. Jude. And she gave me that and I took the bath every day at about the same time. I had to go eighteen days. She told me to follow what she told me."

"Was this to bring Gregory home safely?"

"That's right. She told me that Gregory would come back and love me and never leave me. And sure enough he came back. He wouldn't leave me even when we were separated. He came around, made sure what I was supposed to have.

"See, a lot was going on. My grandmother didn't even tell me about it but this lady knew something was going to happen to

Gregory. She told my grandmother this before it happened. She knew something was going to happen to Gregory but she didn't know what. That's why my grandmother couldn't tell me. My grandmother told me in March. That's when she broke down and told me."

Tyhessia tired of the milk and began to squirm and Jackie slid her to the floor and Tyhessia crawled along the floor and Gregory jumped down from a chair and started crawling after her. "So she gave me two candles for the children. She gave me these candles to burn. One is St. Jude, a white candle, it's to keep evilness away from you, to keep people from doing wrong to you; and the other is a conditioner. It's a black candle. I don't know what it is but it has a very nice fragrance to it. The black candle is to clean up all the evilness, the evil spirits that people work on you. It keeps them away.

"And I burned the candles and each day I felt a little better. I have certain things that I carry around and on me to protect me from my in-laws. I have a special paper I'm supposed to keep, and on the paper I have my name on it. And I'm supposed to wear that in my left shoe, with a dime in it. And that means that as long as I wear that in my left shoe they can't step on me, they can't get next to me. And then I have a little pouch of orange beads. They cost ten dollars apiece. You can't see them in the U.S. And they are very hard to get over there in the West Indies. But everything started going all right after I got those candles and started burning them."

She talked about her in-laws, about her fear and distrust of them, and their distrust of her. "My mother-in-law called me on the phone a while back and she spoke very nice to me. She hadn't called me for a long time. She asked me how I was and she said she was glad she was able to talk to me. Then she started to talk about the funeral and what had happened. Then she really told me what was going down. All I wanted to do was do it all by myself. She told me they felt as if they were left out and that they were in the dark, and that my family could have had a little respect for Gregory. My family at funerals doesn't sit down and cry or anything. They rejoice. They drink a lot. I didn't go for it myself. My mother-in-law, when they came here, she found fifths of whiskey all over the table, things like that; this is what my family does. She said that at the least I could have asked them to help me with the funeral and things like that. But at the time I wasn't thinking. I wanted to do it all by myself. Like a lot of things that went down, I wasn't thinking about it."

She told about how, on Valentine's Day, she had gone to the cemetery and put her heart on the grave and the next time she came back she saw that her heart had been ripped apart and that someone had put palms and a cross on the grave. She was convinced that her in-laws had done it. "I started to write my mother-in-law a letter telling her she better go to confession for what she did. Whoever did it. It really hurt me inside when I went out there and saw what they did to it."

Her mind seemed to float off in a direction of its own, like a boat that has lost its mooring. Tyhessia was screaming and Gregory was jumping on her and she seemed not to hear anything. She was back there at the cemetery. "Gregory's mine more than he's theirs even though they brought him into this world. But when he married me he gave them up. And they see my flowers and they take them off. That's not going to help him by putting palms on his grave. If he's meant to go to heaven, that's where he is. If he was meant to go to hell, then that's where he is. He was too good," she purred, her voice dropping lower and lower. "I know he's watching down over me, my guardian angel."

It was easy to find the house because of the shingle outside the door: "Dr. Matthew Iammatteo, Chiropractor." The Iammatteos live on a busy street on Staten Island, on the fringe of a large shopping area. It is a small, two-story house. Dr. Iammatteo has offices downstairs and upstairs he lives with his wife and their four children.

Two days after seeing Jackie Foster for the first time, I met Adelaide Laurie. She greeted me at the door, Adelaide and her dog Buster, a black-and-white-spotted short-haired retriever who was barking and carrying on frantically. Dr. Iammatteo explained that the dog was not well, that ever since Adelaide and Rocco had put him in a kennel in November when they went to Florida, the dog had turned neurotic; now he was stalking shadows. "He's always going around the floors looking at shadows," said Dr. Iammatteo, a cheerful-looking, husky man in his mid-forties who is built like a weight lifter. Bursting with health, he provided a rather striking contrast to his niece, who wore a simple black dress with a heart-shaped gold locket around her neck, dark stockings, black hair parted in the middle and pulled back into a bun, whose face was as pale as marble and who was sniffling from a cold. She sat on a couch by herself, a tissue in her hand.

Dr. Iammatteo's children were scattered about and he had thoughtfully turned off the TV set in the living room and left Adelaide alone. There was a neatness and an order to the house, a sense of vitality, too, that contrasted sharply with the widow. She was lifeless. As she talked, her face never changed expression. Her large brown eyes seldom showed animation. It was as if she were still far away. But her cheeks did begin to burn pink when she talked about Rocco's parents.

I wanted to know what had made her stay with her in-laws after her husband's death.

"For the first couple of days I really didn't know what I was doing or where I was. But my grandmother, who is a very good woman, said my uncle wanted to take me. He had even brought the kids to his mother's house. They told my grandmother and she said no. These people have enough grief, she said, talking about the Lauries. Don't take her away because she's the only thing they have left. Leave her there. And my uncle approached my father-in-law. My father-in-law said the same thing — she's all we have. This is all the stuff they told me. So I stayed with them. I thought it was the right thing to do. I would have stayed with them indefinitely, I mean that."

"Did your mother-in-law ever say, 'Look Adelaide, I want you here,' to you or any members of that family?"

"I don't think so. She said to me one day, 'I know the day is going to come when you're going to have to go back to your own house.' She said, 'I don't even really want to think of it because you're all we have.' And I felt very bad. If that argument never had happened I would have been there to this day, I know it."

It was on Monday, March 6, she said, when representatives from the One Hundred Club, a police organization that helps policemen's widows, came and asked about her bills. "So I called my uncle because he had everything at his house. He came just as they were leaving. Then my uncle said, 'Get your coat and come for lunch,' 'cause I never was going out, I was just sitting in the house. So as I left the kitchen to get my coat I heard my mother-in-law start to scream. I said, 'What's going on?' She was yelling at my uncle and she turned around and said, 'And you, I have a few things to say to you.' And she started in. I just stood there and I couldn't believe it. She was saying things I did to hurt her, I did so many things to hurt her. I'd slighted her and I'd done this to her. She told me she resented the fact that the patrol car came for me and not for her or Anthony. Because, after all, they were blood relatives. And I said I had nothing to do with that. They didn't have to pick me up. I would have run to that hospital. So that she resented. She resented the fact that my uncle was with me at the hospital. Because after all he was nothing to Rocco. So my uncle said, 'If her father was alive her father would have been with her. Would you have resented that?' She told me that she was screaming at the hospital, 'I'll never have my son again, but you'll get married again.' And I answered her back — though I don't remember a thing about that. I supposedly said, 'No, you're wrong.' She said, 'Don't tell me that.' She said, 'I can't replace a son but you can replace a husband.' "

The widow went on and on like that, her cheeks burning, sniffing into a tissue. At that moment the most important thing in her life, now that her husband was dead, was this estrangement between her and his mother and father. It was as if her husband, her Rocco Laurie, had been forgotten in the warfare between the injured parties. Indeed, it seemed as if this passion over banal family animosities was acting as a purgative for Adelaide, helping her forget, cleansing the wound a little bit. I tried to bring it back to the dead man, for that was what the argument was all about, really — who had what rights to Rocco Laurie in death? It seemed that the wife and the mother-in-law were staking out positions, making claims to territory where each could live in peace with the memories of the dead man.

Finally, I asked Adelaide, "Well, what about what your mother-in-law said in the hospital? Will you marry again?"

"Me?" she sounded incredulous. "No, never. I'd have to find somebody exactly like Rocco. And there isn't anybody who'd even be close to what he was, everything he stood for, the things he believed in. I wouldn't because once we talked about it and I said, 'If something happens to me what would you do?' He said, 'Well, I'd probably go out of my mind. I don't know what I'd do.' I said, 'Would you get married again?' He said, 'No, I'd probably just stay alone. I'd never remarry.' I said, 'You're just saying that.' He said, 'No, I wouldn't.' And I said, 'I wouldn't, either.' "

Anne Iammatteo apologized for interrupting. A blocky blond with a kind face, she came in with a cup of tea for Adelaide. For a while we just sat there, both looking out the window. It was Saturday afternoon and there was action on the street. Passersby were carrying shopping bags, scurrying around, engaged.

"Will you be going back to your house soon?" I asked.

"I think it's going to be hard. I want to go back to my own home, I really do. I'll mind. I never liked living alone. Linda, my sister, she lives alone and she likes it. But she's completely different than me. It doesn't bother her. I was the type, if I had never met Rocco and married I never would have left my grandmother to get an apartment. I'm just not that way. I don't really like to be alone."

Yet, even living with her uncle's family, surrounded by his children, she seemed very much alone, isolated, adrift in an interior world — far more alone than Jacqueline Foster. There was a barrier of loss surrounding her that seemed impenetrable. First her mother, then her father — both dead prematurely — and now her husband. The barrier was up, thick and full of thorns. She found it easy to talk about her bitterness toward her in-laws, exaggerating the slights she felt they had inflicted on her, glossing over the slights she may have inflicted on them. At least this seemed to give her life more substance. It was much more difficult for her to talk about her own real sorrow.

"I bumped into a woman I know," she was saying, "and she told me how sorry she was. I'm all right as long as people don't talk about it. I can't explain it. I don't know, I don't feel that he's really gone. And I don't think in those other terms until somebody brings it up and then I start thinking that way. 'Cause if I catch myself thinking about it I try to put it out of my mind. And I shouldn't do that. I should face up to it, but I don't.

"Sometimes I don't know how I'm still alive. I mean, I should really have been dead long ago, after everything that's happened. I really don't know. One day I was terribly depressed, so I told my grandmother and I shouldn't have because everything I tell her she gets very upset. She was saying to me, 'You have to start wearing your hair like a young girl, you have to start dressing like a young girl again,' and all that stuff. I said, 'Grandma, can't you understand, I don't care any more.' So she said, 'You have a whole life to live,' and all that junk. So I said, 'Grandma, I hope I don't hurt you by saying this but to tell you the truth I don't care. If something should happen to me, I don't really care. I'd welcome it.' She got all upset. She told me that my father used to say to her, 'Oh, Ma, you're going to live longer than me.' And she wished he never said that because he died when he was forty. . . . I say the same thing to her all the time about me. She's much stronger than me and everything. She doesn't want to hear it.

"The body must be an amazing thing because I find myself doing things — like you eat, like you sleep — but I don't care anymore, really. I don't think I'll ever change. That's my attitude now."

The Iammatteos' oldest boy, Matthew, who was thirteen, came bouncing into the house carrying a baseball glove. Buster began to bark. Suddenly, all over the house, noise erupted. Children were shouting, laughing. The mother was hollering at them, a radio was on. The house had come to life. Adelaide just sat there, staring out into space.

Financially, the young widows had little to worry about. For the first year after their husbands' death each would receive his full salary, and that came to eleven thousand five hundred dollars. After that, until they remarried, they would receive half-salary for life. Each was chief beneficiary of a four-thousand-dollar life insurance policy taken out by the Police Benevolent Association. There was also five thousand dollars in annuity insurance for each widow; that came from the police department itself.

In addition, a private organization, the One Hundred Club of New York — supported by a group of anonymous donors and pledged to help policemen's widows — presented Jackie Foster and Adelaide Laurie each a check for one thousand dollars for immediate expenses. And the Foster and Laurie Memorial Fund, set up by the Ninth Precinct and administered by Richie O'Neill, continued to receive donations from all over the country. Contributions came in from every state, including Alaska and Hawaii. A woman from Brooklyn sent a check and an accompanying note that seemed to express the sentiments of all: "We do not live on an island, as John Donne, the great poet said: 'Every man's death diminishes me.' Therefore I cannot stand by and sustain this devastating shock of our magnificent policemen being cut down. I cry, and I am not a crying person." A year after the murders the Foster-Laurie Fund was almost closed out and Patrolman O'Neill presented each widow with a check for twenty-one thousand dollars.

An odd thing was happening. Weeks and months passed but the names Foster and Laurie stayed alive. Policemen get killed almost every day in the United States. They die, are buried, and soon forgotten except for those they have left behind. But, it seemed, the young police officers, Gregory Foster and Rocco Laurie, would not be forgotten quite so soon.

A couple of months following the murders the New York State legislature, having taken the pulse of the public, began to make some moves on behalf of the two police officers. A bill with a dozen cosponsors was filed in the assembly to rename the Triborough Bridge, a principal New York artery that cuts through three boroughs — Manhattan, the Bronx and Queens — the Foster-Laurie Memorial Bridge. It would, said Assemblyman Ferdinand Mondello (D-Bronx), "honor Patrolmen Gregory Foster and Rocco Laurie as representatives of the many men in blue who gave their lives to make the city a better place to live." Then the same assembly got into a strenuous polemical argument over a much less cosmic suggestion — the wording of a resolution that was supposed to be sent to the families of Foster and Laurie.

The resolution (which passed the state senate without debate) was meant to "express the deep feelings of sorrow and shock of the members" over the killings. But a phrase in the resolution

251

referring to the two patrolmen who had served together in Vietnam and had "survived the violent and senseless war" created an inordinate amount of discord. Some assemblymen were angered by that description; they called it unfortunate and offensive. Others used the resolution as a takeoff point for their own crusades — gun-control laws, court reform, the mandatory death penalty (New York law makes death sentences for cop killers optional, though a recent Supreme Court decision barring the death penalty in the United States makes the New York law obsolete). Finally, in weariness, the resolution was withdrawn because "these speeches no longer pertain to this resolution."

But some of the speeches did pertain very much to questions concerning the deaths of Foster and Laurie: would the murderers be caught and, if so, would they be punished? As time went on there seemed to be doubts on both issues, especially that of punishment. The then PBA president, Edward Kiernan, called for mandatory death sentences for "mad-dog cop killers. . . . No parole board should have the right to turn these animals loose to kill again."

Many people felt the same way — including the widows. Both wanted to see justice done; both believed in the biblical injunction of an eye for an eye, a tooth for a tooth. Both were almost obsessed with the urge for the killers to be caught. Almost six months after his death Jackie Foster had a dream about her husband. "I dreamed that Gregory and I, we were in the car together, and he gave me the gun and he ran out of a basement and he started shooting. He was shooting at men who had shot him. And he had told me this was gonna happen. I could see the place perfectly. About two weeks later I went down to the village to look around and, you know, I found the same spot as in the dream. So I know it really happened."

At first Jackie felt that her husband and Rocco Laurie had been killed because of their activities in the precinct, because they had been extra tough on pushers and people like that. Later on, as more facts came out, she modified her conspiracy theory. But she was no less bitter; she wanted her husband's killers caught and punished.

It was even more so with Adelaide Laurie. From the time of the death she felt only resentment toward public officials who, she believed, were coddling criminals. She was upset because John Lindsay had attended her husband's funeral. She felt that the mayor of New York was no friend of cops and that he was much too permissive. "I think he's a phony," she said bitterly. "I don't think he ever did anything for the police department."

In May of 1972 she attended a ceremony for the widows of recently slain police officers. The mayor was there. "He made this big speech," she said, "and he was saying something about bitterness, and how you can't hold it against any one individual. And maybe it's my imagination because he looked right at me. 'Cause I was sitting right in front of him. And I just gave him the coldest stare."

She went on to talk about a news program she had seen on a local television station. "They were interviewing two colored people who got evicted and they were saying they went to the Civilian Review Board with charges against the cops because they beat them up. And I was thinking to myself, I haven't heard anything about the people who did this to Rocco. Nothing at all. It's like it's completely forgotten. That's why I keep thinking, they did a horrible thing and they're still walking around. It doesn't seem like they're doing anything about it. I don't know. If they are I haven't heard anything about it.

"I believe the way Rocco felt," she continued. "If you take someone's life then yours should be taken, too. It's got to come to that. Otherwise, it's not fair."

Two days after the murder of Foster and Laurie the United Press International received a letter, handwritten on a piece of yellow lined paper. It had originally been sent to the Ninth Precinct by messenger. The letter read:

"This is from the George Jackson Squad of the Black Liberation Army about the pigs wiped out in lower Manhattan last night. No longer will black people tolerate Attica and oppression and exploitation and rape of our black community. This is the start of our spring offensive. There is more to come. . . ." It was signed: "The George Jackson Squad of the B.L.A."

A few days later Police Commissioner Murphy called a press conference and read the following statement:

"A few minutes ago the New York City Police Department

253

transmitted an alarm for nine people. Four of these people are named as murderers of Patrolmen Gregory Foster and Rocco Laurie, and the five others are sought for questioning in the same case.

"This group and a handful of others have been responsible for killing and assaults on policemen, both black and white; holdups and assaults against ordinary citizens and businessmen, both black and white. This small group has labeled itself the Black Liberation Army. There is no evidence to connect these people to others who have used similar names, such as Black Liberation Party or Black Liberation Front, etc. This is a handful of people who have taken it upon themselves to assault and kill police officers and who finance their activities by committing holdups and other crimes.

"What is the Black Liberation Army? It is composed of this small group of militants who do not have an organizational base, and who would like to give some semblance of legitimacy to their homicidal acts. Certainly it does not represent the thinking of the black community, since as a matter of fact these assaults have brought blacks closer to their police than ever before in an effort to combat a common enemy. . . ."

On the second floor of the Ninth Precinct, opposite the cage where prisoners are kept while they are being booked, there is a large bulletin board. In March of 1972 it was filled with circulars, pictures, and physical descriptions of the nine people implicated in the murders of Foster and Laurie:

"Herman Bell, *Wanted for Murder*; Andrew Jackson, *Wanted for Murder*; Ronald Carter, *Wanted for Murder* (a red cross was drawn through Carter's mug shot, and, in red pencil, the letters "D.O.A.," and a "No. 1" with a circle around it); Ronald Anderson, *Wanted for Murder*; Sam Cooper, *Wanted*; Robert Vickers, *Wanted*; Twymon Myers, *Wanted*; Joanne Chesimard, *Wanted*; Paul Stewart, *Wanted*. Through fingerprints left in the getaway car that had been abandoned by the Fourteenth Street subway station, and through backup identification by key witnesses, these nine were implicated in the murders. Some of the nine, it was known, were also involved in the murders of Patrolmen Waverly Jones and Joseph Piagentini. Evidence stretched back to other cops killed and wounded in New York since 1970.

254

The first break in the case came on February 16 with the shooting of two cops in Saint Louis. Four black men had allegedly done the shooting. One of the gunmen was dead. He was Ronald Carter. Two others were in custody, Henry Brown and Thomas McCreary. The fourth, who got away, was identified as Twymon Myers. It was quickly established that Carter had been killed by a bullet from the service revolver of Patrolman Rocco Laurie.

New York Chief Inspector Albert Seedman rushed to Saint Louis. He interrogated Henry Brown, who at first claimed that it was Carter who had Laurie's gun. After hours of questioning, Brown admitted that he had killed Carter by accident — with Laurie's gun — when he fell to the floor trying to avoid being shot. Shortly afterward, the Manhattan district attorney's office announced the first indictment in the Foster-Laurie murders — Henry Brown. Brown was sentenced to twenty-five years in Saint Louis for the shooting of the police officers. He has since been extradited to New York to await trial in the Foster-Laurie case.

In early August of 1972 a man was arrested in Newark, New Jersey, and charged with assault on a policeman "with intent to kill." At the time of his arrest he identified himself as Kenneth Dansby. Two New York detectives went to Newark. They took one look at the prisoner and promptly identified him (fingerprints corroborated their identification) as Robert Vickers.

In September, Ronald Anderson was arrested in Brooklyn.

Then Sam Cooper was arrested by the FBI in Miami.

In November, a suspect who had been arrested by the FBI in connection with an earlier bank robbery in the Bronx was identified as Paul Stewart.

In May of 1973, state troopers on the New Jersey Turnpike stopped a car for speeding. An occupant of the car, a woman, pulled a gun from under the seat and started firing at the police. In the ensuing battle, one state trooper was killed, another wounded, one male occupant of the car was killed, another male escaped (he was later flushed out of a New Jersey marshland). The woman received multiple gunshot wounds but survived. She was identified as Joanne Chesimard who, some felt, was "the soul of the gang."

In June of 1973, acting on a tip, police stormed an apartment in New York City. They seized Andrew Jackson.

In August of 1973, Herman Bell was captured in New Orleans. So, of the nine originally wanted in connection with the murders of Foster and Laurie, one, Carter, was dead; six, Vickers, Stewart, Anderson, Cooper, Chesimard, and Jackson were in custody. Twymon Myers was still at large. Herman Bell, it had been established, could not have participated in the killings of Foster and Laurie, but he was indicted in connection with the murders of Jones and Piagentini. Henry Brown, a man not on the original list, was in prison, under indictment. Other new suspects still at large were Melvin Kearney, Avon White, and Fred Hilton. A fourth "new" suspect, Woody Green, was killed by detectives in January of 1973 in a shoot-out in a Brooklyn tavern.

And so the case was far from closed, and justice remained to be administered.

No one was more frustrated than the police of the Ninth Precinct, the friends of Gregory Foster and Rocco Laurie. "If they ever get caught in the Ninth Precinct," Jim Liedy said, referring to the suspects, "they'll hang them. They'll kill them. These guys won't be taken alive so you have to kill them. There was one guy in the black liberation movement. They got him in the Bronx on another shooting. This guy, forget it. This guy's supposed to be so tough you could take his skin off him and he still wouldn't tell you anything. If he was in the station house and there was twelve cops there and this guy was standing there and you gave him a gun . . ." Liedy paused, his eyes bright and hard, "he'd try killing the twelve of them knowing he was going to get killed. That's the type of person he is and that's these guys. I spoke to some detectives; these guys think they're really in the army, like the ones fighting the French or the British. Paul Revere. It's not like the Black Panthers. These guys are the worst of them. They broke off of the Panthers. They wear boots, they wear army fatigues, that's how you can always tell them apart. . . ." Liedy said that the police had no luck infiltrating the Black Liberation Army. "You have to know the guys," he said, "and you have to put a bullet into somebody. That's how tight they are."

So there was the frustration in knowing that these guerrillas were still loose, that they were free to go after other cops. And there was further frustration because of the feeling among cops that even if the cop killers were caught and tried, they might still avoid punishment.

"Let me ask you a question," Bobby Cruz said when I visited the station house in the late summer of 1972.

Four members of the Anti-Crime Unit were in their small office on the second floor. They were all dressed for the street — dungarees, colored T-shirts, beads, and beards. It was warm and they weren't on duty yet and some of their guns were visible, sticking to their shirts or bulging out from their back pockets. One had his strapped to his leg. "Are you going to interview Murphy on this?" Cruz was referring to the police commissioner. "Well, if you do happen to see him through your investigation, ask him why he's got sixty detectives assigned to the Gallo case (Joey Gallo, a prominent Mafia figure, had been killed several months earlier) and ten assigned to the Foster-Laurie case. Ten detectives."

"They've got this guy in Newark," Larry Cummings said, "and only on a fluke because he shot another guy."

"Personally," one of the other cops broke in, "I tell you that's the only way they're going to get the rest of them, by accident."

They talked about specialization, and how it might have hampered the search for the killers. Detectives were then assigned to their own division rather than being attached to a particular precinct. Bobby Cruz felt the old way was better. "Now I'm not going to go into the pros and cons of specialization," he said, "but my personal feelings are had the detectives been assigned to the Ninth when this incident took place (specialization had come into effect a few months prior to the killings) it might have been different. Now, we had a tremendous rapport with the detectives up here in the squad. Being that it is a shit house, cops tend to get closer together. You don't find this solidarity in other precincts.

"If the Ninth squad had been on duty that night when Foster and Laurie got gunned down they would have been able to respond a lot quicker than they did. A good detective, if he's worth his weight, has a lot of informants on the street, he has a lot of contacts, he has a lot of people he can get in touch with when an incident like this does take place. This is what we needed right

257

here, here in the precinct that day — guys who were familiar with the neighborhood, familiar with the people in the streets, who could go over and communicate with them and find out this information.

"We had strangers who didn't know anything about the Ninth, didn't know anything about what was going on over there, didn't know any of the people."

He paused to light a cigarette. "Some homicides can only be solved in the first two or three hours after they happen. Most of them are crimes of passion. In a situation like this one, where it was an out-and-out shooting, an out-and-out deliberate murder, you're not going to get information unless you have people out there who know the civilians. 'Cause most of these people are hip to the ways of life. Things that happen down here don't happen in the Eighteenth Precinct, or Nineteenth Precinct. Down here where the nitty-gritty stuff is, these people know when they walk over to a cop and talk to him they have to be careful to see who's watching them, who's listening to them. And they'll only talk to a friend and they're not going to talk to a stranger. My belief is had the detective squad been here, then more information could have been gathered in these two, three, four, five hours after the shooting took place."

"Oh," one of the cops said, "I would personally like to see each and every one of these guys or whoever is involved."

"Personally," another said, "if one of 'em walked in the station house with his lawyer, I'd still shoot him."

Recalling the brutality of the murders, the police officers grew somber. A heaviness seemed to enter the room. I felt an added weight mixed in with everything else, the weight of menace. Menace hung in the air.

"I want them to get the same kind of treatment," Cruz was saying, "that they gave Foster and Laurie. I took my oath as a cop. I know somewhere in the back of my mind that someday, somehow — maybe it happens today, maybe it happens ten years from now — I will be faced with a certain type of confrontation where I will put my life on the line against somebody else, an armed robber or a mugger or what have you, somebody in the process of committing a robbery. I can dig that. I say, okay, fine. I can accept that. But to be gunned down like you're two dummies standing out there, to come from behind at you. . . . I can guarantee you if those bums were facing Foster and Laurie it would have been the other way around. These weren't the kind of cops who backed down from anything. Good, solid guys. And I think their personal records speak for themselves."

"When the policeman is on the street doing his job," another cop spoke up, "he cannot lose a battle. He must win."

"To be gunned down like that," Cruz continued. "I'd seen their bodies. I also saw their clothing and everything. And to me that wasn't fair. That's not the oath that I took. I don't mind sacrificing my life, putting my life on the line because of the job, I swore to do. But not like that. I didn't swear to do it that way. I would like to see whoever shot Foster and Laurie come and meet me face-to-face, or any one of us face-to-face, and we'll give them the same opportunity — no better. We'll put the gun in their hands and we'll give them the benefit of the doubt. You can kill me, fine, but you're goddamn right I'm going to try and kill you. That's the way I personally feel."

"That's the way we all feel," Cummings said.

"To come in from behind on a cop, a cop who's walking his beat, come in and gun him down and not even giving him a chance. . . . That's not straight pool."

"I know one thing," Cummings said, "with the system the way it is today, had these bums been brought to trial and confronted with this in the court of law — I guarantee it just about — they would walk scot free. They would get away with it."

"You've got a rule book," a cop started to say.

"Yeah," Cummings said. "See, we have to go by the rules and procedures, we have to go by the codes of procedure. We have to go by the penal law and everything. Fine, okay. We understand that. We know that. And I don't want to see the law in this country and the law in this state go completely haywire and be thrown out the window. I'd like to see the law followed.

"But when you turn around and see these guys — we who have got some standards — and we bring these guys in and we see what the system does, you know. . . ."

"They go out the front door."

"You realize you can lock a guy up for robbery, or one with a loaded gun and resisting arrest, right?" Cummings's voice rose, he began to speed up his words. "And after that the case goes to the grand jury and the guy's indicted by thirty-seven people on those charges. Robbery one is up to fifteen years. Do you realize that he can go into the courtroom and cop out, cover all jobs and take it from a B felony — the highest is an A felony — go from a B felony to the lowest, the A misdemeanor and take a year and cover all charges."

"And I'd hate to see what happens in the Foster and Laurie case," Cruz said.

"We locked up a guy for murder," Cummings continued. "You know what he got? He took a plea. He got five years."

It was time to go on duty. The men of the Anti-Crime Unit covered their guns with their clothes and walked out of the room, wondering about their jobs and a lot of other things.

T een-agers were playing outside, black and white, boys and girls, congregated outside the apartment building, talking and laughing and possibly making plans for the evening. It was a warm, late-summer afternoon but the heat was not oppressive and in this integrated middle-class Queens high-rise-apartment complex people seemed relaxed and reasonably friendly.

Darryl Anderson greeted me at the door and invited me in. He was wearing a white T-shirt, light chino pants, and boots. He had a moustache and a small beard. He was slight and slim-waisted, with crinkling, alert eyes, an open face, and a nose that looked like it might have been broken more than once. Jim Duffy, tall and husky, with a neat moustache and a gentle face, smiled and shook hands with me. A little girl of about eight peeked in the living room and ran right out again. Anderson's mother came in to be introduced. Music was flowing softly from the stereo set. The apartment was furnished tastefully, with thick carpeting, sectionals and soft chairs and sofas, and modern art on the wall. Anderson and Duffy, two cops, two old bachelor friends of Gregory Foster, were drinking and picking at peanuts in a bowl.

"Was he a good drinker?" I asked.

"He always used to say he was going to drink me under the table," Anderson replied.

"He could never do that," Duffy said, "not against Darryl."

"I could hold my own," Anderson said, grinning. "Let's put it that way. And, in fact, the last conversation I had with Greg, he was telling me about the Ninth, you know, he was telling me what he wanted to do, stuff like that. And he was also telling me, 'Yeah, I'm going to drink you under the table.' I said, 'Promises, promises.' I said, 'You're always telling me you're going to do that.' "

Anderson paused and his eyes became somber. Duffy stirred in his chair. "And, like I say, it was bad news. You know, you don't go visit a person as much as you should. I mean, that's all of us. You don't figure a person's going to die. You tell yourself, he's not going to die. If I can't see him this week, I can see him the next week, the week after, something like that. And this is really . . . Not only his dying hurt, but this also hurt me because I said now — lots of times I said — I should have went to see him. . . . I should have, but I didn't. . . ." His words trailed off and were picked up by the roar of a plane making its approach at LaGuardia.

"Do cops drink too much?" The impersonal question seemed to rouse both men.

"Drinking is a bad thing some cops have," Anderson nodded. "There are so many things you have to put up with, and so many temptations, and so much danger. Drinking makes it easier for some cops."

"What about women?"

Duffy laughed. "You see a lot of women out there."

"You have the women," Anderson said, "and they just seem to be attracted to the uniform. And, like you hear the old thing that sometimes you can't beat them away with a stick — sometimes you *can't*, you know, really, you can't. And it's very bad because you can maybe resist it for a month, two months, but it's a constant bombardment, every day. There's always some woman wavin', saying hello, how are ya, I want you to come up, have a drink with me or something like that, you know. I mean, how much strong will does a man have before you say, aw, what the hell, one time ought to do it. So it's very bad on a marriage."

"I feel this way about it," Duffy cut in, "being a cop, it's very bad being married. It's the kind of a job if you are married or do

261

have a steady girl friend you can come up with a lot of excuses: 'I got to go to court,' or 'I got to put in overtime.' . . . Excuses that you can use."

"What about Greg?" I wanted to know. "Was he involved this way?"

"Hmmmn. Well, let's put it this way" — Anderson lifted his eyes to the ceiling, smiling, "He had his young lady friends. Yeah, he used to talk about some girls."

"You got to remember, though," Duffy interrupted, "he was crazy about his wife."

"The only thing he regretted about his marriage was that he shouldn't have done it that young. Understand what I'm saying?" Anderson said, pulling on his cigar. "He felt he was too young and she was too young. Because if you — I was going to say, if you could talk to Greg — he would have told you that he really didn't enjoy life. Why? Well, he came out of high school, he got drafted, and after he came out of the service he got married. So there was never a time when he wasn't under some type of supervision, with some type of restriction."

"Really," Duffy said, switching back to the topic that fascinated all of them, "I don't even know a cop that's married in my precinct that wouldn't actually look at another woman. It's impossible because they're there, especially now it's the summertime."

Anderson leaned forward in his chair. "You go on one of those disputes or something. You walk in that house and she's gonna throw on a bathrobe, right? She don't care. Because you're a cop, you seen all the stuff.

"Like I say, Mr. and Mrs. Jones. Mrs. Jones, nice-looking woman, about twenty-something years old, right? To the outside world she's happily married. You been to her house five times within the last week on a dispute and she's fed up, right? Right away her affection goes from her husband . . . maybe her husband's not making enough money, maybe he doesn't have a job; you have a job, a steady job, you're making money, you have position, you have a little power to bend. So her affection goes from her husband to you. You see? All right, so then you snuff that out, but then there's Mrs. Smith and Mrs. and Mrs. and Mrs. and how many Mrs. are you going to say — hey, like you said, how much is your willpower? Maybe when you start to say, I can't take it no more." Anderson laughed and Duffy joined in.

"Like I say," Anderson stood up, stretching. "There's always extracurricular activity. Let's put it that way."

Darryl Anderson works in the Eighty-first Precinct, which is the Bedford-Stuyvesant section of Brooklyn. Jim Duffy is in the Seventy-third, also in Brooklyn, partly Bedford-Stuyvesant and partly Rockaway.

"I started as a foot man," Anderson said, "which we all started as. You know, the cold nights when your feet are so cold that you can't feel them. Then I got a sector car, and now I'm with Anti-Crime."

"I work steady four-to-twelves," Duffy said, "by the pool in the summer. In the winter I have foot posts and I fill in the radio car, but I prefer to work this tour rather than work around the clock because those twelve-to-eights take a lot of starch out of you."

"They call it the dog watch," Anderson laughed, "and believe it or not, that's what you do a lot of times, watch dogs. Bedford-Stuyvesant has got packs of dogs, and about three o'clock they start waking up."

"Like Greg's precinct," Duffy said. "As you know, the Ninth Precinct is a very busy precinct. But it's a funny precinct in a sense. Like, Bedford-Stuyvesant, where we work, is mostly black, very few whites. Where he worked you had blacks, Puerto Ricans, you still had whites in there, and you had the hippies or the zippies or whatever they wanted to call themselves. And they were being set upon by the neighborhood. And you had people coming in from other neighborhoods. You just had a whole conglomerate of things thrown into one place and that's what really made it busy. But he never complained about the work, the business. It was just some of the things that went along with it."

"He liked the Ninth," Anderson said, "but he wanted to go to Forty-one. If you know something about Forty-one it has the nickname 'Fort Apache,' the South Bronx. He wanted to go there because it would be easy for him traveling."

"But he always wanted to go to work, he always liked the work."

"Everybody seemed to want to be busy. You could feel dead in a quiet precinct. You just dread the thought. Even now, like they have a new career path where you work two years in a high-crime precinct and then you can put in for a transfer."

Duffy said, "The only thing Greg didn't like down there, he said they were getting a lot of supervision."

"Well, everybody was. We all talked about it. Everybody was getting a lot of supervision. They had the Knapp Commission, you know, the whole thing. Me and Foster and most of the guys would stand around and talk. And to hear about all those guys that were supposedly on the take! These things were an affront. They were an affront to everybody. Because you know — hey! — I know that I never pocketed anything. . . . What's all this? One guy said he was supposed to be making as much as two thousand dollars. Hey — where?"

"This wasn't Greg at all." Duffy thought a moment. "He wanted this job. I think if you offered him money to quit the job, he wouldn't quit."

"He wasn't that type of guy. He wouldn't take a dime. And when he got killed there was some guy that really got me mad. If I could have got my hands on that guy I would have broken his neck. He said that, yeah, Foster was taking and deserved to be killed. It was on television, some local hood. I know it for a fact — he would never take, he would never take at all."

Duffy spoke softly. "He used to tell us that he was happy there on the job. Some guys, they become cynical, but he was happy. He wasn't all contented with the Ninth Precinct but he was happy being a cop, very happy being a cop."

Did cops really like their jobs? I had heard so much and seen so much that contradicted what these two young police officers were saying. "What's it really like being a cop now, especially being a black cop?"

"Like, at the pool where I work now," Duffy said, "there's a Black Panther headquarters across the street. It's called the Gunsmoke. Like, the slightest little incident that happens, if a kid comes in and he's climbing on the fence and you tell him to get out of the pool. Well, if they see it they want to know why you told the kid to get out of the pool. Everything has to be explained to them. It's rough on that point. They want to know everything, what's happening, why you did this, why you did that, and you feel that your job is hard enough without having to explain to them and your bosses, too."

His mention of bosses turned Duffy in another direction. "The bosses get on you more now than what they used to. When I first came to the precinct it seemed to be more pleasant. But now it's not as pleasant as it was."

"You know what it is?" Anderson said.

"There's more petty stuff than anything else."

"This administration has made an all-out attempt on corruption." Anderson talked with his cigar clenched in his teeth. The words came out slurred. "The thing is, they would go far and wide to lock *me* up, but pushers and stuff like that, you know, they're not going out to the full extent to get them. And this is what makes a lot of guys mad, a lot of guys frustrated."

"Like I say," Duffy cut in, "the job today, you just don't get the enjoyment that you should get."

There was a silence in the room for a moment. Anderson relit his cigar. Duffy groped for peanuts. "You have people out there," Anderson said, "they think it's like 'Adam 12.' They put that on, that's not a cop's life, it's not a cop's life at all. Number one, they never show you how it is when you go on a dispute, when the first minute you walk in the door someone says, 'I didn't call you, MF.' "

"Right, right," Duffy said enthusiastically.

"Hey, you know, they don't say, 'Come in, Officer.' It's, 'Hey, I didn't call you, MF. And don't come in my house.' And the wife's back there screaming. She wants you to come in. See? So now you have to make a decision if this is this man's house. Do I come in or not? Well, nine times out of ten you go in — one way or the other. Either you're gonna go in when he stands up or you gonna go in on the guy's back. It's up to him. But I'm saying, these are the things that you have to do."

There was a reference to a young boy who had been shot on Staten Island, a young black boy, killed by a white police officer. "All right," Anderson said, "you may not agree with what this cop did in that case. Number one, none of us were there. I could Monday-morning quarterback all day long, you see, but until it happens to me. . . . But I'm saying this: to tell a cop you have to be reasonably sure before you shoot — you can't do this. Because every situation is different. A guy may have a gold watch in his hand, like Jimmy was telling me one day about this happening. To him it might look like a knife. Because you're off in a distance. What do you do then? You see? What do you do then? Do you stand there and get up close to him. Maybe it is a knife. Just because a man's three feet away and you hit him with a gun doesn't mean you're gonna stop him. We had a sergeant killed on the job for that very reason. The man was six feet away from him. He got too close and he shot him and the guy still had enough momentum so that when he started to fall he plunged the knife in and he killed the sergeant."

"Is there a pretty good comradeship now between the black and white cops?"

"Well, it depends still, see," Anderson said. "It depends on a basis of ghetto precincts. You're not gonna hug and kiss the guy. Figure this much — hey, we face some dangers, we have more percentages of dangerous situations in a day than maybe a precinct that's not as busy. We may not like each other but we got to stick together. Because I have to depend on him and he has to depend on me. Because even if you call for assistance, by the time assistance gets there if you don't depend on each other you both can be in a world of trouble.

"In that way," Anderson went on, "it throws you together. The busy precincts will have a better relationship between cops. You have to stick together. It was like that in the Ninth. But I once worked in the Hundred-and-sixth when I was in the academy. That's in Ozone Park. They got like coffee klatches. This group of guys won't speak to that group of guys. These are white cops. Hey, what is this? In the precinct I work in everybody speaks to each other. No problem.

"The black cop, he's thrown into a situation that is really hard for him. He's thrown into a situation where he's trying to clean up the communities that he either comes from or he lives in. Lots of black cops live in the Seventy-three, live in the Seventy-seven, live in these precincts, right? And on the other hand they call you Uncle Tom and a Coconut — black or brown on the outside, white on the inside. All these kinds of things, right? The only time you're ever called brother, which is to me an overused word — I agree with Gordon Parks when he said one word he wished they'd

266

strike out is 'brother' — the only time you're ever called that is when the cat wants to use you. He's committed a crime, now he becomes brother. Before that you were a pig MF."

Duffy held up an arm. His face became animated. "I remember the time, you know, I had a red, black, and green liberation color ring on. And we caught this guy that snatched a black woman's pocketbook. So he's sitting in the back room, so he looks at me, he says, 'Man, you should take that ring off because you're no brother.' So I looked at the guy. I said, 'Hey, listen, it's *you* that's not the brother. You snatched the pocketbook from a black woman and you're black and this is supposed to be your sister and you're telling me that I'm not a brother?' And he looked at me and he didn't say nothin' more. But this is the sense that people have, Okay, so I'm black and you're black. You understand me and let me go. You can't do that."

"You can't do this because statistics and basic common sense show that most crimes perpetrated by blacks are against blacks because that is the one they come in contact with. So how can I let this man go in good conscience? This is the same thing Foster had to face when he was out there. How can you do these things in good conscience? So, again, like I say, you're not on the popular side. Again, black cops are a closed group, an enclave, and they very rarely hang around with anybody else *but*. . . .

"A lot of blacks look at the police department: instead of trying to get in there to make changes, if they feel it's really that bad, they've got to look at it as the enemy. And you're not going to beat the police department, not from the outside. From the inside, maybe. But not from the outside. You ain't gonna do it."

"I've had people, little kids, come up to me and say, 'Hi, hello, how are you?' Like that. And an older boy'll come by and say, 'Hey, don't talk to cops, don't talk to 'em?' " Duffy shook his head, uncomprehending.

"Not even other kids — their *mothers*, their mothers will say it." Anderson's face filled with concern. "And you did nothing to bring this on, you did nothing whatsoever. You just trying. You're a thin line trying to keep this whole city from going to hell."

"But, see," Duffy said, "they see your own forces don't back you up — right?"

"So why the hell should *they*," Anderson said. "Who cares? He's only a pig. I have a thing about names like pigs, niggers, and stuff like that. Those are the curse words, see. Because once you call a man a pig, a nigger, or something like that, you're taking away from him being a man. Ya see. You're calling them something else besides a human being, so therefore if you kill him — I killed a pig, I killed a nigger, I killed a kike, I killed a mick, or something like that — you haven't killed a human being. You've killed something less than that because you've made him something less with these words. And these are the words that I hear that I resent. I don't like no kid calling me pig. Call me a pig, I tell him his mother's one."

Everyone laughed, but without much conviction. "How did Gregory feel about all this?" I asked.

"He felt basically the same," Darryl said. "He wasn't going to let people walk all over him. He had a job to do and Gregory believed in doing his job. I mean, he wasn't straight by the book. None of us is straight by the book. I mean, they got laws on the book that you wouldn't believe. Like, you're not supposed to drive around with your ashtray open in your car. I mean, you don't go by that. You go by use of discretion. And this is what he did."

"Most black cops, we live in the city. We haven't moved out of the city. There are some that have but most of 'em live in the confines of the five boroughs. We have to live there. Our families have to live there, we want to make it better, right? 'Cause they can't walk down the street if we don't make it better. So it's a personal thing, and this is it with all the guys. Greg was that way, too."

"This is the way he felt," Anderson said. "He felt he wanted to make things better. He wanted to do things, and in doing things he wanted to see something good done for his work. Which you don't see on this job."

"The night after he was killed," Duffy said, "my father says, 'Oh, you don't need to be on this job.' "

"Oh, yeah, that's what you hear all the time. It's a cop-out. They want you to quit all the time, whenever something happens. If you got a girl friend, you got a mother and a father — anybody — they always want you to quit, to quit. . . . But you can't do this, you just can't do it. "It's a funny thing about a cop's job. Once you get it, it gets in your blood. And you just can't get it out, no matter how you try."

"You know," Duffy said, "a lot of guys say, 'In twenty years, in fifteen years, I'm quitting.' That twenty years comes around — heh, heh, well, 'I'm not really ready yet, I think I'll try . . .' "

"You never stop being a cop."

"You never stop."

Why the attraction, why? This is what I found so hard to understand. It had never been explained to me by anybody, not in all my visits to the Ninth Precinct, not in all my talks with police officers who knew Foster and Laurie. Now these two young black officers, two proud young men — they were closing in on the question. They were reaching toward the sweet center of their profession, the essence.

"Here's the thing," Anderson was saying, a limp cigar clutched in his teeth again. "I guess maybe we're all a little psycho. Because natural instinct tells you that when a man's got a gun, run the other way. We run toward him, right? And it's just something . . ."

"And you always want to be the first car there. That's the whole thing . . ."

"You always got to be first. Like sometimes I've been on a man with a gun run, and, you know, I'm a bachelor and stuff but I want to be the first one up there. I'm going in first because I got to go through the door first. It doesn't cross your mind that you can be blown out of that door backwards. You just want to be the first one in. Why? Who knows?"

"Turn a corner," Duffy laughed, "you see a car there, you say, 'Shucks, beat me to it.' It's humiliating."

"Then we laugh about it, we laugh about the dangers and stuff. It's just a feeling. Like you love to hear a robbery come over the radio, two men with guns. Oh, boy. Now, who in their right mind says, 'Oh, boy, two men with guns?' Hey, you should be going the other way." Anderson laughed. "It's a thing, you just want to get there."

"And then when it's unfounded you seem depressed, you know, aw, shucks . . ." Duffy's voice trailed off.

"Even though you are nervous," Anderson said. "You are nervous. Don't get me wrong. Because it's a fact that most cops have holes in their stomachs by the time they're twenty-six, twenty-seven. By that time they got ulcers, something like that. Because you're living with constant pressure, 'cause you run into that building, right? You got this thing in your stomach, it's like a knot. But it's not gonna stop you from entering that building. You're going in in spite of . . . hell, maybe, I don't know, maybe it's too prove to yourself you're a man. Maybe we all got to do that in some way, shape, or form. But you got to do it."

"You remember the night two cops got shot up in your precinct with a shotgun?" Anderson nodded. "We was down by the pool. It was five minutes to twelve, and we was just about ready to get off, we're down at the pool. Where this occurred was maybe six blocks away. We hear the thirteen come over — 'We're pinned down.' First thing my partner says, 'Hey, man, you want to go up there?' I says, 'Yeah, okay, let's go.' Where it's not really our duty to respond there because we're unequipped, for one thing. But on a thirteen, I don't care if you're at one end of the precinct, you're gonna try your best to get down. . . ."

"I heard Jimmy Gedney's voice — he was in the academy with us. I heard that he was pinned down behind a car and he ran out of ammo. I said, 'Oh, wow, let's get the hell up there!' So we just jumped up there, grabbed a car, said, 'Come on, let's go.' We went up there.

"It's something that you can't take away. Like, you hear another cop's in trouble — thirteen. You got to go. You have to go. You're not going to stand there and wait for nothing. No boss in the world could tell another cop. . . . I've seen it done. A boss will say, 'Don't go.' He can't stop you, because you know another cop's in trouble. That's the only thing you got left on this job, and if you can't protect another cop you might as well get off. That's the way we feel about it."

"There's good parts to being a cop," Duffy said. "Like, sometimes you go on aid cases and you help somebody, and some people do respect you and say thank you. There's a lot of people that even though they may be two percent in the community out of the one hundred percent that are for cops, that two percent still makes you feel good that it's really worth it being there. You feel good, like if a kid is lost and you get him home, you feel good for a whole week, you can take all kinds of criticism for a whole week long.

"I think all cops ask for is just when something's done, just to have someone say thank you, and it'll make you feel a helluva lot better. 'Cause every day you're out here trying. You're trying to do the best you can with what you have."

Anderson kept bouncing reasons at himself — pros and cons, good and bad — trying to dissect the nature of his job. And, still, he could not pin it neatly to the wall. "It's a tough life, though," he said, the downs taking over. "You're damn sure it's a tough life. Like I say, you got to be a little masochistic to accept it because it's tough. Your hours are bad, the working conditions stink. Like, a lot of people have a nice desk and air-conditioned office. You're working conditions are terrible. That precinct that me and him work — after a certain hour there's no place to eat. You can't even eat in certain places, you have to go to another precinct. So working conditions is bad, right? And then the way people come off. But even with all that, with all this against you, you still want to be a cop. And I know the proudest thing in my life was when I was sworn in. I felt — hey, I felt ten feet tall. Nobody could tell me I wasn't something."

"Did Gregory feel the same way?"

"Hey — if I felt ten feet, he felt twenty feet."

The question of Gregory Foster's death came up.

"Neither of us ever thought he would die," Duffy said. "He got through Vietnam, he was smart, cool. He had a good partner. Working with a partner like Laurie, when you work with a partner that you know, you both look out for each other, you feel more secure."

"Sure."

"You always feel better, and like the time it happened. When nine, ten o'clock rolls around you say, 'Oh, wow, another hour, two hours, to go and I'm going home.' "

"You always feel you're going home," Anderson said. "That's another thing. Hey, you even turn to your partner — 'What you doing after work?' 'Oh, I'm going to see my girl friend,' 'I'm going drinking,' 'I'm going to do this or that.' But you always say, 'I'm going somewhere,' or 'I'm going home.' "

"When did you hear about it, Darryl?"

271

"I had heard it on the radio. I was on vacation but I was coming home. I had been in Brooklyn and I heard it over the news that two patrolmen in the Ninth Precinct had been shot. That's all I heard. I didn't hear anything else. So the first thing that hit me — I knew Greg was in the Ninth Precinct and I said, you know — 'Hey, this can't happen to a friend of mine.' So I turned it off. At about two forty-five Larry Chiles called me up and he says, 'I got bad news for you.' I said, 'What?' So he says, 'Greg's dead.' So, you know, disbelief. First thing I asked him, I said, 'You're bullshitting me.' That was the first words. He goes, 'No.' He says, 'I wouldn't kid you on something like that.' And I just. . . . For about a minute or so I just couldn't say nothing. Just couldn't believe it. You don't believe it, you don't believe it at all.

"It's a shame, a shame. A man goes out there, goes out and fights for his country, comes back, right? Goes out here." Anderson pointed to the window. "Because he always said another reason why he wanted to be a cop is because he figured he could do something for his people. Like we all do. And to go out there and have some guy cut him down from the back. . . . You know, because he always said if it ever came down to a fight with the gun, he ain't gonna lose."

"You know, this is the way we all feel. But when you get hit from the back there ain't nothin' you can do."

"We have a thing when we come out of the academy," Anderson said. "We all know that if you get in a bank robbery you're liable to come out of it on the dead side. Or if you come upon a scared person that just committed a homicide, you're liable to get yourself shot. You're prepared for these things. You're not prepared to die, but you're prepared for these things. These things you accept when you raise your right hand and get the shield. But you're not prepared — no cop's prepared — to be shot in the back. To be shot in the back like a dirty dog. For what? For what?"

"We saw the bags," Duffy said, pain in his face, pain in the remembering. "They had their jackets. One of 'em had on the winter blouse. We saw the bags laying over in the corner, like they were ripped and bloodied, stains all over them, and the bags were bloodstained with the holsters in them, and the rest of their clothes. You say, 'Oh, wow, my friend was wearing this a couple of hours ago and it wasn't like this.' And to say this is his uniform.

272

We went and got fitted for the uniform the same day, and to look at them. It's really...."

"You start to cry. I can tell you, you break down and cry, you get up there and see ... Then you get on the street and you see part of his head, part of his skull — the flesh was still left on the street. I remember Duffy went to his precinct and I went to mine to tell the guys what had happened and I just got through it, I just got through it because I was ready to break down and start crying. This was right in front of the roll-call room and they knew it and I'll never forget, it was quiet, guys in there were absolutely quiet. And his precinct the same thing. It was just too much."

"But I couldn't finish. I was crying...."

"It was just too much, just to much to take."

The room was silent. Even the outside was hushed. You could hear Anderson's little sister in another room but her chatter seemed restrained.

"You know what makes you feel so bad?" Duffy went on. "At the funeral. Like, even sometimes when I think about him a lot I close my eyes and see visions of him, the way he looked at the funeral. I'm sorry that they even opened the casket. They should have kept it closed because he just didn't look the same."

"You could see the scars where the eyes were put back together. I said, I don't know why they kept that casket opened."

"The false eyelashes on one of his eyes."

"I'm so sorry that they opened the casket."

"When we left the academy," Anderson said, his eyes moist now, "we never got to see each other as much as we should have. That's the one thing he regrets and we all do. At his funeral we made a thing that we should at least get together — at least once a year or something, just get together with families. Just sit down and have a date because you never know when one of us ain't gonna make it."

"I tell you one thing," Duffy said, "if he was still here today I betcha I'd go see him every day."

"I don't know about that," Darryl said. "I know I'd see him much more."

"I just feel so bad about it."

"I know I'd see him much more often than I know I did when he was alive."

"Greg was a real nice guy, a helluva nice guy."

"He was good. From all the problems that he had, he weathered them pretty good. You know, he stood up under them and he still got what he wanted."

It was like in a church, the two of them going back and forth, responsive reading out of the Bible. Both men's eyes were red. It was Darryl Anderson who roused himself first, who began to smile, a thought coming to him, a sense perhaps that he had better put Gregory Foster in perspective.

"To me," he said finally, "he was just a guy with his faults, like we all have. I wouldn't build him up to being no angel. He had his faults like we all do. He was a *man*. And by a man, I mean he accepted responsibilities that were put on him by society, and he took 'em. And a lot of times he got knocked down like all of us. But you got to get up and you got to dust yourself off and you can't quit. You can't quit. He wasn't a quitter."

It was dusk now and there was little more to be said and, getting up to leave, I couldn't help but think of another conversation I had had, with Rocco Laurie's friend, Brooks Matyi. Because what Matyi had told me about Laurie was what Anderson and Duffy had just finished telling me about Foster. And maybe, among them all, I had been given the answers I sought about Foster and Laurie, about police officers in general, about other things, too.

"This was the night before Rocco's wedding," Matyi said. "I asked him where he was going to be a cop. I figured it would be the Staten Island police force. He said no, he wanted to be a New York City cop. I told him that was crazy. I said, 'Sure, go into training but transfer over to the Staten Island police force.' And he said, no, he felt he could do a better job over there. And he wanted to be over there in the city. Every time I went to see him after that I told him he was crazy for going over there, especially when I found out what area he was in. I said, 'Get out of there, get a transfer. He wouldn't do it. I guess he was happy where he was; he felt he could do a job there.

"I think he was the kind of person who would go where he thought he was needed the most or could do the best job. He was very unselfish and very idealistic. He had very high morals and goals and he felt he would not be making the most out of his goals as a policeman in an easier area. He wanted to be where the work was the hardest."

Perhaps, then, Matyi, and Anderson and Duffy, were telling me that, in the end, the good cop is the one who goes where the work is the hardest. Because that is where he fulfills himself, that is where he becomes a man.

I wanted to tell these two fine young men my thoughts, because I thought they would understand, but I had taken too much of their time and they had told me so much. I shook hands with both, wishing them well, and left. And, out in the street, in the fading light, black and white teen-agers were still playing, listening to music, and smiling to each other. And the air was clean and cool.

I t was more than a reasonable New York day for late January. The temperature ran up over fifty and most of those who wore mackinaws or leather jackets in the East Village had them open. Members of the Anti-Crime Unit from the Ninth Precinct were on the roofs overlooking Fifth Street, peering down onto the scene through hazy sunshine that kept them warm. They were on the roofs because, in a few minutes, on this twenty-sixth day of January, one year minus one to the day when two of their comrades, Gregory Foster and Rocco Laurie, were shot to death, the widows and other members of the family would come outside the station house to watch the unveiling of a plaque in honor of the two policemen. The police were more than a little worried about the situation because, lately, people were shooting at cops. Eight cops in New York City had been shot at during the week. Police were blaming the Black Liberation Army. Larry Cummings said as he went out on the street, "I don't like it, I don't like it at all. It's hairy out there."

The block between First and Second Avenue was filling up. A contingent of marines trooped off a bus and began to form on the street. The marines wore their dress uniform and they all carried rifles. Half the police squad had on their leather jackets and leather gloves. The other half wore the traditional blue uniform. All of their shields were half-covered with the black mourning bands. Jim Liedy, who that night had helped pick up Laurie and driven the dying cop to the hospital, was in the group.

Inside the station house, in the reception area, sat the two widows. Adelaide Laurie wore her black-belted dress, her little heart locket around her neck, her black hair pulled back tight in a bun. She sat there lifeless, staring at nothing. The contrast between her and Jacqueline Foster, who sat beside her, was rather startling. Jackie wore a stylish beige dress. She was wearing a wig with the upswept look. She drank coffee and smoked cigarettes. Her mother sat beside her. From time to time she would lean over and talk to Adelaide. Adelaide would listen and occasionally nod her head.

In another corner of the room Gregory Foster's parents milled around. Their second son was with them, a fine-looking young man in an Afro and granny glasses. He had a camera slung over his shoulder and he was taking pictures. Then Mr. and Mrs. Anthony Laurie came in, followed by their son, Anthony Jr., and his wife Kathy. Mr. Laurie was dressed in a dark suit, white shirt, and striped tie. He had put on weight and looked well. Mrs. Laurie had just had a cataract operation in one eye and was about to have one in the other and her eyes were tearing and her face was pouchy and had a heavy pallor. They walked over to the opposite side of the room from their daughter-in-law, without acknowledging her presence. Adelaide Laurie did not look up.

"Citizens of New York, the two men whose memory we honor today are veterans of two wars. As marines Rocco Laurie and Gregory Foster served in Vietnam. Walking patrols together through the steaming jungles of South Vietnam, they and their fellow marines fought to preserve our country and the world from the menace of Communism. Serving as New York policemen, patrolmen Laurie and Foster were again walking patrol together. This time it was a sidewalk in the Ninth Precinct. Their enemies were violence and those who try to make a mockery of law and order. The conflict in Vietnam will soon be over but the struggle which claimed these two fine young men, the struggle to preserve peace, law, and order at home, is still with us. It is up to all of us, every race and creed, to insure that the respect and honor on the streets do not just become a dream or a groundless hope, but a way of life. In memory of Rocco Laurie and Gregory Foster let us commit ourselves to making this a reality."

They stood out in the street, listening. Adelaide Laurie gritted her teeth, clutched at a handkerchief. One strand of curl fell down the side of her face. She was holding tightly to Jacqueline Foster's hand. Jackie's face was serene. Her left hand fingered a button at the top of her coat. Her mother-in-law and father-in-law stood beside her. The parents of Rocco Laurie, and his brother and wife, stood a distance away. The marine guard and the police stood stiffly at attention. People from the neighborhood gathered around, listening. Mostly they were old people, the ones in that area who believed in the police. Another speaker talked of a Foster-Laurie Education Fund for youngsters living within the Ninth Precinct. The fund would be administered by the National Marine Corps Scholarship Foundation. "This plaque," the speaker said, "will remind all who pass, that each day and night, men patrol the sidewalks of New York at the risk of their lives."

Then a priest moved to the microphone. "Almighty and Eternal God, Father of all mankind, we are gathered here this afternoon to honor the memory of two brave policemen who gave their very lives in the defense of the people of this city. We ask Your blessing on the plaque we raise in their memory. . . . Pour Your blessings on all policemen in our city who put their lives on the line every hour of every day for our well-being and safety. Watch over them and protect them as they perform their daily tasks. And if it should be Your will that they be called upon to make the same supreme sacrifice may they make it as generously and as unselfishly as the two men we honor today.

"Bless also, Almighty God, the wives and families of these two brave men. Grant them the strength and faith to accept this overwhelming loss of a husband and father. Let them have the consolation that their loved ones did not die in vain by making this city once again a safe and sane place in which to play, work, and to live. . . ."

The families went back into the station house after the brief ceremony, after they had looked at the plaque. Inscribed on it were the words: "In memory of Patrolman Rocco Laurie and

Patrolman Gregory Foster, slain while on patrol in the Ninth Precinct, January the 27th, 1972. They served their country in Vietnam as United States Marines and have given us in death the shining example of racial brotherhood that makes us proud to claim them as members of our band of brothers."

The marines and the police marched to Avenue B, to the corner of Eleventh Street. A stand had been erected over the sidewalk where the two men had been killed. Two floral decorations stood on either side of the platform. The marines, with their color guard, and the police came to attention. Behind the police dignitaries was the old sign: "Shrimp Boat," the entrance to the place still barred. The people of the precinct watched without expression — Puerto Rican men and women, blacks, white teenagers in beards and flowered shirts. Three boys from the Cool Ones were there, too. One of them wore a Heckle and Jeckle shirt. They all had basketball uniforms with them. They had a game to play in the afternoon, but they stopped to hear the ceremonies.

Wreaths were placed at the exact spot of the murders, the marines fired a twenty-one-gun salute, aiming in the air. As the spectators looked up, they could see men standing on the roofs, the Anti-Crime Unit, and then it was over. Everyone moved back to the Ninth Precinct headquarters.

Sandwiches had been placed on a table in the recreation area and there were soft drinks and coffee and cake. Police VIPs milled around with the guests. In a half hour the mayor would be there and the ceremony would continue. Annie Laurie, the mother, looked around, squinting through eyes that seemed to see only a blur of blue. In her old, jaunty manner she said, "If Rocco was here, he'd say, 'What's all this business?' " The widows were back in the same seats they had occupied at the beginning of the afternoon. Jackie Foster talked to people who came over to her. Adelaide Laurie barely acknowledged anyone's presence. It was almost as if she were *not* present; the physical body sitting there, twitching, sniffling; but the rest of her gone. She was polite when people spoke to her, but barely reachable.

A few days before the first anniversary commemoration both widows talked about themselves and the changes in their lives and what the year, the terrible year of sorrow, had done to them. Jackie Foster had her children and sisters, and now her in-laws were seeing her again, taking the kids home with them on occasion, and Jackie was through her isolation. She was twenty years old and there was a hard, tough resilience in her. She would endure, she would endure anything.

"This is the last one I'm going to," she said firmly. "He's fading away but every time the call comes it all comes back and it makes me feel sad and down. I don't think about him as hard as I used to. I mean, it's still there in a way, but it is not keeping me down as much as it used to. I'm able to get along. I can live with myself. I feel like a heavy burden has been lifted off me."

She was asked a cold question: Would she feel bad if she knew that her husband was unfaithful to her. "Yeah, of course. Any wife would. I had a feeling he was at the end. I'm putting two and two together. I had a feeling that he was. It don't bother me, though, because I know I had him. He was mine just the same — no matter what he did — 'cause Gregory loved me.

"I know Gregory loved me." Her voice grew stronger. "He had to love me with what I put him through. I guess that's why I stay sick half the time, because I regret so much. I'm feeling sorry for myself and how I treated him at one time and then when I tried to make up to him it was too late."

She said that she had given up the voodoo and the white magic. Someone had given her a book on positive thinking and it had helped her gain perspective. "I'm growing up a lot," she said. "I've matured a lot. And I have my children." She wanted to see them grow up to be good children. She was asked if she would like little Gregory to be a police officer.

"No, definitely not. I'd do everything in my power to stop him. It's too dangerous and I've had one tragedy in my life and I couldn't take another one, not with someone close to me."

"For a long time," Adelaide Laurie was saying, "I didn't trust anybody. It's just the way things happen to you and I guess that's basic human nature. You get very defensive. You don't want to be hurt any more. You don't want to be bothered anymore." She sat in a friend's living room. She was wearing her customary black but she had on a wig and the curls came down to her shoulders and it gave her face a youthful appearance again. And she had rouged her cheeks. She was trying, and that was encouraging.

"I'm not that bad now," she said. "I'm getting on much better, getting out of my shell. I know my uncle was worried about me because I was sitting in the chair all day and I didn't talk, I didn't move, I didn't do anything. And he used to say, 'Show some emotion. Show hatred, show love, sorrow — show something. Don't just sit there and do nothing.' He would say things to make me mad and he couldn't even get me angry.

"I really thought about killing myself. But I'm such a coward, I couldn't go through with it. And Rocco never believed in things like that. He would be so disappointed in me. There are times when I think — even now — how easy it would be to go off the road with the car or something. And I weigh it. But then I ask myself, what would he do? What would he think of this? That's why I think about him all the time.

"Jackie Foster called me one night, trying to cheer me up. She said, 'I'm young, I have two children, I'll get married again some-day.' She said, 'My husband told me I should get married if anything ever happened to him, and you should, too. After all, you're young.' I said, 'Please, don't say that to me. I don't want to hear that.' And she said, 'Well, after all, you can't be alone for the rest of your life.' She said, 'I feel that you should get married. It's what he would have wanted.' I don't think that's what Rocco would have wanted. He told me once, 'If you ever get married again I'll come back and haunt you.' I asked him what he would do if something happened to me 'cause that was the week we had just seen *Love Story*, so we were both all choked up. And he said, 'I don't think I'd be able to live. . . .'

"In a way," she went on, "I wish it had been me because I think he would have handled it better than me. He thought of everything, really. Three months before this happened he took out insurance on the house and when he told me I said, 'I don't want to hear. I don't want to hear it. Nothing is going to happen but I don't want to hear about your insurance.' And he said to me, 'if something happens to me how will you pay off the house?' He said, 'I've got to do it.' I said, 'I don't even want to talk about it.' He said, 'All right, I won't talk about it, but it's here — I'm doing it.'

She said she was sleeping a little better now. "I try not to let myself think about it. Like, if it's creeping up, I push it away. I won't let myself think about it." But there are times when she is not strong enough to cut it out of her mind.

"I still, like at night, I don't fall asleep right away and I think I can hear the doorbell ringing and I see the two policemen standing there. The dog is barking and it's chaos and I remember everything." Suddenly, she was transported back in time, riding to the hospital, the memory opening up on her, pure and bright. "I can remember standing there and somebody came and shoved a watch in my face and said, 'Is this your husband's watch?' And I looked up at him and I said, 'I don't think so.' I looked at it and it had a black face and I knew that wasn't his. . . . All these things — people talking here, talking there. Why is the commissioner here? What would he be doing here? A nurse crying. She was trying to console me. She was crying so much that she asked another nurse to take over and she walked out. I can remember her crying. . . ."

She broke off the reverie, returning to the present. "I'm so busy I don't have a chance to do much thinking. Now I dread the weekends. Before, I loved the weekends, being home, but now they drag. They go by so slow, I hate it. I crochet. I do that. That's about all. The girls at work want me to go here and go there but my heart's not in it. Even my priest, he said, 'Now, in my country — he comes from Portugal — the women wear black for one year and then they start to break it off a little bit.' So I said, 'Well, Father, it has to come from me. If I don't feel that I want to wear any other color then you know it has to be what I feel.' I'll be twenty-five next month," she said, smiling for the first time. "An old lady. I feel old, I really do."

They were seated now on the main floor of the station house. On one wall were the two plaques, draped in a black shroud. Three others, uncovered, were arrayed in the same row along the wall. An American flag, centered among the plaques, was tacked on the wall above them. Captain Edward Rogers, who was now Deputy Inspector Rogers, introduced the police commissioner.

Murphy talked about the "two men who made the ultimate sacrifice to protect the people of this city." Then he introduced the mayor, John Lindsay. "I think," Lindsay said, "that the most vivid memory I've had in the many years I've been in office was the tragic night one year ago when I heard of these two brave policemen who gave their lives for the protection of their community."

Jackie Foster and Adelaide Laurie sat together holding hands, both weeping now. When the mayor finished, Deputy Inspector Rogers asked for the escort to bring the widows up to unveil the plaques. They stood on either side of the drape and Rogers pulled the string. The drape fell away and the two plaques were visible with a bouquet of bursting red and white carnations and purple flowers between them. Monsignor Dunne, the police department chaplain, rose to bless the plaques, and the mother of Rocco Laurie, standing now, began to moan.

The widows received miniature plaques from Inspector Rogers and he kissed them both and then another police chaplain rose to perform the benediction.

The guests were escorted back to the recreation room. Mayor Lindsay, dapper as always in a dark blue suit and wide, flowered tie, came by once more to pay his respects. The widows were seated where they had been all afternoon. Someone went up to Mrs. Laurie, the mother, who was wiping at her eyes.

"Well, the worst is over."

"The worst will never be over for us," she said.

Gregory Foster's brother came over to Adelaide Laurie, bent down and kissed her. So did the father. Then Mrs. Foster, in her black coat, bent over Adelaide and spoke to her. Adelaide grasped Mrs. Foster's hand and held on.

"I have thought so much about you all these months," Mrs. Foster said. "I wanted to come and pay you a visit but I didn't know what your reaction would be." Adelaide Laurie just listened. The mother continued. "You have to be strong. And, remember, you're younger than your in-laws. You have to learn to give in a little bit, and if you do I'm sure they would give in, too." Adelaide nodded twice and Mrs. Foster kissed her and was gone.

An hour later everyone was gone and the Ninth Precinct was

back to normal. A young man, handcuffed, was being booked at the front desk. Behind the desk was the only sign of what had recently transpired — the two fresh plaques and the flowers between them. The plaque on the left had a photograph of Gregory Foster, a head-and-shoulders shot, a serious look on his face. Underneath the picture the legend read:

In Memory of
PTL. GREGORY FOSTER
SHIELD 13737
9th Precinct
Slain in the
Performance of Duty
On January 27, 1972

On the right was the other plaque. Rocco Laurie had a half smile on his face. Underneath his photograph were the same simple words:

In Memory of
PTL. ROCCO LAURIE
SHIELD 11019
9th Precinct
Slain in the
Performance of Duty
On January 27, 1972

The flowers were removed the next day. The plaques are there permanently, and there is room on the wall for more.

EPILOGUE

A week after the killings a new team took over the sector that had been Foster and Laurie's. Eugene Lewis and John Raftery are both bachelors. Lewis is thirty-four, Raftery, twenty-eight. They were in the same class together at the academy in 1969. They have worked together before. Lewis, who is six-foot-three, comes from Richmond, Virginia. He lives in an apartment in Spanish Harlem. Raftery, who is six-foot-six, is a native New Yorker, living now with his parents on Staten Island. Lewis and Raftery were walking Avenue B, from Fourth to Fourteenth Streets when, one summer night, I did a four-to-twelve with them.

At three-thirty in the afternoon Gene Lewis sat in the small room that belonged to the Neighborhood Police Team, his feet propped on the desk. His partner hadn't yet arrived. Lewis was wearing a short-sleeved denim shirt and blue flared slacks. He had thick black hair in the form of a mild Afro, bushy sideburns, and a full moustache. Granny glasses completed the look of the modern urban black cop.

Lewis had walked the same post before, with another partner, and the first thing I wanted to know was whether it had changed since the murders of Foster and Laurie.

"It's about the same," Lewis said, lighting up a cigarette. "The junk is still there and the thieves are still there — real small-time thieves that would take a camera, mug you, for any amount of money.

"Only one change that I've actually seen — and I don't know if it's because of police work or community relations or just an upgraded intelligence level on their part. They don't want to fight the cops out in the street any more. They'll fight someplace else. I think that's what's going on. You can see it in the street gangs; they're beginning to unify and it's not a riot any longer. You get a few skirmishes here and there but they're so slight that maybe you say it's a family fight. They have large families, these Spanish people, and a family fight might consist of twenty people. You couldn't really call that a riot. But other than that it's the same. The Neighborhood Police Team has helped, but the Neighborhood Police Team can help only those who want to be helped, and there is such a slight number of these people down here. Other people enjoy seeing things the way they are."

"Do you like being on the Neighborhood Police Team?"

"It's so diversified. You find yourself as a referee in the street. You got to tell yourself once in a while you're still a cop. You see, every day, the same people. So, consequently, you're going to say hello and they're going to say hello." He laughed abruptly. "Some of them don't want to see you at all, 'cause of something they're doing that they don't want you to know about, especially early in the morning."

A young cop opened the door of the room, looked in, and popped right out again. Outside, several prisoners were lying inside the cage. Fans were whirring everywhere. It was a hot, late-summer afternoon.

"I think every man on the team," Lewis was saying, "wants to accomplish something. It's this thing about trying to bring back a kind of trust in you. It's pretty hard going out there and you're being judged collectively every minute. Sometimes the only thing you have to rely on is the few people that you know on the block that are all right. Well," he said, pausing to clarify a thought, "you can trust them. You can draw the line for every-body. Even out there on the street you have to draw the line. The civilian, see, he doesn't know the whole thing. But you as a cop *and* as a civilian, you know both sides of it. That's one of the advantages."

Another advantage, I suggested, might be the gun.

"Not the gun. The gun is not really an advantage to you other than having a gun. 'Cause most of the people out there, if they're after you, now they won't miss. If they're out there to get you they're not going to miss you because they're going to set you up. They're going to stalk you down like an animal, and that's what's going to happen to you. Even the best cops go."

That brought it back to Foster and Laurie and the big question — why them? Gene Lewis did not have the answer. "I don't believe that someone set out to shoot two men in the back like that. These two young cops were aggressive but not the type of cops that would cause someone to hate them. I never read either one of them that way. They were both very dedicated guys. They had their problems like everybody else. They might bitch about them a little bit — bitch at home, bitch along to my partner, bitch along to me. But they were not the kind of guys where you'd say, 'I don't like them, I don't like these guys.' You wouldn't say that. I had just talked to Foster a couple of nights before. He seemed pretty uptight about something, I don't know. It was pretty cold that night. I think I had gone off to stop by the theater and I stopped to talk to him. I think he was working by himself a couple of nights in a row. The night was cold. It was quiet. The only way you could depict his attitude that night was as bitching it off as a cop.

"Sometimes I get uptight — shit, I'm getting out of this precinct. That's when you come to the point where you can't see yourself doing anything. At least if you're a garbage man or something, you go down a block, you can turn around, and empty the garbage out. You can see that you accomplished something within that block."

Raftery was supposed to meet Lewis in the Neighborhood Police Team room but still wasn't there. "He may have gone upstairs to dress," Lewis said. "He drives in from Staten Island. I plan to bring him up to my neighborhood. He heard how bad it was. I just want to show him what it really is to live in a congested area like that. I think it all helps to understand exactly the plight of these people down here. And they're all not bad. I find myself guilty of saying fuck them, too, sometimes. I'm guilty of it too but I don't maintain this attitude; it happens sometimes when I see things and I can't do a damn thing about them. And I know people are going to suffer for it and I can't do nothing half the time. And I feel — fuck. Then you straighten yourself out. I gotta go dress." He picked himself up. "See you downstairs."

Lewis introduced me to John Raftery downstairs. Raftery is so tall he stoops. He has short brown hair and a small moustache. He is a soft-spoken New Yorker with an understated sense of humor. As I walked with the partners down Fifth Street toward their post, Raftery talked about the time he and Lewis worked in civilian clothes in Anti-Crime.

"With me and him riding around, people used to just look at

us and laugh. They knew who we were. One day I got out of the gypsy cab and one woman said to me, 'You're the police, aren't you?' 'Yes, I am.' What could I say?"

"They know us, anyway," Lewis said. "From Avenue B to C, they all know us."

"Well, after all, we walked the post for a few years. We were in the same academy class and the same company and everything. We started June of '69. We got out in October of '69. We came here."

The partners reached Avenue B at Seventh Street and started to stroll slowly up the avenue. The street was crowded and some of the street people looked strangely at the cops, wondering about the civilian who walked between them. "It should be a full moon tonight," Raftery said, "so you should get some action."

"I was home last night," Lewis said. "I kept hearing sirens and looked out the window and I looked up — there's that moon. I knew it."

Raftery chuckled. "I saw that moon last night as soon as I turned out and I said it's going to be a fun evening. I had guys walking up to me singing, people trying to save me with prayers. I was walking around late, three girls start talking to me, so next thing you know — ba-boom, ba-boom! — the garbage cans are going over, bottles are breaking, there's a fight going on."

"I was off," Lewis said. "I had a big weekend, a big swinging weekend."

The partners continued walking. They passed Eleventh Street. On the other side of the street the Shrimp Boat sign was still up, but the place was closed tight, a barred gate at the entrance. I had an urge to cross the street and examine the sidewalk to see if the stains were still there, if there was any sign at all that the bodies of two policemen had lain on that piece of concrete. But the partners walked on. They talked about their vacations and about arrests they had made.

"That one case I had, the guy was locked up for sodomy," Raftery said.

"He was gay?"

"I couldn't read the thing on the yellow sheet so I said to him, 'What does this say here?' It was like S-O-D, you know, I couldn't read the rest. 'Oh that,' he says, 'I'd rather not talk about it.'"

They laughed and talked more about their work. "We've never really had any bad altercations," Lewis said. "You do what you have to do. But if it's something you can adjudicate on the spot then you should do it without compounding — like, if you make the wrong moves, say the wrong thing, you mostly compound because people are very touchy in certain situations. We're very lucky that we're able to talk to most of these cats. We work the post. We know who the troublemakers are. We know exactly what they are capable of doing most of the time. And once you let them know where you stand they won't pull no bullshit."

They talked about other cops in the Ninth, about one in particular who, they felt, overreacted to situations.

"He must have watched 'Dragnet' or something like that before he came on the force," Raftery said.

"He's pretty thorough, though. He'll do the job. But he'll fuck up on you, too. I had to explain to him one time that all black people with beards — you don't stop them for suspicion. He's from Queens. This is his first dealings with an area where you got more than one nationality."

"I spent half my life," Raftery said, "thinking that brown people were a different nationality. Then I went in the army. You can tell the average cop who hasn't been in the army."

Lewis mentioned the cop he had just been talking about, and others. "These guys are missing that little quality that would get them over a hurdle, knowing how to approach people of different nationalities, understanding them not to the point where you make a damn fool out of them, but you pick it right up quick and understand these people's actions, their motives. If you been in the army you don't forget these people you met in the army. You know, all white and black, all Puerto Ricans. You learn how to deal with them, even the name-calling and shit like that."

As he talked, Lewis kept looking around. They stood easily on the corner but they saw everything. "I don't hold a grudge against a guy for calling me a black-ass nigger. I hear that shit all the time. People come to me and John and refer to other white people; they say, 'You know, man, them whiteys, they're motherfuckers.' Right to John. I mean, like they don't think they're insulting him and they'd come to me the same way. Like a black dude or a white dude and say, 'These fays, man, they ripped me off.' This shit don't faze me. It don't faze him. People will come up and if it's a white person they'll talk to John. Sometimes the black person won't talk to me. All right. I won't let them divide us. I'll say, 'Is this police business?' They say, 'Yeah.' Then I say, 'Okay, we both have to hear this if it's police business.' If it's anything else, 'Excuse me, John, talk to the broad,' or whoever it might be. But not if it's pertaining to police business. 'You talk to both of us at the same time.'"

"You noticed how he mentioned the broad, you see." Raftery grinned.

He said, "You can't do the job the same way here as you can in some small town in New Jersey. For that matter, even Queens. Like, the other night when you were on vacation, I was over here on B and Ninth Street." The partners were standing now on the corner of Tenth Street, bordering Tompkins Square Park. "All of a sudden this guy is smashed on the ground and I turned around. I thought the guy was drunk or something. I said, 'Hey, what's the matter?' And there he was, lying facedown. I turned the guy over. Holy Christ. He had a hole in his chest like this. Somebody shoved a knife in the guy. I thought he was going to go south, but from what I heard he made it. Oops, there's our scratch." A patrol car had driven up and Raftery walked over and his memo book was marked by the lieutenant who was driving the car.

Just then a boy rushed out of the park. "Officer, a dog bit my friend."

Raftery and Lewis walked fast into the park. There was a group of children milling around, and a couple of adults. The boy in the center of the circle, who was about twelve years old, was crying. He showed Raftery his arm. The bite had punctured his skin. His mother was somewhere else in the park with her other children. They told the police officers that it had been a German shepherd, off the leash. The owner had just let the dog at the boy.

"You going to shoot the dog?" a boy asked.

"No, son," Raftery said, "we're not going to shoot the dog. Where do you live?" he asked the boy who had been bitten.

"Seventy East Eighth Street," a woman answered.

"Got a phone?" He shook his head. A small girl in the crowd came over to the crying boy.

"I got bit by a rat when I was a baby. From the ceiling he jumped on my stomach. I didn't cry," she said reassuringly.

"You cried," another boy said. "Her aunt upstairs went away for a weekend and they left the water running and the whole ceiling fell down."

"And I saw it crawling on her," a woman said, "and I screamed and the rat got scared. We shot it."

"You shot it with a gun?" Lewis asked.

"Yeah, my landlord shot it and then he came for the rent."

Raftery suggested that the woman, who was a neighbor of the bitten boy, take him to the clinic nearby. "Does his mother have to go with him?" she said.

"Well, if we can't find her, what are we going to do, right?"

"Let's wait a minute until the mother comes," Lewis suggested. "It's not that bad. Let's see if we can find the mother." Just then a boy came up to Lewis. "Hey," the cop barked, "you're not supposed to put your hand on the gun."

Finally, they spotted the mother and a couple of kids ran over to her and she came running up. She spoke no English and the other woman explained what the cops had suggested. The whole group walked off to the clinic.

The cops watched the army of children leave. "The kids sort of make your day sometimes," Raftery said.

"Save your day," Lewis said.

"Yeah, you get about ten of them come up to you. Ask you the same questions — 'Does the whistle work? And what do you carry here? Where's your handcuffs?' Except last night I was walking along and one of the kids was up in the window. 'Hey, you flat-footed bastard,' he yells. So I ignored the remark. It's nice to be appreciated."

They talked about the girl who had been bitten by the rat, how matter-of-fact it seemed to her because all she knew, her whole life, was this neighborhood.

"No matter how much money you could put in a ghetto area," Raftery said, "what can you do with it? Rehabilitate the area, or are you going to rehabilitate the people?"

"Yeah," Lewis agreed. "What are you gonna do with the people? I found most of these people don't know that the system is, they don't know what the system is doing to them. They're not articulate enough to explain it to you and they're not smart enough to understand it themselves.

"I've heard dudes refer to this place as the real drop head," Lewis went on. "Like, you're not accepted anyplace else, you can always drop in here and get yourself squared away. You drop in to sell your dope, to take off a few people, to live with your wife or something; if she's white and you're a black dude you'll get no trouble down here. Vice versa, too. So I think this seems to be the melting pot for all different nationalities of people who can't make it on the straight side of the street. And they come and go so often that you can't really establish any kind of contact or draw up any plan to counteract their attitudes 'cause they're only here for six months, then they're gone. It's the elderly who stay here more than six months."

"What's killing it is the kids," Raftery said. A breeze had risen now as the partners walked out of the park in the fading light. The noise seemed to be picking up — dogs barking, yells of children playing on the street. "I can't see the kids going straight because nobody sets an example, I mean a good example, for the kids."

"Take that school down there," Lewis pointed toward P.S. 71. "It's a shame. Grown-ups see kids breaking windows and they don't say one thing, you know what I mean? There's no sense of responsibility. I'm almost ready to think that most of these people down here have lost all hope. I think most of them seem to think, oh the hell with it. So they vent their hostilities on the police department in most cases. They're so uptight over different areas of society that this is the thing; they hate the cop. I had very vicious cases of people very militant for no reason. But when they come to a time when they really need you, some of them mellow. That's why it's so hard to just . . . like, when you see a guy who's acting up and you walk up to him and say, Look, man, why don't you knock it off?' He's having an argument with his wife or something."

"We get these all the time," Raftery said.

"That's the advantage of working the same post all the time. We worked Avenue C, we knew who the disputes were. Like the broad down there in 620, Maria. And then across the street, Mary. We know them, we know their husbands. We'd go down there, tell them, 'Come on Charles, come on, man. Let's get the fuck out of here. Come on, come and swap at us for a while.' "

"Go have a drink or something."

"Then the broad says, 'You keep the motherfucker out of here 'cause I'm going to kill him if he comes back tonight.' So we tell him, 'Look, man, don't go back there tonight.' "

"The women down there do numbers on men, too," Raftery remembered. "You were there that night, Sixth Street and Avenue C. We had this drunk come over to us, so this woman, Mary, walks up. She wears a T-shirt, that's the way she dressed. Bang, she lays into the guy. The guy falls on the sidewalk. 'Leave them cops alone, you fuck,' she says."

They both laughed. "We took a woman to Bellevue one time. This is no lie, she had cut a couple of men with a butcher's knife. I took her out to Bellevue. The doctor told me, 'I'm letting her go.' I said, 'All right, just give me a ten-minute head start.' 'Cause she's telling me she's going to kill me, too."

"Let's go get some egg-drop soup," Lewis said. It was nearly eight o'clock and the partners weren't scheduled to have their dinner until ten-thirty. We walked along the east side of the avenue. On the corner of Ninth Street we ran into a man named Duke, a short, stocky black man who had been drinking. "He's a bullshitter," Raftery said to me, "but he's a nice guy."

"How you doin', Duke?" Lewis said.

"I went to court."

"You went to court today?"

"What happened to you?" Raftery said.

Duke told a long, involved story about how a man walked past him with a gun and said he was going to shoot him. He did, but not before Duke pulled out his own gun and started shooting. "The judge," Duke said, "he told me, 'I'm giving you bail of five hundred dollars.' I said I don't even got five hundred pennies."

After he left, Raftery said, "That must be a tough way to go through life. Every year you get shot or stabbed."

"Every year he gets shot, either shot or stabbed," Lewis affirmed. "Every year."

The sign said "Chow Mein" and it was on Avenue B between Tenth and Eleventh streets, two doors from the Shrimp Boat, maybe a hundred paces from where Foster and Laurie had been ambushed. The restaurant was dingy, dimly lit. The Chinese waiter's apron was very dirty. One other couple was in there eating. I slipped into a booth, the two police officers sat across from me. They both took off their hats. They were wearing the summer blues, the denim work shirts. I had no appetite. My thoughts were on Foster and Laurie, the gunfire that had taken place just yards away from where I was sitting. Night was coming on and I had trouble concentrating on the partners' conversation. I felt a sudden chill.

"I am going to try and study for the sergeant's test." Lewis was talking about police work and how he got into it and where he thought he was going.

"I guess I'm an older guy, older than most when I came on the job. I was working in radar for six years. I was working for the New York State National Guard, radar technician, making ten-six, eleven, doing all right. Then one day I just got sick of it. I just got fed up. Radar's a lot of strain on you. So I resigned one morning. I didn't have no job yet. All right, the hell with it. So I had taken some tests and, surprising enough, the same night I got a telegram from the post office. So in two days' time I was working again. So I worked in the post office about three months. I was getting sick of that when the police department job came. I went down and took some tests. So then I forgot about it and here it comes.

"This job has its moments of doubt for me," Lewis said. "But it's the best I can do right now, to make this type of money. I enjoy some aspects of this job, I really do. You have the sense of doing something humane. You're able to help people who need help and you're not on the outside looking in, you're exactly into what's going on in this city, in this area, anyway. Then you've got that certain element of danger here, keeps your adrenalin going."

I felt my adrenalin flowing at that moment. Now it was dark outside. Strange faces kept peering into the restaurant. They seemed to be looking at the men sitting there.

"Keeps you healthy in a way," Lewis continued. "You don't lay down on this job. You can get other jobs, get over into the office somewhere where you can type all day, but you're out here in the street, keeps you alert. You come close to something."

"Okay," Raftery said, "don't talk no more. I'll see you in church." He was enjoying the soup.

"It changes your life," Lewis went on. "It changed mine. I tell you, the job has changed me around."

"How did you become a cop?" I asked Raftery.

"Well, I was driving a truck before I came in. I was in the army from '65 to '67. I wound up driving a truck when I got out. I figured it was kind of boring and I figured this might be interesting, more interesting than driving a truck, anyway, so I made the move."

"It pays so much to have a partner you can trust," Lewis said. "I know if John stops at two stores he ain't out there to pick up no dope. Nobody ain't going to be giving him no five dollars or shit like that stuff. He's going to do what's necessary to do at the time and that's it. 'Cause some guys on the job, you don't want to work with them for the simple reason you don't know them. You don't know what this guy's situation is, his family or his financial situation or just his makeup. He may be in some bullshit that you'd be implicated in by association. That's the hell of a bust to take. Some guy might be on the take or something. . . . That's the only thing that stings me every now and then. It really gets to me when someone questions my integrity or my personal honesty on the job. It throws me into the barrel with everybody else because somebody else took some money. They look on me and say shit."

"It is a little embarrassing," Raftery said.

"I know right after the Knapp Commission this morning, I was going to court on the bus and everybody's reading about police corruption. I turned around and I felt like this. Women started clutching their pocketbooks tight."

"You turn around," Raftery said, "and you feel like saying, 'Hey, look, pal, there's thirty thousand cops. I can't answer for everybody. You answer for yourself.' If the guy's black I said to the guy, 'Can you answer for every colored guy there is in New York? Of course not. Then I can't answer for every cop. Just worry about yourself.'"

"So we have a little thing," Lewis said. "Like, if we're locking up a black guy he starts hollering prejudice and we laugh at him. If a white guy is saying it we laugh at him because he's wrong.

If he's committed a crime or an infraction of a law and he's going to cry prejudice, we know we're not treating this guy unjustly. So we're able to laugh at him."

Lewis pulled the door open and held it for me to go first. Raftery stepped aside, waiting, too, being polite. I stepped out into the night. There were no shots. Nothing. We walked together up the avenue, past the Shrimp Boat. There was a sudden moment there on the street when I had the awful feeling that I was stepping over bodies, over Foster and Laurie. I looked down quickly. There was nothing to be seen on the sidewalk. The moment passed quickly and I was ashamed of my vision, and my fear.

We went as far as Twelfth Street, then turned around and walked back down the avenue. Near Tompkins Park the partners saw someone waving at them. They ran into the park. A small, conservatively dressed Puerto Rican was pointing to a teen-aged boy who was sitting on a bench, his head down, talking incoherently, nodding.

"He's out on speed," Lewis said immediately. Raftery used his radio to call the precinct and summon an ambulance. They tried to talk to the boy. He mumbled but could not lift his head. The park was dimly lit. Off in a corner, young men, naked from the waist up, were playing on a small basketball court. Men and women walked through the park, some together, some alone. A middle-aged white woman with blowsy blond hair, and wearing a dirty summer dress, was sitting on a bench near the cops, her two German shepherds on a leash. I sat down on the same bench, glad to rest my feet. Suddenly, I felt a strange rustling sensation around my pubic area. At first it didn't connect. Then it came to me that the woman with the dogs was fondling my genitals. I got up hurriedly.

"Hey, what are you doing?"

Raftery and Lewis laughed. "This is Ruth. She'd do that to Mayor Lindsay if he came near her."

"How long have you been doing that?" I asked.

"Since I was a young girl. That's my way of introduction, instead of shaking hands."

I didn't know what to say. "Keeps from getting monotonous, right?" she said.

"What's that?"

"Keeps from getting monotonous, grabbing a little cock once in a while."

The cops were still laughing when the ambulance pulled up. They lifted the boy to his feet and half-carried him to the ambulance. They started to walk on the avenue once again.

They tried to explain the demographics of the drug culture in the East Village. "There's plenty of heroin and cocaine around," Lewis said. "But the younger kids are usually up on speed and marijana. Marijuana is a vice-squad deal, especially in this park. The stuff is very easy to get down here, 'cause everybody is dealing something. But you can't say the crimes are caused by junkies. I think most of the time a lot of these crimes, these rip-off artists, are young people, twelve to sixteen. They're not really addicts. But you do have a lot of addicts here. It hasn't changed any. When we first got down here the hippies had just begun to leave. But the hippies were never engaged in hard drugs. They were always in smoke, LSD. But these people here are mostly graduates. The older ones are into hard drugs."

Lewis and Raftery started walking toward Fourteenth Street. It was time for dinner. "See," Lewis continued, "there are so many problems here that *that's* the reason why you don't have the response from the neighborhood that you would get in another neighborhood that is not as drug orientated. Everybody you say hello to is either a junkie or on the methadone program. Most of the incidents they clean up themselves. Something happens, somebody gets ripped-off within a certain circle, they deal out the punishment.

"You see," Lewis said, talking earnestly now, Raftery beside him, listening, "if we wanted to dive into things we could dive into them. But we're not here for that purpose, really. These people who need us, they can come right up to us. They know we're gonna help 'em. So this is all a part of being out there, letting them know we can be approached and we're not the animals they say we are."

We ate in a luncheonette on the avenue at Thirteenth Street.

299

They both had grilled ham and cheese sandwiches and milk shakes. Raftery was talking about his brothers and sisters, all married but himself. "The last one that I heard was a cop in my family," he said, "was my grandfather in Ireland."

They thought about what they would really like to do; both mentioned sports. But then it got back to the job and its sorrows. They had passed Eleventh Street and Avenue B again on the way to eat and I thought of what had happened there. I asked them if they ever thought about it.

"Every time I pass the block," Raftery said, "the thought enters my mind. But I guess there's a certain amount of danger in any job. Sometimes, after a thing is over you think about it. You go on a gun run or something like that, you think to yourself, one little slipup, you know. . . ." He stopped talking to eat.

"Certain jobs," Lewis said, "you feel the fear, a burglary in progress or something. I'm going into a dark building, I don't know what I'm looking for but you're able to handle it, especially if you're with someone you know. You don't have some other cop coming in the other end shooting at you. The first couple of minutes you don't know. Like one night, four men with shotguns, shots fired, right? We have no friends down on Tenth Street, right?"

"It was Tenth Street," Raftery nodded.

"We have no friends down there, right? So there's an element of fear there when you don't know where it comes from. Or you hear the bang, you go down."

"We were greeted well, though," Raftery said.

"Yeah, with a bottle off the roof — *bang!*" Lewis gulped down the last of his milk shake. "It's a beautiful thing to do something for people, but like sometimes you know that you have to lean on them a little bit. Some of these guys out here, too, they do the mean jive, they may be pulling that bullshit here in the street. You walk up and tell them about it and they know — they *know* — the next time they're going. Then, after, if they want to fight, they get a fight. They get everything they want. If they want to be treated like men, they act like men. I mean, I'm not going to give them something they're not going to give me."

The moon was up and it was warm and the street was calm. Full moon or not, it had been a quiet night. Raftery walked on ahead while Lewis stopped to talk to two black women sitting on a stoop; addicts, he told me later, but good women otherwise. On the corner of Eleventh Street and Avenue B, the northeast corner (Foster and Laurie were killed on the southeast corner) Mark Tuft appeared from nowhere. Tuft was the sixteen-year-old boy who had witnessed the end of the murders from the window of his parents' apartment, overlooking the avenue. Lewis introduced the boy to me. "He's writing a story on Foster and Laurie."

Tuft played it as though he had never seen me before, though he had. "I knew them both. They were great."

"Everybody is somebody except me," Lewis said.

"Well, you weren't around," Tuft said. "You changed beats."

"You know I was down here before, working with Charlie. You act so stuck up now. As soon as John R. came around here you brightened up. Foster came, you brightened up."

Tuft laughed. "Foster used to come around when he didn't have to work. He used to come around and stay with us."

"I drop by when I don't have to work."

"Yeah, you stay here and talk to us, right?"

"I used to come by and you all were in the movies looking at all those sex pictures."

"You see," Tuft laughed, talking to Raftery, "he didn't do that."

"Well, you got to understand, Gene is kind of old."

Tuft thought for a moment. "Yeah, that's right. Foster was younger. We used to tip him all the time and he used to listen to that. Tell him all the gossip that was going around here. He and Laurie used to want to try to get into things which we told them would be dangerous if they did. Foster'd just say: 'Well, we'll see what we can do.' "

The cops shuffled their feet, looking over the neighborhood, their tour almost over. "He was real nice, though," Tuft said. "Seems like everybody in the neighborhood, you know, everybody loves him, mostly the kids. And his friend, too."

Tuft used the present tense — loves him — but neither cop picked up on it. It was time to start back to the station house. We crossed the street and passed over the piece of sidewalk that had held the two young men in life and in death. "We have our moments of fear, of dying," Lewis said, as if he had read my thoughts.

Raftery took off his cap and wiped his brow. "I'm happier than I was," he said, thinking of his past.

"Me, too," Lewis said. "I'm glad I came on the job, too. We have our moments."

The night was almost over for them and they had survived and tomorrow they would be back.

Acknowledgments

First, my deepest gratitude to the wives — Jacqueline Foster and Adelaide Laurie — without whose full and generous cooperation there would have been no book. Others were unsparing of their time and memories, especially Mr. and Mrs. Anthony Laurie, Sr., the parents of Rocco Laurie; Rocco Laurie's brother, Anthony, and his wife, Kathy; and Dr. and Mrs. Matthew Iammatteo. I am indebted to my friend, Ed Hymoff, who showed me the way in the Vietnam episodes, and to the Marine Corps for their help, especially to Gunnery Sergeant Dick Mescal who, along with his staff, found for me the key men who served with Foster and Laurie. Among those who talked freely to me were Gunnery Sergeant Gerald Lester, Dale Duke, Michael Brown, Steve Breneisen, and Peter Wood. Special thanks to Brooks Matyi, who opened his heart to me. The police of the Ninth Precinct were friendly and cooperative throughout. My special thanks to patrolman Richie O'Neill, who opened all the right doors. And grateful thanks to Patrolmen Jim Liedy, Joseph Cloke, Earl Kirwan, John Raftery and Eugene Lewis. And to two patrolmen not of the Ninth, Darryl Anderson and Jim Duffy. To those who live in the precinct and were willing to talk to me, especially the "Cool Ones" and Mark Tuft, my thanks. I am grateful to my editor, Roger Donald, for his wisdom in helping to make this a better book. Final thanks to Lydia Paglio, who transcribed all my tapes and began to see patterns emerging long before I did.

— AL SILVERMAN